CW01084015

BELOVED CHILDREN

BELOVED CHILDREN

History of Aristocratic Childhood in Hungary in the Early Modern Age

edited by

Katalin Péter

CEU PRESS

Central European University Press

First published in Hungarian as "Gyermek a kora újkori Magyarországon" *by*
MTA Történelemtudományi Intézete in 1996

English edition published in 2001 by
Central European University Press

An imprint of the
Central European University Share Company

Nádor utca 11
H-1015 Budapest
Hungary

400 West 59th Street
New York, NY 10019
USA

Distributed in the United Kingdom and Western Europe by
Plymbridge Distributors Ltd., Estover Road, Plymouth PL6 7PZ,
United Kingdom

ISBN 963 9116 77 7 Cloth

Library of Congress Cataloging in Publication Data
A CIP catalog record for this book is available upon request

Printed in Hungary by Akaprint

TABLE OF CONTENTS

LIST OF CONTRIBUTORS

István Fazekas PhD, Delegate of the Hungarian National Archives in Vienna

Judit Fejes PhD student, Central European University, Budapest

Ildikó Horn PhD, Associate Professor, Eötvös Lóránd University, Budapest

Katalin Péter DSc, Senior Fellow, Institute of History of the Hungarian Academy of Sciences, Professor of History, Central European University, Budapest

ACKNOWLEDGEMENTS

The authors are indebted to the Hungarian research fund OTKA, who supported the project "Childhood in History", on the results of which this book has been based. We also wish to acknowledge the support of the Institute of History of the Hungarian Academy of Sciences, where our research was conducted. The authors and the editor are indebted to our reviewers Ralph Antony Houlbrooke, professor of history at the University of Reading and Andrzej Wyczański, professor of history at the Polish Academy of Sciences for their useful comments.

SOME PRELIMINARIES BY WAY OF INTRODUCTION

THE TITLE chosen for this book, *Beloved Children. The History of Aristocratic Childhood in Hungary in the Early Modern Age,* makes reference to a quite normal state of affairs: parents are generally expected to love their children as a matter of course, and there are very few people who would confess to not loving children in general. There is good reason why kissing babies is a widely used weapon during election campaigns. As to ancient times, we read in the Bible that the pharaoh's daughter rescued the child Moses because she felt pity on seeing the apparently abandoned baby. Or again, in the story illustrating Solomon's wisdom, we read of a mother preferring to give up her son to a woman falsely claiming him as her own, rather than letting the child be cut in two. Today, cases of child abuse or gross neglect are high-profile news precisely because they contravene norms that we regard as innate in human beings. So why should there be anything strange in reading about "beloved children" in early modern Hungary? Common sense suggests that people in that period would have loved their children naturally, as they have done throughout history.

However, for the few who happen to be interested in scholarly research in this field, expectations are somewhat different. Firstly, they will be aware of the debate in which parental love, as expressed by parental care, has a history like any other phenomenon. Secondly, they will know that world-wide homogeneity in terms of family structures and family feelings has been brought into question. While both these areas of discussion have antecedents in earlier scholarship, the discourses on them were constructed in the 1960s. This was a particularly fruitful time in the field of historiography, when many areas of study were opened up or reopened. It was a lively period in historical research, as it was for most elements of culture in Europe, on both sides of the Iron Curtain. The Beatles can be regarded as a symbol of those years—Beatlemania was probably the first common experience after the Second World War that united young people on both sides of the continent, and young people in the US.

The debates within historiography concerning the family are a more prosaic fruit of the atmosphere of those years. In the West, studies on the history of childhood apparently concentrated on the awareness of East European differences. The family structure discourse centred around the problem of whether or not Western Europe, due to certain demographic peculiarities, should be regarded as a unique part of the world. The two discourses, which have had their separate history for the last two or three decades, have been described in detail in the introductions to all the books relevant to these topics.

In terms of the history of childhood, however, the controversies have become less intense—to the extent that already several years ago Hugh Cunningham could write a rather detached account of the various opinions held.[1] The history of the family reached this same stage more recently with the publication of a book by Leonore Davidoff, Megan Doolittle, Linet Fink and

Katherine Holden.[2] In contrast, as to the question of European uniqueness the climate on that front would appear to be as hot as ever. One of the leading experts in the field, Richard Wall, declared that particular discourse to be hopeless in as early as 1983.[3] However, three years ago, more than thirty years after the whole question arose when John Hajnal equated Europe with Western Europe, Maria Todorova, the distinguished American scholar, still felt so strongly about it that she declared certain attitudes in the debate "pathetic". She was referring to historians who "demonstrate that their areas bear if not all, at least the majority of characteristics which allows them to be squeezed into the 'European' rubric".[4]

Such is the problem faced by researchers into childhood in Hungary. On the one hand, they have data that are regarded as "European" or "Western". On the other hand, they are fully aware of living neither in Norway nor in the United Kingdom. On the whole, *Beloved Children* does not fit into the discourse on Europe. Nor does it fit exactly into the discourse on parental care.

In order to align itself with the latter, it would have to identify the point when active parental care began. From that time on parents, and society in general, did not merely regard childhood as a special phase in the life of the individual, but acknowledged that they were responsible for the physical and spiritual welfare of their offspring. This change is to be looked for in around the sixteenth century. Even Linda Pollock, the most eminent advocate of the concept of childhood being a natural phenomenon with only the intensity and content of parental care changing in history, did not refer to sources of earlier times.[5]

In Hungary, however, it is evident that one cannot start exploring the history of any phenomenon using written sources. Written culture began here very late compared to the West—that is, at the turn of the first millennium AD. Most people automatically pick up a dictionary of historical etymology when looking for the first use of a word that indicates the earliest existence of a notion. Looking up the modern Hungarian word *gyermek*, "child", is fruitless, since it is of uncertain lineage.[6] The words *anya* (mother) and *apa* (father), however, are at least two thousand years old, with the word and notion *anya* probably being the older.[7] As these words make sense only in relation to offspring, the social unit of mother, father and child must have existed among the peoples of which the Hungarians, or rather their forbears, formed a part at that time. Among the oldest words in the language are *szeretet* (love) and *játék*, a word that can mean anything in connection with playing.[8]

Since the linguistic evidence pointed to early parent-child relations, and even to the possibility of mutual feelings of love or of parents allowing their children to idle away their time in play, it seemed worth looking further. The easiest way to do that in Hungary was to turn to the time when the Hungarians, at the turn of the ninth and tenth centuries AD, arrived in the Carpathian Basin and began to settle.

This process is known in Hungarian as *honfoglalás*, literally translated as "taking up home". Apart from the grammatical origin of the word, however, the term *honfoglalás* expresses powerful emotions. The word used in most translations, that is, "conquest", is equally emotive, but from the opposite point of view. With such contradicting emotions in play, this period has excited much interest and has become one of the best-researched epochs of Hungarian history. The research has been mainly archaeological, and evidence has been found in the form of grave sites and objects that were buried along with the dead for use in the afterlife.

However morbid, investigations into grave sites are particularly effective in providing evidence for historical attitudes towards childhood. Firstly, they tell us that children were not neglected in death. They were buried, and various artefacts, according to their social standing, were interred with them to be taken into the next world. This could be seen as a symptom of an attitude that did not discriminate between adults and children, were it not for the fact that children's graves were distinguished by a unique feature. While the graves of adults contained tools related to warfare, hunting and work in general, children's graves contained nothing similar.

The children's graves investigated included those of well-off children as well as less elaborate graves that apparently belonged to the children of servants. Many of the graves had been robbed or were incomplete. The most important difference between children's and adults' graves, however, could be established. No matter how elaborate or simple the items found in the graves, the children's graves never included objects that suggested warfare, work or hunting.[9]

The conclusion is obvious: if children were not involved in adult activities in this world, and if they did not have to work, then there was no reason for them to appear as adults in the next world. It should be pointed out that even children who were already old enough to ride a horse were not pictured as adults after their death. Only a horse and tack were buried with these older children, if their social standing required it, but never weapons. Traces of the graves of babies have disappeared, most probably because the items buried with them were perishable.

All in all, the archaeological evidence of the conquest period points to the same conclusions as the earlier linguistic data. The archaeological findings merely enable us to consider sociological factors revealed by the graves but not by linguistics: it was not only among the social elite that childhood was regarded as a special stage of life.

Nor was the existence of the mother-father-child unit contradicted by the archaeological findings from the conquest period. The most striking discovery seems to be the fact that the burial sites must have been planned well before the actual burials took place. This is suggested by their consistent arrangement. The richest graves are always found in the geometrical centre, surrounded by the graves of others in order of decreasing wealth. Females were either buried in one area at the rich person's side, with the males in the area opposite them, or male, female and child graves were found on both sides of the richest person, with the richer on one side and the less wealthy on the other. The supposition is that the person with the most abundant grave items was the head of the group that used the same burial site. This supposed head was generally male, but there were also women among them.

The sites were obviously planned on the basis of the different relationships between the people who intended to be buried at the same site. They were clearly conscious of the hierarchy and the relationships among themselves. The relative place of each individual in the social structure must have been permanently in evidence, otherwise they would not have been able to inter the dead exactly according to their position in society, and in the family.

When not buried between a female and male body, children were buried nearest to the head of the group, irrespective of gender. To my mind this indicates the prestige in which childhood was held. Nevertheless, it was more common to bury children between the two persons who were most probably their parents. The obvious question arises as to which of their children was buried with the parents, and to this we have no answer. If we assume that each couple had more than one child, we can suppose that their other children were buried in the rows of males or females when not interred nearest to the richest person. As a rule they were buried in separate graves.

If a man and a woman were interred side by side, usually also in separate graves, the woman's grave was always located to the right of the man. The only explanation for this seems to be that they formed a couple. Gyula László, an expert in this field, arrived at the conclusion that monogamous couples and their children constituted the group that used the same grave site. They were perhaps relatives, an extended family, and their servants.[10]

In the language of the discourse on parental care, this means that childhood was regarded as a special stage in the life of the individual. Children were seen as individual beings and society cared about their needs in the next world by providing them with the necessaries for it. In other words, parental care was extended to the realm of the afterlife, which has later emerged in the form of care for the spiritual needs of children. As to parental care for physical needs, grave items yield no information about that. We only know by linguistic evidence that the *bölcső* (cradle) was used for young children well before the conquest period.[11] The word could refer to a sling for carrying the infant or a light piece of furniture for her or his safekeeping during the day or night, as in all cultures that have borrowed this most practical piece of childcare equipment from the nomadic peoples.

In summary, parental care in the sense of social and parental responsibility for the child's fate in this world and the next can be established by clear evidence from the beginning of history. Inevitably, the form of that care must have changed. Indeed, every aspect of life must have been changed in the course of the long process in which a nomadic people adopted an agricultural lifestyle. They moved from airy tents to closed buildings; they had to learn foresight in the event of a bad harvest or other disasters; and they established a kingdom that functioned by the rule of law. Finally, they adopted Christianity.

If there is one single period in the country's history in which changes in parental care should be studied, it is the ninth, tenth and eleventh centuries. How great a change was it in popular attitudes when parents started taking their children to be bap-

tised to ensure their salvation instead of burying them with provisions for the afterlife? How did parents react to the new duty
or possibility of sending children to school instead of preparing
them for life by their own example? How did society react when
the first Christian king, St Stephen, declared the main obligation
of his bishops, the representatives of the recently established
church, to be the protection of widows and orphans? Did they
see this simply as delegating common social responsibility to
the church? Or was the protection of a family that had lost a
father a new idea for them?

In spite of the importance of such questions, the discourse on
childhood has traditionally been constructed along different lines.
This is perhaps because the time before Christianity belongs to the
distant past of the history of Western Europe and, in the eyes of
historians, has no bearing on modern notions. Or perhaps it has
something to do with academic etiquette. Whatever the reason,
Beloved Children has been written in the knowledge that parental
care and social responsibility, like the responsibility of parents,
for the well-being of their offspring in this world as well as the
next belong among the most ancient attitudes.

In deference to the existing debate, however, the early modern period has been chosen for this book. At the outset of the
project the authors were unsure whether they would be able to
find written sources concerning intimate and emotional relationships. The discovery of such sources was a welcome surprise.
However, since the review of those sources took longer than
expected, it was decided to focus the studies on the aristocracy.
The sources relating to aristocratic families are much easier to
handle than evidence relating to peasants and their concept of
childhood. Nevertheless, their attitudes could also have been
illustrated using the data as well.

As to the discourse on Europe, we preferred to leave that
out of consideration. There seemed to be no sense in entering a

debate that has become, as it were, a conversation among the deaf. On the other hand, nor is there any sense denying that there are huge historical differences between the countries of Western Europe and Hungary. After all, we are talking about a people that arrived late from the depths of the Ural Mountains in a region that had been regarded as the outskirts of civilisation in Antiquity. To give only one point of reference, their arrival took place three hundred years after the first building had been constructed at the site of Canterbury Cathedral and after the pope had appointed the first archbishop of Canterbury.

Meanwhile, a long dissertation could be written about the meeting of cultures, whether in the form of encounters between travellers, diplomats or young people from Hungary studying abroad. In the introductory remarks to a book called *Beloved Children*, however, a less scholarly approach is probably permitted. On this point, we refer the reader to the works of George Mikes, an eminent Central European among the British who spoke his mind about the latter with hilarious success. Mikes's collections *How to be an Alien* and *How to be a Brit*, published by Penguin, have run to several editions. It would be delightful to have a similarly light-hearted account of how a person from the West feels in this part of Europe.

For light-hearted should be the keyword here. This should be equally true for the debates and differences between cultures. The tedious quarrel about who and who is not European, intellectualised according to an abstract notion of progress, should be turned into a fruitful conversation about individual human beings. However, that is beyond the scope of these preliminaries to *Beloved Children*.

The point I would like to make here is that we are not debating the fact that people from all walks of life in early modern Hungary lived among circumstances that can be regarded as traditional. At the same time we find no attitudes of fatalism, no lack of feeling between spouses and no evidence of neglect in parent-child relationships—except in deviant cases, of course. While we acknowledge that there were differences between Hungary and England, for instance, in terms of life during that period, it should be stressed that positive emotions were not the privilege of advanced societies.

To begin with, mortality was certainly high by today's standards and this was a bad sign for the future of the population. On the other hand, high mortality rates meant that the population tended, on the whole, to be young. This can be illustrated by data on people who were regarded as adults, that is, who are referred to in the sources as adults with respect to their status within the family. This method of investigating the problem of age was chosen in the absence of sources providing demographic evidence.

Out of a group of 97 seventeenth-century peasant women, known by name, age and marital status, 9 were in their teens, 81 in their twenties to forties, and only 7 aged fifty or over. The oldest was sixty-one. From among a group of 60 married men, 46 were below fifty and only 14 were over that age. The oldest was seventy. Out of a group of 241 unmarried men, 13 were in their teens, 24 were aged between twenty and twenty-two, the vast majority were between twenty-three and thirty, and only 2 of them were over thirty. As regards marital status, from among the 97 women 88 were married or widowed at the time they were mentioned in the source we used.

The figures show that among 404 adults of both genders living in the seventeenth century, known to us by name and encountered in the most varied of circumstances, there were only 21 over fifty years of age, and 22 were in their teens. The vast majority were between twenty-one and forty-nine years old. If conclusions can be drawn from such a small sample, this suggests that we are dealing with a young population.[12]

In spite of the size of the sample, the figures are valuable since they have been newly discovered and are based on contemporary sources. In the absence of contemporary sources providing information relevant to age evaluation, the normal method of approaching the question of age is to project twentieth-century statistical data onto the historical period in question. Here, the figures have been extracted from various non-statistical contemporary sources after years of painstaking work. Although the sample is too small to allow statistical conclusions, the data attached to them, along with a few similar cases bringing the total to 473 in all, point towards some puzzling perspectives.

To put it briefly, men were at a disadvantage in the marriage market throughout the seventeenth century. It was common for both men and women to marry several times, after having been widowed, but there were certain social norms and demographic factors that limited their range of choice. The social expectation was for spouses to be of roughly the same age, the man being slightly older. An age gap of ten years was tolerated in the first marriage as well as the third or fourth. However, a bigger age difference, such as that between the Paxi couple where the wife was fourteen years younger than her husband, was exceptional. As to having a younger husband, this happened rarely and the age gap was no more than around five or six years. We found evidence of only one husband who was more than ten years younger than his wife.

The normal state of affairs, as suggested by the literature on traditional societies in general, was for an adult to be married. Individuals who were no longer regarded as children were referred to as unmarried—in other words, society hinted at their readiness for marriage. When a girl reached the age of about fourteen she became a *hajadon*, a female who goes bareheaded, that is, who does not wear the headscarf of a married woman.

Boys were given the equivalent designation of *nőtlen* at the age of about eighteen. This marks the point at which they were regarded as being of marriageable age. The actual marriage, however, usually came much later.

As a rule, girls were married off at between eighteen and twenty. Among the 88 married women known from our sources there were only three below the age of eighteen. One of them was fourteen and two sixteen. At the other end of the scale, we know of one woman who was single at over twenty, a certain Anna Bencze. At the age of thirty-six she was referred to respectfully as "honourable virgin". Men were married for the first time at between twenty and twenty-two years of age. We know of two men who were single at over thirty. One of them remained a bachelor for good, devoting himself, according to the sources, to bringing up the offspring of a deceased brother. The other man mentioned as a bachelor in the sources may well have married at a later date.

The details given above indicate that although people did not marry as early as might be expected on the basis of modern data projected onto history, they were in fact married much earlier than their counterparts in western countries.

Hidden behind this apparently simple fact, however, are many potential consequences influencing the general atmosphere within society. There is a huge advantage in beginning sexual life openly, with general approval, approximately at the time when the individual feels the urge to do so. It seems unnatural for people to spend their best and most fertile years in celibacy—or at least feigned celibacy. Surely this caused tensions between the sexes? And should it not be regarded as an advantage for children to have young parents? Those who start a family at around thirty, who may have acquired set habits during a relatively long period of single life, suddenly have to change their lifestyle completely for the sake of their child. Does this not make their concept of childhood different from attitudes held by people for whom being an adult means having children as a matter of course?

Inevitably, these are questions to which we can provide no answers. We have posed them here in order to indicate that life in a traditional society could perhaps have been a more relaxed experience for the individual than life in a society labelled by historians as more "modern".

We found no evidence among women of fear of childbirth, probably because in a society where women gave birth at an age when they were most suited to it biologically, notions of fear did not develop. On this question, our attention has been called by a Western expert to the fact that children were born at much shorter intervals in Hungary than in England. The only plausible explanation seems to be the more active sexual life in Hungary. There must inevitably be a substantial difference between the sexual behaviour of partners who start a family at around the age of twenty and those who are only allowed to do so some ten years later.

Marriages often took place at an even earlier age among the aristocracy, the focus of our studies in *Beloved Children*. It appears that the higher the status of the family, the younger the couple at the time of marriage. The lifestyle of members of the aristocracy, however, can hardly be compared to that of the peasants. The relationship between the two social spheres, that is, between the aristocracy and the peasants who worked on their estates, remains an important area of research. There were inevitably changes in this relationship in the eighteenth century, although this is merely a suggestion for a further area of study.

PRACTICAL INFORMATION

Our aim is not to provide an exhaustive survey of childhood in aristocratic families. Instead, we have chosen to present four situations that we regard as typical in early modern Hungary. Two chapters contain case studies, one of them exploring the kind of scheming that went on in connection with the arranged marriages of three of the Esterházy children. We considered this an important topic since it is characteristic of the period under discussion. The planning of marriages often began very early: families might even begin discussing the marriage of an unborn child. Marriage contacts were exploited in many forms in the aristocratic society of the time and, as in all strata of society, it was only the married who were regarded as fully functioning adults.

The second case study concerns the education of the children of Count Ádám Batthyány I, an eminent personality in the history of Hungary. The education received by his sons is of general interest, since it was typical of aristocratic boys of the time. The children would initially be taught at home before going on to study at educational institutions abroad, in the company of a large entourage like that which accompanied the young Batthyánys. Despite the careful selection of tutors and classmates, young aristocratic boys often fell into bad company or were unable to achieve good results. The fate of the Batthyánys also reveals that not every aristocratic child became a leading politician.

The study on orphans has been included since being an orphan was a common experience in early modern Hungary. On this subject, in the absence of appropriate sources, we were unable to carry out demographic research. There is no way of knowing the number of mothers or fathers in any given generation who died before they were able to bring up their children. Our picture of the situation of orphans had to be composed in a mosaic-like fashion, from snippets of information. It is for this reason that, unlike the other chapters, this one includes mention of lower-ranking—merely noble rather than aristocratic—families. Data referring to the aristocracy would have been insufficient to allow us to base a study exclusively on them.

Finally, a separate chapter was written on the subject of children under the age of ten, because it seems to us that this period of childhood can be regarded as a distinct sub-period. At this age children usually lived with their parents or grandparents, that is, at home in the wider sense of the word. Another important finding was that the upbringing of girls and boys under the age of ten was apparently more or less the same. As the relationship between parents and children this young was especially intimate, family emotions were directly accessible, and writing on the subject was a real pleasure.

A NOTE ON TITLES AND NAMES

Members of the aristocracy in early modern Hungary used or referred to titles only rarely. The reason behind this probably goes back to the status of their counterparts in the Middle Ages. Before the sixteenth century a family or an individual was regarded as socially prominent, *előkelő* in Hungarian, by social consensus. She or he was granted certain royal favours, invitations to court and to the sessions of the Diet, appointment to high offices, the right to keep an army, or the gift of large estates. The main requirement, however, was to have a substantial body of followers who provided political support for the lord and gave assistance to the lady in his absence or in widowhood, for which they received various social, political and financial rewards. Everyone in the society was aware of who the *előkelő* were. Titles were not needed, since everyone was expected to know their status.

The idea of granting titles by royal charter was introduced by the Habsburg kings. Some great lords of the realm were apparently uncomfortable with it. It is characteristic that the oldest families, like the Zrínyis, did not receive titles by royal charter—their high standing was too obvious. They, a very few exceptional families, became the members of the new aristocracy by their natural status as *előkelő*. It was looked at as vulgar to flaunt one's titles.

The lowest title—*báró*, or baron—was never used and was not even referred to, although it was the prerequisite from the first third of the sixteenth century onwards for belonging to the aristocracy. The next highest titles—*gróf*, roughly corresponding to count, and *herceg*, roughly meaning prince—were used on certain official occasions, although in everyday life individuals were rarely referred to or addressed using such terms, except by people of much lower standing. In *Beloved Children* we have made the concession of applying the titles count and prince from time to time in order to help the modern reader, who is accustomed to seeing members of the aristocracy mentioned by their titles. However, the consistent use of such titles, let alone the use of the title *báró*, would have been so much contrary to contemporary customs in Hungary that we have refrained from it.

In terms of names, there are two peculiarities in Hungary. First of all, if someone was granted a title it did not mean that they changed their name. For example, Sebestyén Thököly, who started out as a merchant, remained Thököly throughout his rapid rise in status, as a nobleman, a *báró*, and a *gróf*. The Thökölys did not become princes, but the Pálffys, for instance, did, although they too continued to use the name Pálffy.

The other important point to make with respect to names in Hungary is that married women in all walks of life and in all periods of history have retained their maiden names, officially or unofficially. This can be regarded as the rule among aristocratic ladies in early modern Hungary, who never adopted the names of their husbands. One of the most outstanding personalities of the time was referred to, even on the official portrait of her painted for the Nádasdy family gallery, as "Countess Orsolya Kanizsay, beloved wife of Count Tamás Nádasdy". We have no knowledge of a single personal letter by her signed in her married name or including a reference to either her husband's or her own title.

In the present volume we have adhered to this common practice. Women, mothers and grandmothers are generally referred to by their maiden name in *Beloved Children*. The names of their husbands are only mentioned if the context requires it. This is doubtless unusual for the English reader, but it cannot be avoided.

The Editor

Notes

1 H. Cunningham, *Children and Childhood in Western Society since 1500*. London, 1995.
2 L. Davidoff, M. Doolittle, J. Fink and K. Holden, *The Family Story. Blood, Contract and Intimacy, 1830–1960*. London, New York, 1999. (The book also deals with the history of earlier times than those indicated.)
3 Richard Wall, "Preface". In *Family Forms in Historic Europe*, ed. R. Wall, J. Robin and P. Laslett. Cambridge University Press, 1983, IX.
4 M. Todorova, "Zum erkenntnistheoretischen Wert von Familienmodellen. Der Balkan und die 'Europäische Familie'". In *Historische Familienforschung*, ed. J. Ehmer, T. K. Hareven and R. Wall. Franfurt/M, 1997, pp. 283–300. (I am grateful to Susan Zimmermann for supplying me with the text of the forthcoming English translation.)
5 L. A. Pollock, *Parent-Child Relations from 1500 to 1900*. Cambridge, 1996, p. 215.

6 *A magyar nyelv történeti etimológiai szótára* I-III. Editor-in-chief L. Benkő. Budapest 1967–1976 (hereafter Szótár), I, 731.

7 Szótár I, 159, 162.

8 Szótár III, 731; II, 266.

9 Gy. László, *A honfoglaló magyar nép élete*. Budapest, 1988, pp. 132, 144–146, 159, 162, 165. (Another book by the same author, with a similar title and also translated into English, is a much shorter, popular edition of this work.)

10 Ibid., pp. 132, 141, 146–147, 149–150. 160, 165.

11 Szótár I, 365. *Magyar néprajzi lexikon* 1–5. Editor-in-chief Gy. Ortutay. Budapest 1977–1982, I, 362–365.

12 K. Péter, "Szerelem, házasság a Hajnal-határtól keletre". Manuscript for the forthcoming volume *Ámor és Mámor*, ed. G. Szabó.

HISTORICAL BACKGROUND

THIS BOOK is on children from aristocratic families who, either because of their parents' position in society or as a result of their own efforts as adults, were closely involved in the politics of their day. We therefore considered it appropriate to include in the volume a brief historical outline in order to provide a context for our remarks about the care and position of children in this period.

In the stories we are told that aristocratic children were often sent to the court in Vienna. A father's care is illustrated in a description of how, on receiving news of his child's illness, he rushes home from the Diet in Pozsony to be at his child's side. We see the prince of Transylvania involved in correspondence concerning his little son's holiday even while he is reconsidering the western alliances inherited from his predecessor, and so on. Readers who are unfamiliar with Hungarian history might well be puzzled as to why Hungarian aristocrats sent their children to Vienna, and why the Diet was not held in the country's capital. It might also be difficult for them to understand why the little-known prince of Transylvania was involved with the question of western alliances at all…

The illustrations might also cause some confusion. The buildings pictured here are similar to those in which the better-off families among the English gentry lived during this period, although the captions tell us that these were the homes of the greatest dignitaries in the kingdom of Hungary. The reader surely requires an explanation as to why these people were so poor.

Finally, in a text dealing with the age of the Reformation and Counter-Reformation, why is there no mention of whether these families were Protestant or Catholic? Why were their children not treated according to the advice given by their own denomination? Surely the reader requires answers to these questions.

It is for this reason that the following historical background has been provided. Its inclusion is not intended to suggest that the study of the children themselves is of less importance than the history of wars, poverty, or denominational allegiances. Instead, it has the practical aim of pre-empting the kind of questions highlighted above.

In fact, it would be impossible to separate the historical background from the subject under discussion. The period covered in this book represents one of the most difficult eras in Hungarian history. The people of the time experienced the collapse of the great medieval kingdom, and their lives were lived out amid war and destruction. It would not be at all surprising to learn that the care of children was considered unimportant—but this is not the case. The title of the present volume captures contemporary attitudes exactly—children were loved, or at least the social norm was for them to be loved.

As a final justification for the inclusion of this historical background it should also be pointed out that in the early sixteenth century, the beginning of the period discussed in this book, the population and the territory of Hungary were not identical with the Hungary of today. The country's present borders were established after the Second World War, while in this book we are dealing with the very different Hungary of the sixteenth and seventeenth centuries. In those days there were no tensions between nationalities. People simply spoke different native languages.

THE KINGDOM

In response to the first and most straightforward of our questions, the younger members of the Hungarian aristocracy were sent to the court in Vienna because this was the seat of the king of Hungary. This situation had come about gradually after 1526. It was in this year that the Ottoman forces won a major victory over the royal army at Mohács, near the Danube. The young King Louis II, who with his queen, Mary of Habsburg, had been at the head of a cultured and convivial court in Buda, the country's capital, also met his death in this battle. Many of the country's secular and ecclesiastical lords lost their lives alongside him.

Following the battle the enemy left the country, but the tragedy at Mohács made it clear that the Ottoman Empire, a long-time threat, had chosen the line of the Danube as the goal of its westward expansion, which implied a dark future for Hungary. At this realisation the remaining Hungarian politicians divided into two parties holding opposing points of view but both seeking external support. One of the parties, whose ultimate goal was the rule of a national king, counted on the country's traditionally good relations with Poland. The other party attempted to gain the support of Emperor Charles V by the election of a king from the Habsburg dynasty.

Of the two, it was the national party that acted more quickly. Hardly two months after the battle of Mohács it elected as king János Zápolyai, the brother-in-law of Sigismund I, the king of

Poland, and one of the wealthiest lords of Hungary. A day later János I (John I) was crowned with the Holy Crown.

The Habsburg party acted less swiftly. It lost a great deal of time before electing as king Ferdinand I, the brother of the emperor and the brother-in-law of King Louis who had died in the battle of Mohács. They were only able to get possession of the Holy Crown from the other party much later, thus Ferdinand was crowned almost a year after his election, in November 1527.

It is important to emphasise the coronation ceremony itself, since it had huge significance in the contemporary consciousness: by the Holy Crown, during the coronation ceremony, power was vested in the king by the country. This meant that until King John's death in 1540, the country had two kings because two kings had been crowned. The size of the territory over which power was actually exercised varied, as did the allegiance of the subjects. Nevertheless, the two kings ruled in one country.

Finally, after the initial irresolution of the Habsburg party and at the cost of many internal struggles, Ferdinand I emerged victorious, although he did not provide help against the Ottomans. In 1551 he succeeded in gaining possession of the Holy Crown. This brought to an end the struggle for the kingdom. Ferdinand and his successors, who were duly elected and crowned, became the kings of Hungary. The lands that were ruled by them were regarded as the kingdom of Hungary, also known as Royal Hungary.

However, the Habsburg kings rarely spent more than a few nights in the country. Their seat was in Vienna, but they also spent much of their time in Prague and in the territory of the German Empire. This was because when Charles V distributed his estates between his son and his brother in 1555, the head of the Austrian house, Ferdinand I, who was already king of Hungary and king of Bohemia, was made Holy Roman Emperor as well. This was how children, young people and adults, members of the Hungarian aristocracy, became part of the multi-faceted society at the Vienna court. The loyalty due to the dynasty, whether heartfelt or feigned, prompted a great many subjects to attend the court from various countries.

THE FALL OF BUDA

The next question to be addressed is that of the capital city. The city of Budapest only came into existence in 1873. Before this date Buda, with its medieval royal castle, had been the capital, while Pest had been considered an insignificant town. However, sessions of the Diet could not be held in Buda during the period covered by this book, since at that time it was the seat of the sultan's representative.

Buda had been taken by Suleyman the Magnificent in 1541 without a single sword being brandished. At the time it was in the hands of Queen Isabelle, the widow of John I, and her followers, and was being besieged by Ferdinand's army. The sultan came to Isabelle's aid and defeated the emperor's army. Throughout the siege and the battle the queen remained in the castle.

Before returning home, Suleyman expressed his desire to meet Queen Isabelle and her baby son, John II. While the audience was taking place in Suleyman's camp at the foot of the Buda hills, his soldiers entered the castle. By the time the meeting between the sultan, the queen and her retinue had ended, the castle gates had been closed. Queen Isabelle, her young son and her entourage were trapped outside.

What followed was one of the saddest episodes in Hungarian history. Suleyman the Magnificent declared that by taking the capital he had taken possession of the whole country but was graciously prepared to hand over certain parts of it to Ferdinand and to John II. While he himself established a *vilayet*, or province, with Buda as its centre, Ferdinand would receive the western part of the country and John II the eastern part. Both of them were to pay a tax, in the form of a "gift" to the sultan.

The legendary luck of the Habsburgs did not desert them even then. First of all, it became clear that the Ottoman Empire, at least for the time being, had no wish to extend its borders west of Buda. Meanwhile, the Habsburgs had obtained control over the Hungarian territories neighbouring Austria, so that even in the event of an attack by the Turks, the enemies of Christendom, the fight could be taken up in this region. Ferdinand, who had not set foot in Hungary for years and who had moved the Hungarian administration to, or near, Vienna, lost very little and was not personally affected by the sultan's fateful decision.

Isabelle, on the other hand, found herself in a dramatic situation. Barely a year earlier had she given birth to a child, the long-awaited successor to John I, in the traditional seat of the Hungarian kings in Buda. King John I had been absent at the time the child was born, dealing with a pro-Ferdinand uprising in the eastern part of the country, Transylvania. Before long the king was dead and his son, while still a baby, was elected king in his place. However, the election had no bearing on the situation created by the sultan. According to his decree, the widowed queen was only permitted to go to that area of the country where only recently there had been uprisings against her late husband's rule. She obtained some ox-drawn carts and set off with her infant son and a few followers. They slowly wound their way in the very direction from which the Turkish armies had entered Hungary.

Since 1526 the Ottoman armies had often appeared in Hungary: even the victorious sultan himself had visited the country on several occasions. The wars between the two kings and their followers would have lured him even if he had not already been looking for an opportunity for westward expansion. John I had asked for, and received, help from the sultan against Ferdinand I several times. Prior to 1541, however, the sultan had always withdrawn his army in the autumn. By taking Buda he had declared his decision not to allow the uncertainty in Hungary to continue any longer. In the central, fertile areas of the country, the Ottoman Empire arrived to stay.

Nevertheless, it is not necessary to discuss this settling-in process in greater detail for the purposes of the present study on aristocratic children. These children would probably have been unaware of the fate of those living under the Turks since the nobility had fled as one from the territory occupied by the Ottoman Empire. Highborn children would have had no idea of the unimaginable hardships that had to be endured by those who had nowhere to run. While it cannot be denied that some landowners organised settlements, moving peasants to their protected estates in other parts of the country, the population in general was predominantly left to its fate.

On the surface, the local administration of the Ottoman Empire was set in place. However, a struggle for survival was taking place at a deeper level. The ecclesiastical and secular leaders of the settlements had to maintain contact with the foreign authorities, learning the tricks of coexistence. Occasionally whole villages would move to inaccessible marshland out of the reach of the Turkish soldiers and tax collectors. Then, when the danger was over, they would return to their former dwellings. The churches continued to function, as did some schools. Occasionally, and with enormous difficulties, Christian students from the territory under Ottoman rule managed to make their way to western universities.

THE PRINCIPALITY OF TRANSYLVANIA

The princes of Transylvania were occupied with the question of western alliances, since the west European enemies of the Habsburg dynasty regarded them as natural allies. This situation emerged gradually, like so many other phenomena in early modern Hungary.

The story began in the Middle Ages when Transylvania, as an individual legal component of the kingdom of Hungary, was under the rule of an official appointed by the king. It was he who convened the assembly of the Estates in the province to manage local affairs. However, the secular and ecclesiastical lords living in Transylvania, like nobles from all over the kingdom, were also invited to participate in the Diet called by the king and held in Buda or its environs. The name Transylvania, used in most modern languages, comes from the Latin and expresses the province's location in relation to Buda—it lay *trans silva*, that is, beyond the forest. Transylvania, surrounded by the Carpathians, was divided from the rest of the kingdom, and thus from Buda, by a richly forested range of mountains.

When the country was divided into three by the sultan, not only Transylvania but certain counties lying to the west of it were granted to John II. Initially, attempts were made to rule the eastern part of the country from territories lying outside the one-time province. However, these attempts did not prove successful. Isabelle occupied the palace of the bishops of Transylvania in Gyulafehérvár, and the town became the centre of this part of the country, which continued to have an uncertain legal status.

The country's uncertain legal status, in this context, refers to the fact that the decision made by the sultan in 1541 was carried out but never made law in the country's statutes. Suleyman I had split Transylvania and the territories annexed to it from the kingdom, but in the minds of contemporaries it continued to belong to the Holy Crown and would remain part of Hungary for a long time to come. Initially, it was referred to according to its medieval status. The term Principality of Transylvania emerged after the death of John II, who was known as king but who had merely been elected, never crowned. His successor as the ruler of Transylvania and the territories annexed to it was István Báthory, who became king of Poland in 1575. Báthory's change of status meant that his Hungarian dominion received the name Principality of Transylvania. After all, the king of the mighty Polish kingdom could not govern anything less than a principality.

Although the Principality of Transylvania came into being as a result of political decisions, its subsequent history was strongly influenced by ideological attitudes. For instance, there would have been no real obstacle to prevent complete submission to the sultan. However, every subjective reason was against such a course of action. Virtually everyone held to their conviction that the tripartite state of the country and the independence of the princes of Transylvania from the king of Hungary were only transitional. This situation would only last until the "Turkish yoke" was shaken off. However, by a fascinating twist of history, by the time Turkish rule was in fact shaken off in the late seventeenth century, during the reign of Emperor Leopold I, also king of Hungary, this attitude had been superseded. Politicians in Transylvania at that time had no wish to restore the rule of the Holy Crown over the principality, but submitted to Leopold as emperor.

For a hundred and fifty years or so, the princes of Transylvania came almost exclusively from the ranks of the Hungarian aristocracy. Several of them belonged to the Báthory family, with its many branches, which had estates both in the kingdom and the principality. Prince István Bocskai, at the turn of the sixteenth and seventeenth centuries, had spent most of his childhood in the royal and imperial court. The Rákóczi family, famous in Hungarian history for many reasons, also started off on the side of Vienna. Zsigmond Rákóczi, who was the first member of this family to become prince of Transylvania, had been a captain in the royal castle of Eger. He earned his wealth as a military supplier for Rudolf II and received a title from him. From among the better-known princes, Gábor Bethlen was the only exception in that neither he nor his ancestors were given a title by the king. The Bethlens had not been regarded as a significant family, and it was only after 1541 that Gábor's father managed to make a real career for himself in the principality. He was favoured by István Báthory. Prince Gábor Bethlen's brother, however, received a title from Matthias II, emperor and king of Hungary, before he also became prince.

Thus, the public lives of those magnates who eventually became princes of Transylvania usually began at the Diet of the kingdom. Their debut in public life took place as young members of the Upper House and they were eventually elected as princes by the Diet of Transylvania. As princes of Transylvania they no longer attended the sessions of the royal Diet, although they had the right to do so. The princes were represented through envoys, who usually played a significant role in the sessions of the royal Diet.

It is important to clarify these issues in detail, since to readers who are not familiar with Hungarian history it might appear strange that in this book early modern Hungary includes Transylvania. On this point we have followed contemporary thinking according to which, besides the kingdom, the principality of Transylvania and even the territory under Ottoman rule was regarded as Hungary.

Thus on the occasions that the princes of Transylvania appeared in the kingdom at the head of an army they did not do so as aliens. They fought for a national kingdom against the kings elected from the Habsburg dynasty. With hindsight, we know that their efforts were in vain. However, in certain situations people had reason to believe that victory was near. Nor were they alone in this belief. There were frequent occasions on which the western enemies of the House of Habsburg also expected the fall of the emperor. At such times they were keen to form alliances with the princes of Transylvania.

POVERTY

The disadvantageous situation of the country meant that there was real and extensive poverty in early modern Hungary. All that reached this region were reports of the discovery of America, which, with its ever-growing demand for everything from rope to paper, had set certain countries in Europe, such as Holland, England and France, well on the way towards industrialization. None of the beneficial effects of that discovery reached this far. Nevertheless, the discovery was regarded as a great event in Hungary, too. There was much talk of it, of the newly encountered exotic peoples and the enormous riches of the New World, but the whole matter was looked at with a certain—understandable—detachment. Even the most enterprising in Hungary had no hope of participating in the emerging world economy.

Some of the economic opportunities that arose in the wake of such discoveries did have an impact on Hungary during the sixteenth century. After the turn of the century, however, Hungary was only to suffer the disadvantages of the new economic order. It was in the seventeenth century that it became clear that Hungary and the countries surrounding it, the region that is today referred to as Central Europe or south-east Europe, would be left behind by the economic progress of western Europe.

In the sixteenth century, when industrialisation and world trade began in western Europe, the pace of progress made an impact in Hungary, too. It was not so much that industrial opportunities increased, but that demand for agricultural products grew. Landowners, towns and wealthier peasants all took advantage of the situation, delivering grain, wine and beef to the markets of the great western cities. Although there were problems due to the distances involved, the trade was immediately beneficial. Then trouble came in the form of the general European crisis at the turn of the century. Goods that had been delivered over great distances suddenly had to be returned—or destroyed, if returning them was not worthwhile. Foreign trade came to an end. Whoever was able to become self-sufficient did so, and everyone tried to avoid spending money.

It was the landowners who emerged in the best position—or, rather, it was they who did the least badly. They had serfs whose work continued to provide them with a livelihood. As for the serfs themselves, despite the usual history-book image of them as dull and ignorant people, they proved to be capable of satisfying the landowners' new needs. Peasants by birth, they also turned their hands to playing music, working in mines, building palaces, bird catching, or working as nursemaids in aristocratic households.

Thus the aristocracy managed to weather the hard times. By Hungarian standards they were even rich. We have no knowledge of any owners of large landholdings who did not have the means to modernise their medieval castles. More surprising is the amount of energy they invested in order to live in comfort despite the hard times.

The modernised castles remained fortresses to the outside observer, surrounded as they were by strong walls and moats. On the inside, however, there were arcades and balconies giving onto the castle's inner courts and gardens. The various areas of life were kept separate. On the lowest level of the castle were the smiths, cooks and general staff. Further up, there remained medieval-style rooms for storing household supplies and large quantities of food, although now the residential quarters rarely opened from them. Storehouses were also constructed next to the castles. It was also common for the family's private residential quarters and the offices of the head of the family to be in different wings.

The great hall very probably divided the public space from the space reserved for private life. It was here that the whole household, members of the family, their guests and the most respected of the servants probably ate together at several tables. Uncertainty about the everyday use of the hall results from the fact that although we know the household was in the habit of taking meals together, the layout of sixteenth and seventeenth-century castles is not easy to reconstruct, since they were largely rebuilt in the eighteenth and nineteenth centuries. As they stand today, there is one large hall. Formerly, however, there could have been other large rooms in which people ate together. From contemporary descriptions we know that apart from a common dining hall and some rooms that were adjacent or giving onto it, the male and female members of the household had their rooms in different quarters.

Besides the space shared with the household as a whole, the lady of the house and the head of the family certainly had their own bedrooms. A servant would sleep in front of the lord's bedroom in a corridor or a small room, but we have no information as to whether a similar arrangement existed for the lady of the castle. The existence of separate bedrooms is mentioned beyond doubt in several inventories. Normally the lavatories opened from them. The information contained in contemporary letters, however, suggests that couples usually slept in the same bed. As yet, no data have been found as to whether they retired to one of the bedrooms together in the evening, or visited each other only after the rest of the household had gone to sleep. This must have been dependent on many factors.

The other members of the family probably had only one room. Younger children shared a room with their nurses or tutors, and the older children with their servants. It appears that they used the same room during the daytime when necessary. According to all the existing data, however, members of the family spent their time together during the day.

DENOMINATIONS

In the present volume there is very little mention of the denomination of the families discussed. There is a straightforward explanation for this: in terms of attitudes towards childhood and in relation to the children themselves we found no religion-related differences among the various denominations.

This should not be surprising. In Hungary the concept of childhood and the idea of the exceptional status of the child had taken shape well before the onset of the Reformation, that is, before the emergence of denominational differences. The fact that there existed a very broad concept of childhood is attested, at the eve of the Reformation, by a text with the most unusual of origins.

In 1514, at the nadir of the history of serfdom in Hungary, the members of the Diet, incensed at the peasants' uprising that had recently been cruelly suppressed, passed a law containing some extremely strict regulations regarding serfs' obligations and restricting all the rights they had previously held. According to the severest of these measures they became "tied to the soil". This meant that serfs lost their freedom to move from one estate to another. In practice, serfs were denied the opportunity to use their labour as a bargaining tool in order to obtain better conditions. Previously they had been able to threaten a landowner with departure or promise another work in the future. In short, they had been able to change their terms of service and move from one place to another freely.

In spite of its severity, however, the 1514 law made a clear distinction between children and adults. In one paragraph it was stated that "if a mother takes her son with her on account of his tender years, the boy is obliged to return to his former dwelling place on reaching adulthood or a marriageable age".[1] This meant that if a mother, under the specific circumstances defined in later articles, mainly as a widow, chose to move, her infant son was to be allowed to leave with her and could only be claimed back once he had reached adulthood.

With the passing of this law the landowners, who enjoyed unlimited power over their serfs, restricted their own rights over serfs in childhood. Even though peasant households relied on the work of children from a very early age, there is no suggestion that the child serf had any obligations towards the landowner. Female children are not mentioned in the law, perhaps because they had a natural right to remain with their mother and this right was too obvious to receive special mention in the law. The provision stating that "girls...can freely marry and move"[2] clearly refers to daughters who chose to stay in one place together with their mother.

The concept of childhood in Hungary can be traced back even further in time. Here, however, the main point is that it already existed before the Reformation. In theory, attitudes towards childhood could have taken different forms among families of different denominations. In reality, however, it did not, most probably because of the very peaceful onset of the Reformation in Hungary. The period that comprises roughly the sixteenth and seventeenth centuries could be referred to as the time of conversions.

To begin with, the Reformation was a very slow process. While in western Europe the decision to adopt or reject it was in the hands of the highest secular authorities, in Hungary Protestant church organisations emerged without rulers being involved. The vast majority of the population of all three parts of Hungary had become Protestant by the 1570s, under Catholic kings, Catholic princes and Islamic sultans. During the sixteenth century there were only nine years, between 1562 and 1571, in which the ruler of Transylvania, John II, who had grown up a Catholic, adhered to Protestant tenets.

Thus religion was clearly a private matter. In Hungary, the secular authorities did not demand that people declare their religious affiliation, as happened, for example, several times in England. Conversion to Protestantism, mainly in the case of the aristocracy, was an individual decision. It was indicated more often than not merely by invitations of evangelically minded preachers to the churches of aristocratic estates, or by the family going to church instead of worshipping in the chapel of the castle. Data on these changes are hard to discover. Later on, from approximately the turn of the century, conversions in Royal Hungary took place in the opposite direction, although this did not happen in Transylvania or in the territory under Ottoman rule.

From among the Protestant subjects of the Catholic Habsburgs, however, many members of the aristocracy converted to Catholicism in the seventeenth century. These changes in religion are easier to trace since the people concerned made rather a show of their conversions. In the case of magnates, conversion usually took place by means of a declaration before an assembly of priests. However, we have no indications as to the changes in everyday life that resulted from the change in religion.

The reason for the lack of differences between the members of different denominations in secular matters is most probably to be found in the fact that people of that period were not separated by real religious borders. The conversions and re-conversions that took place during the sixteenth and the seventeenth centuries meant that some people changed religion several times, and it was common for families to include members of different denominations. Nor was it rare for one generation of a family to belong to a different denomination from the next.

A number of very good examples of nearly all the phenomena connected with religious conversion can be gleaned from facts scattered throughout the chapters contained in the present volume. These mainly concern Count Tamás Nádasdy and his family, several generations of which are mentioned in the course of this book.

Born in 1498, Nádasdy himself clearly began life as a Catholic. However, by the 1530s there were many Protestant intellectuals under his patronage and he employed Protestant preachers in many of the churches on his estates. At precisely the same time, in 1534, the count married Countess Orsolya Kanizsay in a Catholic ceremony. Even in the 1550s Nádasdy married off one of his nieces in a ceremony conducted by Catholic bishops. His wife, who was born in 1521 when evangelical teachings had just reached Hungary, also began life as a Catholic, but in a letter to her husband written in 1554 she quotes Calvin almost verbatim. As a widow, she chose Lutheran tutors to accompany her young son to Vienna. This son, Ferenc Nádasdy, attended the court from the family's palace in Vienna.

Ferenc Nádasdy was a Lutheran, educated by a father who might have been converted—if he ever really did break off relations with the Roman Catholic Church—at the age of forty at the earliest. As to his mother, Orsolya Kanizsay, it is hard to say whether she regarded herself, after conversion at some unknown date, as belonging to the Calvinist or the Lutheran denomination. His children represent the only undoubtedly Lutheran generation in the whole Nádasdy family. They were brought up by parents who were both born Lutherans.

In the next generation, another Count Ferenc Nádasdy, the great-grandson of Tamás, converted to Catholicism at the age of around twenty. The decision was influenced by Miklós Esterházy, a new convert himself. Esterhazy had earlier converted his wife, Krisztina Nyáry, the daughter of a staunch Calvinist couple. Nádasdy's bride, Countess Júlia Esterházy, was thus clearly Catholic by birth.

As a result of the many conversions and mixed-denomination families, the Catholic children of Júlia Esterházy and Ferenc Nádasdy had, in the middle of the seventeenth century, a very mixed group of people to take care of them. One set of grandparents was entirely Lutheran, the other Catholic, converted from different Protestant denominations either as children or adults, and only one of their parents was born a Catholic. It would be impossible here to list by denomination all the aunts, uncles, other relatives and servants of the children who came into constant contact with them.

It seems safe to say that there was no single family, from any of the social strata, in the Hungary of the sixteenth and seventeenth centuries, which belonged entirely to one denomination. We cannot even be sure that the example of the Nádasdy family, in which mixed marriages took place but were not characteristic, is among the best examples for a period when mixed marriages were in fact common. Examples could be cited of Lutheran or Calvinist children whose aunts were nuns and whose uncles were high prelates. The most famous Roman Catholic Church dignitary, for instance, Péter Pázmány, was also a convert from the Calvinist faith.

This should not, however, imply that there was no hostility between the different denominations. There were some very sad cases within families in which wives rejected their husbands as a result of their religion, or girls forced to feign conversion in order to be able to make a marriage convenient to their parents.

The beginning of the last third of the seventeenth century saw the onset of a most brutal Counter-Reformation in Royal Hungary, authorised by the Catholic king. By that time the process of conversions among the great families had ended. The vast majority had become Catholic.

It was only in the eighteenth century, after one or two generations of clear denominational status had been established, that distinctly different Catholic and Protestant attitudes towards children emerged. These attitudes, along with many other circumstances including the departure of the Turks and Transylvania's new status, were characteristic of a period very different from that discussed in *Beloved Children*.

In this book we are dealing with a period when it was natural even for the highest-ranking men to hug their children and for the most high-minded ladies to take their little sons along with them if they protested against being left at home. Whether the same was done in the eighteenth century is another question. It is generally accepted among historians that the forms of social communication became more formal at that time. The task of finding out the impact of fastidious etiquette on attitudes towards childhood, or the reasons for its emergence, lies with students of that period.

Notes

1 1514, article 21, paragraph 3.
2 1514, article 21, paragraph 1.

CHAPTER 1

THE FIRST TEN YEARS OF LIFE

CONCEPTION

THE MOST direct contemporary reference to the conception of a highborn child in the early modern age can be found in the extensive autobiography written by János Kemény in the mid-seventeenth century. According to stories told to him by his relatives, Kemény's father had "woken up to it" early, after a night spent in revelry, and he had been conceived as a result.[1] The event had come to be part of the family lore since clearly there had been witnesses to it: in flight from war, Kemény's parents had, at the time, been sharing a room with several other families.

To approach one's wife after a night spent drinking was doubtless not uncommon. However, the presence of others in the room at the time was very much contrary to the norms of the day. Society at that time regarded the sexual life of married couples as intimate and private. In his memoirs, written in the early eighteenth century, Miklós Bethlen was quite ready to inform his readers about his sexual experiences with prostitutes. However, he was more reserved when it came to sexual relations with his wife, arguing that "…it is not becoming to write about my bedchamber…"[2] A similar reticence can be discerned in a letter written by Pál Telegdy in 1588 to his bride, Kata Várday, on the subject of their approaching wedding night. He contrasts the public character of the wedding with the intimacy of their first night together. While they would both suffer embarrassment during the day, Telegdy promises Kata to "tuck up our shame in the dark of night".[3]

In keeping with this kind of attitude, it is not surprising that marital sex is rarely discussed in contemporary documents. Couples simply do not mention their sexual relationship in their letters. However, it seems that sexual intercourse was generally considered to be an opportunity to give and to experience pleasure. Proof of this can be found in a letter dictated by Éva Thököly to a clerk. She obviously regarded the idea of being her husband's primary source of pleasure as self-evident: "You will kill your own joy, the person on whom it primarily depends…if you kill me, a poor orphan."[4]

Nevertheless, there are various indirect references to the actual sexual act, which hint at good as well as bad experiences. In 1642 Ferenc Keglevich and Erzsébet Erdődy were involved in a lengthy and complex lawsuit in order to have their marriage dissolved on the grounds of sexual incompatibility. Keglevich made accusations of "sorcery", while his wife blamed his impotence for the failure of the marriage.[5] One can only suppose that they must have experienced a great deal of suffering before deciding to face the publicity of a divorce case. In contrast, András Jakusich's wife obviously found great fulfilment in her marriage. Just three months after her wedding, which took place in February 1608, she asked her father, Palatine György Thurzó, to move for the passing of a law by the Diet "to prevent newly married men from leaving their homes without their wives during the first two years of marriage". We know of the request from a letter sent by the bride's mother to her husband, the palatine.[6] As the highest dignitary of the Estates he was certainly in a position to propose bills. However, this particular request was conveyed to him simply to inform him of his daughter's happiness in marriage.

György Thurzó was himself happily married. He wrote to his wife in the eleventh year of their marriage, when they already had nine children, that "I would rather have you in my bed than a bed-warmer, my sweetheart. The Good Lord will surely allow us to see one another soon and embrace in good health."[7] Their daughter Zsófia was born a year after the letter was written. Since we know that Thurzó was rarely absent from home for long periods it is doubtful whether her birth was the outcome of the happy reunion referred to in the letter. However, many children were doubtless conceived when husbands returned after a long absence. Miklós Esterházy made the following, characteristic, contribution to the discussion surrounding the probable due date of his child in 1626: "...I do not know how you are counting the months, but there are surely at least three more weeks to go, since it was on the thirtieth day of March that I returned home from here at that time," he wrote from Pozsony in November.[8] His calculations were proved correct when the child was born on 31 December, exactly nine months after the return home mentioned in his letter.

Most commonly, however, the beginning of a pregnancy was dated with reference to the ceasing of menstruation. Countess Katalin Thurzó, for example, the wife of István Thököly, wrote to her mother in the spring of 1622, when, after the death of her infant son, she was hoping to become pregnant again: "The women here keep comforting me by saying that I am surely with child again but I cannot believe that, for the monthly sickness is on me every month." She was in no pain, but promised to let her mother know if and when anything "happened".[9] Nor did she have to wait longer than two months. On 13 January 1623 Katalin wrote to one of her aunts: "I am expecting any hour now what the Good Lord has promised—the arrival of the new guest in our house."[10] There were to be many more opportunities for her to experience the joy of expecting a baby. There are references to six further pregnancies at more or less regular intervals after the birth of her second son.[11]

Regular sexual relations within marriage were obviously common, the proof being the fairly regular arrival of new babies. The history of Kata Zrínyi's pregnancies serves as a good example. She lived with her first husband between 1565 and 1571, that is, between the ages of seventeen and twenty-four. She became pregnant for the first time the year they were married. She subsequently conceived at decreasing intervals of twenty-three, eighteen, seventeen, and twelve months. Between 1577, when she was thirty, and 1585, Kata lived with her second husband, and the rhythm of conceptions was similar. Their first child was born in the first year of their marriage and five live births followed at intervals of twenty-nine, twenty-four, twelve, thirteen, and fourteen months.[12] The fact that these were live births should be stressed, since miscarriages were not recorded in family chronicles—the main source of our information on pregnancies and births—and stillborn babies were very rarely mentioned. Only data on live births are available for the research into the sexual behaviour of married couples.

The family records of the Csáky family are a rare exception. Lord Chief Justice István Csáky recorded the birth of a stillborn daughter,[13] and it can therefore be assumed that records were kept of all the pregnancies of his three wives, with the exception of miscarriages. The large number of entries make it difficult to obtain a clear picture of the facts in the case of his third wife, Mária Barkóczi, whom he married in 1689 at the age of fifty-four.[14] However, with respect to his first wife, Margit Lónyay, there are no such uncertainties. She first became pregnant in 1654, one month after their wedding. Up until 1669, pregnancies followed at intervals of seventeen, nineteen, fifteen, fifteen, twenty-eight, seventeen, twenty-one, twenty-two, and fifteen months. Csáky's second wife, Klára Melith, first became pregnant in the winter of 1672, three months after the marriage. Successive pregnancies followed at intervals of twelve, fifteen, twelve, nine, twelve, and eleven months. István Csáky was nineteen when his first child was conceived, and it can be supposed that his first wife was probably not much younger, since Csáky was her second husband. Klára Melith had also had a husband before Csáky, and between the ages of thirty-seven and forty-five she presented her second husband with ten children, the interval between pregnancies decreasing with each one.

Regularly updated family records reveal that this was a usual sequence of events. A first child was often born shortly after the marriage, then further children appeared at intervals of usually less than, and rarely longer than, two years. When the interval between births was as long as twenty-eight or twenty-nine months, a miscarriage or stillbirth can be supposed to have occurred in between.

Due to the vagueness of contemporary terminology with respect to illnesses, it is almost impossible to determine the numbers of miscarriages. However, the miscarriage of a foetus did not necessarily lead to the death or subsequent infertility of the mother. Miklós Bethlen's two wives, Ilona Kun and Júlia Rédey, are instructive examples in this respect. Between them they gave birth to seventeen living babies, even though Bethlen mentions in his memoirs that his wives had had several miscarriages.[15] Since neither Ilona nor Júlia died during pregnancy or childbirth, these miscarriages must have occurred between successful pregnancies, none of them being fatal for the mother.

All the available information points to the fact that regular, and presumably unprotected, sexual intercourse was common among highborn married couples of the day. Data concerning the pregnancies of Kata Zrínyi during her two marriages, and data for the two wives of István Csáky nearly a century later, suggest two further conclusions. Firstly, the pregnancies of Kata Zrínyi and Margit Lónyay, the first wife of István Csáky, occurred at similar intervals, suggesting that the sexual life of a married couple was probably the same in the sixteenth and seventeenth centuries. The second conclusion is perhaps more important. It is based on the fact that Kata Zrínyi conceived at fairly regular intervals with her two husbands, while the available data indicate a marked difference, with respect to the intervals between pregnancies, between the two wives of István Csáky. Margit Lónyay, Csáky's first wife and his partner in his younger years, conceived at much longer intervals than Klára Melith, to whom Csáky was married between the ages of thirty-seven and forty-five. These facts indicate that the rate of conception must have been dependent on the natural capacities of the women.

It was the woman's biological capacities, in terms of conceiving and giving birth, that determined the number of children in a family. The most radical form of birth control was the death of the woman. Many women died in childbirth or shortly afterwards. This was the fate of both of István Csáky's wives and also of Kata Zrínyi. However, István Thököly's wife, Kata Thurzó, survived eight pregnancies and lived with her husband for a further fifteen years after the last. She died at the age of forty-seven, leaving him a widower. We know of several similar stories. Erzsébet Czobor, the wife of György Thurzó, survived nine live births and lived with her husband for another thirteen years before his death. Éva Thököly, the second wife of Pál Esterházy, survived seven deliveries and conceived for the last time at the age of thirty-two. She lived for another twenty-four years with her husband without bearing further children, and outlived him by three years.

PHYSICAL AND SOCIAL FORMS OF FAMILY PLANNING

Both Erzsébet Czobor and Éva Thököly were still of childbearing age when they suddenly ceased becoming pregnant. A similar situation can be seen in the case of several other women in their twenties and thirties. Their suddenly ceasing to become pregnant at regular intervals was probably not due to ill health, since they went on to live for several more years or decades. In some cases it might be assumed that the husband's loss of virility was to blame. Éva Thököly's husband, Pál Esterházy, for example, was already fifty-six when his last child was born.

On the other hand, many men of that age were obviously still in full possession of their masculine powers. Palatine Tamás Nádasdy was fifty-seven when his son was born in 1555. Another famous palatine, Miklós Esterházy, was fifty-nine, when his last son was born. His wife died in childbirth. István Csáky, who had several wives, fathered his last child at the age of sixty-three.

However, Erzsébet Czobor stopped having children when her husband, György Thurzó, was a mere thirty-seven years old. Proof that this was due to a deliberate decision on the part of the couple can be found in a letter written by Thurzó. During a long absence from home he wrote to his wife on the subject of their children and grandchildren. It appears that he felt somewhat bewildered at the existence of two generations of offspring of the same age, and he wrote to his wife suggesting that it would be better to "forget our youthful fervour and just be called father-in-law and mother-in-law, my dear".[16] All the evidence we have indicates that the couple lived in harmony throughout their married life.

The case of Éva Thököly and Pál Esterházy was very different. Their relationship deteriorated irrevocably in the spring of 1691. There had already been tension between them earlier in their marriage, but it was in that year that Éva Thököly wrote to her husband complaining that "You do not live with me any longer". Her husband must have made some serious accusations against her, for she argues in the same letter that she is "neither a gambler, nor a whore".[17] She went on to give birth to a son later, but it is uncertain whether the couple's relationship had improved temporarily or whether the baby was indeed the fruit of some marital infidelity. Whatever the truth, by early 1691 Esterházy and his wife had clearly adopted the kind of sexual patterns characteristic of dysfunctional marriages. Such couples usually had few children, if any. The contrast with data relating to marriages in which sexual intercourse was regular and unprotected inevitably leads to the conclusion that in unhappy marriages certain methods of contraception must have been used, or couples simply abstained from sexual intercourse.

Although there is a clear connection between unhappy marriages and low numbers, or lack, of children, there may also have been genetic reasons for low fertility. This was probably the case among the Báthorys, rulers of Transylvania, who were hoping to found a dynasty. Nevertheless, all the men in the family remained childless or had only few children.[18] A similar situation, although not as serious, occurred in another princely family of Transylvania, the Rákóczis, where the numbers of children were also small. From the beginning of the seventeenth century until 1660, all the children born to this family were male, with the exception of a single daughter born to Zsigmond Rákóczi.[19] However, since the survival of the dynasty could not be ensured by just one or two boys, it is unlikely that a deliberate choice had been made to have small families. In addition, marriages in the Rákóczi family, unlike those among the Báthorys, were, by all accounts, mainly happy.

In contrast, the low number of children born to another important family was obviously the result of a series of unhappy marriages. The men of one particular branch of the Perényi family, which had produced so many palatines that it became known as the "palatine line", were notorious for being unpleasant and violent. When Péter Perényi was held as a political prisoner by King Ferdinand following the Battle of Mohács in 1526, Anna Nádasdy wrote to her sister-in-law that she would be quite happy if Perényi were never released from prison, for he was a bad husband just like his father, Palatine Perényi, had been. "You must have heard how my lord Péter's father treated his wife and how he treats his own...," she wrote.[20] As for Gábor Perényi, the preacher at the funeral of his wife, Ilona Országh, showing complete disregard for convention, alluded to how much she had had to suffer because of her husband.[21] His vicious behaviour must have been common knowledge. Thus, not surprisingly, Gábor himself was the last of this aggressive line of the Perényi family.

Palatine Perényi and his heirs lived their unhappy lives in silence, while the discord between certain other couples had repercussions throughout the country. The case of Zsuzsanna Forgách and Ferenc Révay was even brought up at the Diet by Révay himself. Although Révay kept his wife locked up in a house surrounded by a triple wall, she was still abducted by Péter Bakich, who, according to the legal documents, had been "spurred on by crazed love".[22] Zsuzsa Forgách was twenty-five when she escaped, and it is hardly surprising that she had had no children by her husband. However, no children were born to her by Bakich, either. She was forty-three when, in 1625, another act of parliament finally cleared her and Péter Bakich of the charge of incest. Prior to this verdict it would have been unwise for the couple to have children; by the time they were cleared, it was already too late.

Any information suggesting that in certain situations people avoided having children should be regarded as particularly significant. Without such data, the high numbers of children born to couples who had regular and unprotected sexual relations might create the false impression that aristocratic families considered children simply as evidence of God's blessing and accepted them as they arrived, one after the other, in the course of nature. However, interruptions in this sequence in cases where there is no obvious biological cause; the low numbers of children, or even the absence of children, in unhappy marriages; and the absence of children in cases where a couple's relationship was considered to have been inspired by "crazed love", all indicate that couples at that time were aware of methods of contraception and made use of them.[23]

This awareness doubtless explains the fact that illegitimate children were very rare in aristocratic families. The unfortunate case of Erzsébet Pográny was an exception. She became pregnant by her fiancé, István Poltári Soós, after the couple's betrothal but before the wedding had taken place. He subsequently married another woman. Her son was declared illegitimate until his father's death in 1659, when Leopold I granted him full legal rights.[24] By this time Ferenc Soós had already reached adulthood. The emperor justified the step he had taken by referring to Soós's loyalty to the crown and to the emperor himself. However, such cases were presumably rare, since in extant letters written during this period there is no mention of highborn unmarried mothers, nor do we have any data with respect to children born within less than nine months of the parents' marriage.

Besides physical methods of contraception, the most likely explanation for the absence of illegitimate children, or at least of any data referring to such children, is the fact that a social form of contraception was also practised. The life of the famous poet and lover Bálint Balassi serves as a good example. He lived in the second half of the sixteenth century, and, like all the other illustrative examples used in the current study, he was an aristocrat. However, as a poet he revealed more than was usual about his private life.[25] It is clear that Balassi's lovers were either prostitutes or highborn married women. The poems he wrote to his lovers are full of passion, but they do not conceal the fact that he only felt secure with women who belonged to one of these two social groups, none of whom would be likely to make him a father. In the case of the women of pleasure the reasons are obvious, while married women were unlikely to allow themselves to be identified as mothers of bastards. Illegitimate children could potentially be presented to their husbands as legitimate offspring.

While Balassi indulged in such love affairs without remorse, others conducted their extra-marital amours in secret. A century later Miklós Bethlen, for example, like Balassi, frequented brothels. The only difference between the two was that, unlike Balassi, Bethlen expressed no feelings of love for the prostitutes he encountered there. Instead, he was filled with self-loathing and, according to his memoirs, never completed the sexual act.[26] Although other aristocrats do not refer in their letters to this aspect of their lives, many of them doubtless had recourse to the services of prostitutes.

It would seem that adulterous sexual relationships with married women were so safe that they were very rarely recorded. The most famous case from the seventeenth century, however, that of István Csáky, a relative of the István Csáky mentioned earlier, became common knowledge. He was known by his contemporaries as the lover of Prince Gábor Bethlen's second wife, Katherine of Brandenburg. Even Csáky's mother, Anna Wesselényi, hinted at the fact in her letters.[27] Csáky and Katherine had no children.

This social method of avoiding the blessing of children was not always without danger. In the mid-sixteenth century, János Török had his wife Anna Kendy beheaded when he discovered her adultery.[28] The wife of Miklós Thököly resorted to sorcery against her unfaithful husband and his mistress, although she too was involved in an extra-marital affair. She was tried for witchcraft in 1662.[29]

Finally, it can be supposed that the safest method of social family planning was to engage in sexual relationships with servants. Anna Wesselényi was alarmed at the sight of her seven-year-old son "catching" maidservants, and told a friend about the incident in a letter.[30] Miklós Bethlen was sixteen when he tried to persuade a nurse to commit "the crime" with him, and he went on to make further attempts with other members of the household.[31] Records of the interrogations during the case against Erzsébet Báthory, who was accused of cruelty in 1610, reveal that she had a lover among her servants.[32] Her case is an obvious example of how aristocratic self-control usually failed in the presence of servants. It can be assumed that aristocratic men fathered children in families of low rank and made no provision for them at all. The opposite is far less likely, although aristocratic women might occasionally have had children by fathers of humble birth who then grew up with the legitimate offspring of the aristocratic marriage. None of the existing sources refer to the presence of bastards in aristocratic circles.

EXPECTING A CHILD

We have discussed the different methods of family planning in detail, since they point to the fact that children were rarely born to aristocratic families without the parents' will. This does not mean that all pregnancies were planned in the modern sense of the term. However, it does suggest that couples refrained from using such methods of contraception when they considered themselves ready to bring up children and when there were emotional or other reasons for wishing to start a family. Noble families in the sixteenth and seventeenth centuries were therefore delighted to learn that a woman had become pregnant and were always eager to be given news of the births of children in other families.

Couples who remained childless were often willing to make great sacrifices in order to conceive. Women often subjected themselves to painful medical treatment. There were doctors who specialised in the treatment of infertility, and one such doctor, Gáspár Szegedi, was practising in as early as the middle of the sixteenth century.[33] He became very widely known and his services were sought by numerous aristocratic families. His most famous patient was Orsolya Kanizsay, wife of Palatine Tamás Nádasdy. The talented doctor, a graduate of the University of Padua, proved successful in this case, too. In 1555, nineteen years after their marriage and after a great deal of heartache, the couple finally had a son, whom they named Ferenc. Miklós Esterházy and his first wife resorted to other means in order to overcome their problem. It appears that Orsolya Dersffy herself found a suitable partner for her husband in order to secure the birth of a child for the family. This somewhat surprising story seems to have been accepted by contemporaries, and its authenticity is supported by several indirect data.[34]

Couples were anxious to have children for several reasons. The most common and understandable of these was doubtless the desire to secure the future of the family and of the family fortune. One of the most irrational reasons was recorded by Miklós Bethlen in his memoirs. He considered that having numerous children was a proof of masculinity.[35] Couples may also have been influenced by the fact that social relationships and social prestige could often be enhanced through the advantageous marriages of their own children. Whatever the reasons for having children, there are many indications that a large and well-cared-for family was regarded as the basis upon which the good reputation of both the mother and the father was built. The various rational and irrational reasons, together with the biological impulse itself, were doubtless combined within the emotion of parental love. We cannot tell to what extent parental love influenced conception, but there is evidence of it in several cases from the very beginning of the pregnancy.

Loving parents often called their unborn babies by pet names. The unfortunate Krisztina Nyáry, for instance, who was left a widow at the age of seventeen, four months pregnant and with one baby daughter already, wrote in a letter of how she had been left alone "with my little heavy one just four months old and my little nine-month-old daughter".[36] We know of no other examples of the use of the name she gives to the child she is carrying—her "little heavy one"; men and women alike usually referred to their unborn babies as their "new guests". The expression was used by György Thurzó in a letter written during his journey to see his daughter at the end of her pregnancy: "…the Lord has promised us a new guest".[37] The palatine was travelling as quickly as possible, in the hope of reaching his daughter before the baby was born. Already himself the father of ten children he had written a little earlier to his own wife, teasing her about "the rumours that God has blessed us with a new guest and new hope".[38] The word "foetus" was also used, but always in the context of expressing joy at the approaching arrival of a child. However, one of the most beautiful phrases was used by a servant, who was informing his master about the condition of his wife and their long-awaited child: "My lady and her good fruit...are healthy", he wrote.[39] This was obviously an allusion to the biblical verse in which Jesus is referred to as the "fruit" of Mary's womb.

The joyful atmosphere of expectation and the positive experiences of expectant women led people to regard a healthy pregnancy as natural. The overwhelming majority of pregnancies were indeed free of complications, and women were generally active throughout. Krisztina Nyáry, for example, visited her husband in Pozsony in 1626 when she was eight months pregnant and stayed there for some time.[40] In 1628, and again eight months pregnant, we know that she was busy with financial matters in relation to the family estates[41] and that she travelled even later.[42] Orsolya Kanizsay, who had had so many problems conceiving, was able to provide for her husband's retinue, sending them provisions just a few days before giving birth. In her letter to Nádasdy she apologises for not having sent similar provisions earlier, adding in jest "I have been preoccupied with waiting for the new guest. I do not know where he has got to, nor when to expect him..."[43] Ferkó was born five days after the letter was sent. Anna Bakich, in a long letter informing her husband about important public matters and domestic events, mentions her pregnancy almost as an afterthought: "I am still very heavy...but I will soon be able to write or send you good news, God willing."[44] Just before the birth of her twelfth child, Kata Zrínyi wrote to her husband about developments in a lawsuit, telling him that he should not worry and that she would arrange everything. The only mention she made of her pregnancy was that "I am heavier day by day", which suggests that her due date was fast approaching.[45]

It appears that Kata Zrínyi, like most of her contemporaries, did not expect there to be any complications, otherwise she would have summoned a midwife or doctor, or both. Some women did so even in the earliest phase of pregnancy. When Erzsébet Czobor was expecting her first child she had no reason to suppose that anything was wrong. However, since the baby boy died soon after birth the family was more careful during her next pregnancy. Thurzó first found a midwife in the neighbourhood[46] and later sent for another midwife who was more widely known and who lived some distance away.[47] On other occasions he sent not only for expert midwives, but also for doctors from Pozsony and Vienna.[48] Many families sent for the midwife only shortly before the baby was due—providing, of course, that the pregnancy had been without complications. This was what happened in the case of Boldizsár Batthyány's wife in 1571.[49]

Fathers-to-be often had to spend a great deal of time far from home, since they were often busy with the administration of their estates or caught up in public affairs. The regular letters they wrote to their wives or to members of the household provide a wealth of information about how pregnancy was experienced. When a midwife or a doctor was needed, it was usually the husband's task to find one. Some husbands advised their wives about diet. Miklós Esterházy even asked for an exemption from fasting during Lent for his wife, Krisztina Nyáry, for fear that lack of meat would reduce her strength.[50] An extreme example of this kind of care is Kristóf Batthyány's intention of taking his wife from one side of the country to the other, during the winter of 1542 when she was in the last weeks of her pregnancy, since he considered the air there better for the mother-to-be during the delivery. In a desperate letter his uncle's wife, Kata Szvetkovich, managed to dissuade him from taking his wife on such a long and dangerous journey.[51] László Csáky, on the other hand, demonstrated not only his thoughtfulness, but also his common sense, when he stayed with his wife until their child was born rather than leaving her to attend the opening ceremony of the Diet in 1649.[52]

THE BIRTH

It is likely that a mother's attitude towards her children depended, to a great extent, on her own age at the time of giving birth, although the shortage of data means we have no conclusive evidence.

The youngest to give birth in this period was the mother of Miklós Antal Esterházy. He was born in 1655 when his mother, Orsolya Esterházy, was barely fourteen.[53] From among the members of the aristocracy she had the highest number of children in this period, giving birth to seventeen surviving daughters and sons. Her last child was born when she was thirty-nine. Some women gave birth even after they had reached the age of forty. Zsófia Illésházy was forty-three at the time of her thirteenth live birth in 1590, that of her last child, Anna.[54] Kata Thököly gave birth for the last time in 1701 at the age of forty-five.[55]

Of course, not all children were fortunate enough to be cared for by their own mothers, since some women died in childbirth or soon afterwards as a result of complications. But Kata Thököly survived many deliveries, she died giving birth to her last baby. Zsófia Illésházy lived long enough to see her tenth child, Miklós Esterházy, as an adolescent, while Orsolya Esterházy died suddenly, two years after the birth of her last child.

Personal letters, the most important source of information about family life, rarely describe the actual birth, so we know very little about how labour was experienced. Since fathers were usually at home for the birth, events did not often have to be described in letters to them. Others were usually informed of the arrival of the new baby in very brief notes. Some sources do, however, occasionally refer to the terrible pain that some women had to endure.

The most horrific case was that of one of the daughters of Count György Thurzó, whose name is not mentioned in the letter that describes her ordeal.[56] In the summer of 1616 she gave birth to a stillborn child, and it was discovered that it had been "dead for two days in the mother". It was reported that she "could have delivered two children at a time with that degree of suffering". The wife of a local pastor was with her, probably as a midwife, but possibly also to comfort her in her terrible pain. It seems likely that the difficult labour was unexpected, since the young countess's mother arrived only afterwards to take her daughter away with her in a cart transformed into a bed. The young woman apparently recovered and went on to have several children. According to the family records none of Thurzó's daughters died in 1616, and all those who were married at that time had several children later.[57]

All that is known about several other young mothers is that they were "not well" for some time after giving birth. Erzsébet Szvetkovich, for example, the wife of Kristóf Batthyány, was ill for a long time after the birth of a healthy son in 1542.[58] Kata Várday was close to death after the birth of her first daughter, Kata Telegdy, in January 1590.[59] After the birth of her second daughter, Anna, in April 1591, she had such severe constipation that even her brother-in-law and her husband exchanged letters about a possible cure.[60]

It is clear that enduring often horrific deliveries indicated an incredible will to live on the part of these women. Regardless of any data we may have, giving birth to eight or ten, let alone seventeen, children must have been terribly hard on both young and older mothers. Some were unable to cope with the strain on their bodies. It was by no means rare for a woman to die in childbirth even before her baby. The wife of István Pogrányi, for example, died in 1627, and all the women in attendance confirmed that the child was "still tossing about in the belly of the woman for two hours". They wanted to take the child out, but they were prevented from doing so by the sister-in-law of the dead woman who wished to deprive her brother of an heir.[61] The form of intervention envisaged by the midwives appears, by the tone of the narration, not to have been unusual. Babies could be cut out of their dead mothers' bodies, but nothing could be done if the child died before being delivered. In 1670 Margit Lónyay died "on the third day after terrible suffering…for she was unable to part with her burden".[62] She was "a silent sufferer", although others may well have suffered with less forbearance. There is no doubt that the main cause of death among women was childbirth or subsequent complications.

The risks connected with bearing children were well known among people of this period. Nevertheless, there are no data indicating fear of childbirth, but countless references to careful preparations for the great event. György Thurzó invited a specialist to his home in 1598. He wrote to his wife that "He knows of methods and medicaments that will help you to have an easy delivery if you take them."[63] Beside the midwife and the doctor there were usually some experienced female relatives and the mother of the woman in labour present at the delivery. People sometimes came from far away to help. In the autumn of 1571 Boldizsár Batthyány's wife travelled a great distance to help a relative in her confinement. The proud father thanked her in grateful letters afterwards.[64] As soon as she received her son-in-law's letter Erzsébet Czobor rushed to the side of one of her daughters who was in labour. "I am busy taking care of her", she wrote to her husband, and the tone of the letter suggests that this was only natural.[65] In the autumn of 1635 László Csáky took his wife, Magdolna Batthyány, to Vienna, for she "had some troubles and had to be taken there". Her mother was with them. They managed to get to the specialist in time. "God has given us a son", was the reaction of Magdolna's delighted mother-in-law.[66]

Letters were often sent to announce the birth of a child, and such letters reveal something of the relief felt by the family after a successful birth. "I would like to inform you that my dear wife has given birth to a son by the grace of God", wrote István Gyulai, in Latin, to Kristóf Batthyány in 1541.[67] In 1608 György Thurzó was delighted to share the news about his daughter, writing that "God has favoured her and blessed her with a beautiful son."[68] On receiving Péter Révay's letter announcing his good news, Pál Czobor's wife replied: "You write that the Good Lord has visited you with a beautiful son, let His holy name be praised for it."[69] "God gave my wife a beautiful daughter on the thirtieth day of last August, praised be His holy name", wrote Pál Pálffy to a friend in 1644.[70] Most of these letters or announcements are solemn in tone, although one exception is the diary entry written by László Rákóczi, in which he records the birth of his daughter in 1656: "God has given us a little Frauenzimmerchen out of His love towards us."[71]

BOYS AND GIRLS

Boys and girls seem to have been equally welcome. However, deep in their hearts all parents expected sons. In 1560 Anna Bakich wrote to her husband, Mihály Révay, promising "a valiant knight to occupy your house".[72] Like many other mothers in that period she was obviously hoping for a boy. György Thurzó, who had already lost two young sons, wrote in his new-year greetings to his wife, Erzsébet Czobor, on 1 January 1593: "May the Lord bless you with a beautiful son in the New Year."[73]

Many years later Miklós Esterházy spoke less solemnly when he wished the same for his wife, Krisztina Nyáry. He informed her that one of their relatives had had a son, and added: "Let us trump this achievement, God willing."[74] His son, István, born to his first wife, was nine years old at the time. Not long after the birth of his long-awaited son, Tamás Nádasdy was looking forward to the next one. In 1559 he wrote to his wife, Orsolya, in response to her request for the release of a certain prisoner, that her request would be granted if she acted as she had done "when God gave Ferenc to this world".

It was common at the time to hope for boys. Nor was the family's attitude in that matter influenced by the number or gender of the children they already had. When a daughter was born, the parents and relatives seem almost to have offered one another consolation. While György Thurzó and his wife, Erzsébet Czobor, were still waiting for a first son, he wrote to her that the daughters they already had were also gifts of God: "May the Lord give them a long life and may we take delight in them."[75] This seems to have been the general attitude of fathers towards their daughters in those days, nor would it have been unusual to console a family in their disappointment after the birth of a girl. In a letter written by one of Erzsébet Czobor's sisters-in-law, Erzsébet is offered consolation after once again becoming grandmother to a baby girl: "I have learnt that God has given my relative a beautiful little daughter. May she be brought up to honour the Lord's holy name and to your and my brother's great delight. We would indeed have been better pleased if the Lord had chosen to give her a son, but one cannot tell the Lord what to do…It often comes to pass that God gives these poor girls husbands who do great services to their relatives, so let us praise the holy name of God for everything."[76]

This hope for good future husbands for new daughters had to be expressed more often in some families than in others; the distribution of male and female children was highly uneven. In the first half of the sixteenth century the case of Bernát Thurzó and Katalin Neydecki, whose marriage produced four sons and four daughters, can be regarded as a rare exception.[77] Similarly unusual was the Felsővadász branch of the Rákóczi family, which, apart from a single daughter, produced only sons for three generations from Prince Zsigmond to György Rákóczi II.[78] It was more usual for both boys and girls to be born to a family, but with a marked difference between the genders of each. Ferenc Dessewffy had six sons and three daughters in the first half of the sixteenth century.[79] Lord Chief Justice István Csáky had two sons and seven daughters by three successive wives in the second half of the seventeenth century.[80] Members of the Esterházy family, which was probably the largest family of the period, kept detailed records of all their offspring. The common ancestor of all branches of the family, Ferenc, had ten sons and three daughters in the sixteenth century. One of his nephews, Dániel, had eleven sons and four daughters, while Palatine Pál had sixteen sons and eight daughters born to two wives in the second half of the seventeenth century.[81] However, the differences must have been evened out overall by the same genetic mechanisms that operate today, which means that a slightly higher number of boys than girls must have been born in each generation.

Given the desire to have sons and the tendency to anticipate the birth of a baby boy, it would be natural to suppose that, as children, boys were treated more favourably than girls. There is no proof, however, of any discrimination within the family, whether emotional or social, between boys and girls. During the sixteenth century both the sons and the daughters of aristocratic families were sent to stay at the court in Vienna or Prague. The social function of this practice was clear to the aristocracy of the time. The wife of Ferenc Batthyány, for example, was annoyed that her nephew, Boldizsár Batthyány, did not visit the Viennese court regularly and she reprimanded him severely: "I have heard that you do not like staying at court…It would be better for you to show the greatest attention both to His Majesty and to the country, for those present at court are far more likely to be taken account of than absent servants."[82] In the same letter Countess Batthyány points out to Boldizsár the example of her husband, but she could also have mentioned Boldizsár's own father, Kristóf Batthyány, who had also been sent to Vienna as a child. He became accustomed to life at the court and felt so at home "in the queen's cage" that his parents had great difficulty luring him home.[83]

At that time the group of older and younger children at the Vienna court comprised both boys and girls. In 1545 King Ferdinand gave Mária Szvetkovich a large sum of money just before she left the court to marry János Choron. The king justified his generous gift by recalling how "Mária has been serving our beloved daughters ever since her childhood."[84] Mária must have met her fiancé at the court, too. It was also decided at the royal court that László Bánffy's daughter should marry Gábor Majláth. Her future mother-in-law referred to her as someone who was in the company of Her Majesty Queen Anna.[85]

Later on, from about the end of the sixteenth century, the visits to the court became shorter, but they retained their political character. István Csáky sent his two-year-old daughter, Anna, to the king's court with her mother in 1629, at a time when he was trying to clear himself of various political charges. He wrote to a friend: "I have sent my wife to His Majesty with my sweet little daughter to represent me there and as a token to show that though I could not send my heart, I sent my most precious treasures instead."[86]

Appearing at court worked in a similar way in the opposing camp. Three-year-old Mária Erdődy occasionally appeared at the court of Gábor Bethlen, prince of Transylvania, the archenemy of Ferdinand. Her mother took her along, since her father wanted his family to be seen among the prince's entourage. However, Mária's mother did not like being there. On one particular occasion she wanted to go home but was detained at the court, and she wrote to her relatives describing how "little Mária is strongly pleading with His Majesty" to let them go home.[87] Some of the letters suggest that Mária, or Marianka as she was known affectionately, usually had her meals in the company of the prince and his entourage.[88]

It also seems to have been quite common for aristocratic fathers to take their children—boys and girls alike—to sessions of the Diet. We know of a parliamentary report written with childlike seriousness by one little boy.[89] We also know that in 1625 the wife of Miklós Esterházy went several times to Sopron, where sessions of the Diet were being held, taking with her his son by his first marriage and her own two little girls.[90] Pál Esterházy, still in his teens at the time, described a ball held during the Diet. There had been so many young ladies there that he could not remember whom he had danced with.[91]

It is very difficult to ascertain whether certain children were given preferential treatment on these occasions. It is likely that they were, since where extensive correspondence is available it makes clear that some children were preferred above their siblings and that parents had favourites. The most famous story is that of Zsigmond Rákóczi, the son of Zsuzsanna Lórántffy and György Rákóczi I.[92] The couple had two sons who survived into adulthood and of the two they favoured Zsigmond from the very beginning. The fact that Zsuzsanna Lórántffy refused to give financial support to her other son, György Rákóczi II, then waging an unsuccessful war against Poland, may even have had some bearing on the course of Hungarian history. In other cases parental preferences did not have such serious consequences. Kristóf Batthyány, for example, had two sons, Gáspárkó and Boldizsár, and the latter was the darling of the whole family. All his whims were catered to. He was given books, fancy clothes and whatever else he wanted. His sensible aunt tried to intervene, in a letter written to a tutor, who was supervising the boy: "Boldizsár should be treated in just the same way as Gáspárkó." She argued that he should not have all the expensive clothes he wanted made for him, "but only clothes of the same broadcloth as Gáspárkó".[93] However, the boy continued to be spoilt and went on to become a highly educated but rather unpleasant young man. As an adult he quarrelled with everyone in his family.

Of course, there is no way of establishing the parents' motives for choosing a favourite from among their usually numerous children. However, it seems surprising that throughout his life György Thurzó's favourite remained one of his daughters, Borbála—who was known by the pet names Babuska, Borbálka or Borissenka—even after the birth of his long-awaited son Imricskó. When the boy was born Thurzó, in an eloquent letter, praised God for giving him a son. His relationship with his daughters did not change at all, and Babuska remained his darling. Once she was in the room, where her father was writing a letter to his wife, so the words he quotes are doubtless recorded exactly. This is probably the only source that reveals how a child addressed his or her father in that period. Asking him to summon her absent mother and grandmother home she calls him "Pane Apka", addressing him in Slovakian, the native language of the Thurzós. Borissenka was not dissatisfied with the company of her "Sir Daddy", but she was unhappy at not being allowed outside without her mother.[94]

MOTHERS AND FATHERS

Fifty years after the incident just mentioned György Rákóczi II described a similar situation. This time the child was a boy, his son Ferkó, and the letter he was writing was to his own mother. Ferkó, he told her, "being present while I am writing", had been asked whether he wanted to visit his grandmother. The boy was delighted at the idea. Ferkó's mother was very probably at home, but he was allowed to stay in his father's room while his father was writing a letter.[95]

These scenes, in which we see Thurzó and Rákóczi together with their young children, appear quite natural, even though these fathers were busy men who had plenty to occupy them apart from playing with their offspring. They were both active and influential politicians. As a member of the Royal Council, György Thurzó was one of the leading personalities of the country at that time. György Rákóczi had recently been made prince of Transylvania and was engaged in renewing his father's and predecessors' western connections.

The fact that these busy fathers cared for their children and were often with them is indicative of typical contemporary attitudes towards children. Children were not seen as the responsibility of their mothers alone; fathers were expected to take an equal share in caring for them. Transgressions of these norms provoked angry public reactions.

One notorious case arose in the Perényi family. Péter Perényi, who has already been mentioned for his reputation as a bad husband, allowed his son Ferenc, then about eight years old, to be taken captive by the Turks in 1532 in order to save his own life. The full details of the incident are not known as the sources contain many contradictions.[96] It remains unclear whether they were taken captive by the Turks together, or whether Perényi sent for his son to replace him as a prisoner, in fulfilment of a promise made in order to obtain his own release. Indignant contemporaries claim that not even the sultan believed such behaviour possible.[97] None of these letters attempted to justify Perényi's deed by arguing that the freedom he had purchased by the sacrifice of his son was used for the benefit of his country or his king.

The general opinion regarding this deed was expressed discreetly by Pastor Mihály Sztárai. A former chaplain to the family, he wrote a biography of Ferenc in which he spoke twice of the sorrow felt by both the mother and the father at their son's captivity. After "the mother and father threw their young child to the savage tigers in a flood of tears", "the father's and mother's hearts almost broke in their longing for their son".[98] Sztárai did not dare to criticise Perényi directly, but in the words he attributes to the boy in the biography he makes his own verdict clear. Pleading with the sultan for his release from prison, Sztárai has Ferenc Perényi say that he will kill his father but spare his mother, because "she shed tears for me when I was handed over to Your Highness, but my cruel father was not sorry for me at all, he had no tears in his eyes. His behaviour showed his indifference, for had he considered me his son and felt even a spark of love towards me, he could have paid my ransom with only half of his vast fortune."[99]

His mother's role in the incident is unclear, nor is it of primary importance here. The case was an exceptional one and met with general condemnation. However, the fact that Sztárai did not differentiate between the sorrow of the child's mother and father, and that in his biography Ferenc expected identical behaviour from his parents and a sacrifice on the part of his father, is revealing of contemporary attitudes. Parents would normally be expected to behave in such a way. Although there were both bad fathers and bad mothers, there was no clear distinction between the roles of father and mother in everyday life.

It was, naturally, the mother's task to see that her children were taken care of. This was taken so much for granted that there is scarcely any mention of it in the letters. This lack of data might even suggest that in large households children were not taken care of directly by their mothers but were left to the care of servants. However, such an assumption would be false. The scattered information available indicates that even the noblest households were dependent on the mother's presence. This is illustrated by a letter written by György Thurzó, in which he refers to the fact that Babuska was not even allowed to go outdoors without her mother. There is also mention of one occasion when the wife of György Rákóczi II was intending to go on a journey but decided to stay at home when her son Ferkó became ill.[100]

Nor was it the case that healthy children were left to the care of servants in aristocratic families. Margit Choron describes how her daughter was faced with a dilemma: although she wanted to visit Ferenc Nádasdy and his family with her mother in the autumn of 1584, she was forced to stay at home because her "old woman" was taken ill and she had nobody with whom she could leave her little son. She dared not take the child with her, for "there are so many illnesses around these days".[101] This suggests that it would have been natural to take the child along, but that, once the epidemic had made that impossible, the "old woman", the head of the women servants, would have been expected to take care of him. In the end the boy's mother did not leave her child with the ordinary servants but instead gave up the idea of her long-planned visit.

On one occasion Orsolya Kanizsay travelled to Vienna without her son Ferkó, in order to meet her husband. Her preparations indicate how unusual it was to go on a journey without her child.[102] On other occasions she took him along, just as other mothers travelled with their children. However, it was also common for children to stay with relatives, often with their grandmothers, if their mothers were travelling. On one occasion Mária Forgách intended to go away without her son, Palkó Révay, but the child cried so much at the strangeness of the situation that his mother took him along with her.[103] Some sixty years earlier Anna Bakich wrote to her husband to tell him that their daughter, Anicska, had stayed with her mother-in-law while she was attending a christening. Both of them were quite happy: "Your mother was delighted to have her and Anicska was very happy to stay with her."[104] An incident from 1561 illustrates how helpless even the wealthiest household could be in the absence of the children's mother. After the death of his wife, the grief-stricken Miklós Zrínyi sent his three daughters to stay with his friend, Ferenc Batthyány. However, he had little idea what to send with them. "I do not know what I should have sent along with them. If your wife finds out that they need anything, please let me know and I will arrange for it to be sent at once", he wrote to Batthyány.[105]

Ferenc Batthyány and Miklós Zrínyi were the most outstanding generals of the day and held important positions in the state, yet their correspondence about the little girls' belongings was by no means unusual. Husbands would often stand in for their wives in exceptional circumstances, such as the illness of the children or of their mother. On such occasions fathers often stayed at home, even if it meant neglecting their official duties. In 1588 István Lónyay apologised for not having answered a letter, saying "my wife and one of my children were very ill and it was not sure which way the Lord would turn their condition".[106] János Telegdy wrote a hasty letter to his brother "late at night" to inform him that he was not able to visit him as he had promised because his wife and child had suddenly fallen ill.[107] In 1643 László Csáky wrote to his mother that he could not suggest a date when he might meet her since his three little sons were ill. His mother, Anna Wesselényi, commented on the situation in a letter written to her other son: "The poor boy doesn't know what to do with so many invalids at home."[108]

It is strange that Anna Wesselényi did not offer to go and help her son and his wife as grandmothers and other relatives usually did. She could perhaps have taken the boys to her own home. Borbála Thurzó even offered to help one of her distant relatives when she learned that he could not attend a meeting of the county council because of the illness of his little son and of the daughter of someone who was staying with them. "I wrote to him, telling him to bring the little girl and boy to my house. I will take care of them and have already sent for the doctor", she wrote to Erzsébet Czobor.[109]

It was also quite common for children to be left with their fathers even when their mothers were not ill. It was natural for a mother to entrust the children to their father when she went to visit someone, or if she was simply travelling for pleasure. Thurzó's wife left their children in her husband's care even when they were ill. On one such occasion he wrote to her that "Our daughters are all better and easier now." Speaking of Babuska, then one and a half years old, he added: "The little one is especially well. I have played with her a lot today."[110] In the meantime, Erzsébet Czobor was staying with her mother, a detail we learn from another letter written to her by Thurzó to summon them both home. In the letter he wrote the following day he tells his mother-in-law that "little Borbálka has been cured by the Lord and you can play with her just as you have done before". He wrote to his wife that "I have given Borissenka a kiss from you."[111]

Several sources reveal that children travelled with their father without being accompanied by their mother. Ferkó Nádasdy, when he was just five years old, went to Vienna with his father. That this was regarded as quite natural is suggested by the letter written by Tamás Nádasdy to his wife at home, in which there is no indication that there was anything extraordinary in the father and the little boy travelling without the child's mother.[112] Another letter refers to ten-year-old Imre Thurzó and his father staying together in a village near Pozsony in October 1608.[113] This suggests that Thurzó had taken his son along to the Diet and that they had found lodgings outside the overcrowded town. In a letter written to György Rákóczi I, his wife asks him to send her absent teenage sons home.[114]

Fathers were expected to take their children to see the doctor and to accompany them to and from relatives, and these were tasks they seem to have accepted readily. Any attempt to shirk such responsibility met with the rebuke of friends or relatives. Kristóf Batthyány, for example, appears to have avoided being with his family as much as he could. He often sent his sons to stay with his uncle, Ferenc Batthyány, and was often unwilling to go and fetch them home. When this happened his aunt would send word that he was expected to accompany the boys' home in person.[115] Much more typical is the kind of behaviour illustrated in the following example. One little girl, named Orsicska, had been staying with relatives for some time, and when the child wished to go home and asked for transport to be sent for her, her father, whose name is not known, went to collect her at once.[116]

Fathers and mothers obviously co-operated in disciplining their children. This is true even of Kristóf Batthyány and his wife, even though their marriage was an unhappy one. Dissatisfied with the pedagogical methods used by the nun, who was teaching their children, Batthyány's wife complained to her husband. The absent father wrote immediately to the nun: "Sister Anna, I have known for some time that you chastise my children, that you are cruel to them and beat them, and that you are alienating them from my family and relatives."[117] Batthyány warned the woman to behave properly if she wished to remain in the service of the Batthyány family. It is surprising that boys of eight or nine should have been entrusted to a woman rather than to a man, but it was quite common to reprimand a tutor if he or she acted against the will of the family.

Harsh corporal punishment was considered unacceptable in aristocratic families of that time. However, milder punishment of this kind was tolerated. Even Tamás Nádasdy sometimes considered it necessary, although he was obviously familiar with rather more subtle methods of discipline as well. He once wrote to his wife to say that although he had bought the present that Ferkó had asked for, the boy should not expect to get something for nothing: "Unless he writes himself next time, or at least signs the letter in his own hand, I shall not send or give him anything."[118] The boy was five at the time. This implies that Nádasdy wished to teach the child—with his wife's co-operation—that human relationships should be reciprocal. The child was only to expect a present from his father if he himself gave something in return. In another letter Nádasdy suggests that his wife should entrust the child to someone who "will spank Ferkó" when necessary.[119]

A spanking was obviously acceptable in aristocratic families, but tutors or nurses who were cruel to the children were repri-manded or dismissed. Pál Esterházy remembered a tutor, who, "being a very rough man, beat me a lot, often three times a day. Finally he was dismissed."[120] The same thing happened to the tutor of Miklós Bethlen, who had beaten and humiliated his pupil. Nevertheless, it is puzzling that parents should have let the relationship between the boys and their tutors deteriorate to such an extent.

It was more common for highborn children to be spoilt than to be treated cruelly. The giving of presents is the most obvious and best-documented form in which children were indulged. It was usually the fathers who gave presents to their children, since they often had occasion to travel to distant towns and provinces.

Children were quite used to receiving presents, as illustrated by the following two incidents. In 1500 the sons of János Korvin welcomed one of their male relatives with the cry: "What have you brought for us?"[121] Nearly a century and a half later, little Pál Esterházy asked the same question of a prelate who was visiting his home.[122] The little Korvin boys were given cakes, while Pál Esterházy received a devotional picture and a rosary.

Cakes and fruit, especially tropical fruits such as oranges or pomegranates, were often given as gifts. Kristóf Batthyány sent his sons, who were staying with his uncle at the time, a gift of chicory.[123] However, the best surprises were always toys. The great-grandsons of Kristóf Batthyány, Bódiskó and Ádámkó, received a big box of toys from their father who was then in Vienna.[124] It was even more common for presents to be given in person. Tamás Nádasdy once sent home "some small presents in a box" for his three-year-old son. He asked his wife to keep them until he arrived home, so that he could give them to the little boy himself: "I often set off so quickly that I cannot buy anything for him and you have commissioned me to bring him a present whenever I am away", he wrote in the letter that accompanied the box.[125]

In the above example it was the child's mother who asked her husband to bring presents for their child. In other cases the mother's role is not so obvious. On their father's return home children were regularly given presents, usually toys. Sometimes children were given gifts by people who in reality were hoping to find favour with the children's fathers by their generosity. There are several illustrations of such incidents in connection with the Nádasdy family. Tamás Nádasdy obviously preferred gifts to be given to his only son than to himself. It was doubtless for this reason that the ambassadors Antal Verancsics and Ferenc Zay brought back "various beautiful valuables" for Ferkó from their mission in Constantinople.[126] An acquaintance in Italy sent Ferkó "some fancy clothes, including some Saracen costumes". There must also have been some masks, for Nádasdy warns his wife to take care lest the child be frightened by them.[127]

Presents given by mothers were probably so common that no mention was made of them in letters. Borbála Thurzó talks about buying toys for her children, who were then staying with her mother, only in a postscript to one of her letters. She probably wanted to arrive at her parents' house bringing gifts with her, as was the custom. She writes that she is sending pomegranates with someone else, but "I am going to bring the presents myself".[128]

HEALTH AND EDUCATION

There is relatively little information about the kind of toys played with at the time, since parents did not mention this common feature of life in their letters. However, Bálint Balassi gives detailed descriptions of boys and girls playing in his *Szép magyar komédia* (Fine Hungarian Comedy). One of the characters, Credulus, recalls his childhood: "When I was a child I often played with other children in a lonely valley…There were usually many girls there, too. They came to play and have fun there. They would make garlands or sing songs."[129]

The occasional references in our sources indicate that children usually played outdoors. A letter of 1654 describes how Betkó Rákóczi, aged three, played ball with her father and some servants.[130] Nearly one hundred years earlier, Ferkó Nádasdy, aged four, was taken fishing by his mother.[131] At around the same time the son of the Blagay family was sent to the royal court "to play with the little princes".[132] Playing was obviously the common pastime for children both indoors and outdoors. Miklós Bethlen mentions a number of games that could be played either sitting quietly or involving physical movement. The latter included playing at ball, playing with a sling, bowling, spinning tops, throwing balls, fighting, running races, jumping, shooting arrows and bird-watching. Indoors, children could play dice, chess, cards or games of chance. Bethlen also mentions that there were other games for older children.[133]

Games played by boys and girls were, by all accounts, fairly similar. Nevertheless, it seems curious that dolls, traditionally the most common toy played with by girls, are not mentioned in the sources. Boys and girls presumably played together, just as women and men shared common pastimes in those days. Families socialised together, although men had their own amusements in inns or with prostitutes. In 1655 László Rákóczi and his wife spent much of their free time together, sleighing, playing music, bathing, watching jousts, shopping by candlelight, visiting the imperial gardens in Vienna, strolling in parks or in the countryside around Pozsony, inviting a German magician and his wife to their house, dancing, dining outdoors with friends, and watching the Whitsuntide procession and the children's running races at Seiberdorf. They attended a fair in Vienna, won a prize at a pleasure ground, and often called on friends. "We had a very good time", Rákóczi often wrote in his diary.[134]

Children and adults clearly found their main entertainment in mixed company. However, the letters, which constitute the most important source of data about private life during this period, are far more informative about the children's state of health than about anything else. Parents constantly informed their friends and relatives of the health of their own children and showed an interest in the welfare of others' children in return. Diseases and their cures were often discussed in detail. Naturally, this does not mean that children were permanently ill.

In the published letters of Orsolya Kanizsay, written to her husband between 1541 and 1562, the family's children are mentioned forty times. On three occasions she describes a child's illness, and on thirty-seven occasions reports that the child in question is completely healthy. One reference appears to suggest that Ferkó had just been cured of flatulence.[135] In other words, according to the letters of Orsolya Kanizsay, her children were healthy the majority of the time. The data in her letters must be considered reliable, since one cannot suppose that a mother would have concealed the illnesses of six-month-old Ferkó from his father or that she would have omitted to mention the maladies of children staying with her, for she openly remarked on her own backaches, headaches and other problems.

In most cases, the available correspondence shows a similar picture—children were, in the main, healthy. Breast-feeding was usually unproblematic, although highborn children were not generally nursed by their own mothers. Rather than referring to women breast-feeding their babies, the letters repeatedly mention inflammation of the breasts among aristocratic mothers. Nearly all reports concerning new mothers mention painful, swollen breasts. In 1613 Erzsébet Czobor wrote the following about her daughter, who had just given birth: "Her breasts are very hard" and "she is burning with fire". "Some water" had already been brought for her from the doctor, but Erzsébet asks her husband to bring medicine since "it is a recurring problem and she is in great pain".[136] However, inflammation of the breasts could be prevented. In a letter of 1591 János Telegdy reprimands his younger brother for allowing Kata Várday's problem to become so serious. According to Telegdy, his brother should have found a cure for his wife as soon as she noticed the first signs of inflammation. He also gave the recipe for a decoction with which the breasts were to be treated.[137]

This kind of inflammation was either cured or proved fatal for the woman in question. It is hard to understand how these women failed to realise that the only thing they needed to do to prevent inflammation was to breast-feed their babies. Neither their mothers nor the midwives and doctors of the day seem to have realised the difference between the condition of those mothers who nursed their children themselves and those who did not. Meanwhile, noble families continued to employ wet nurses.

In a letter apparently written by Kata Szvetkovich, the attributes of an ideal wet nurse are described. Mothers, who "had had many children and had taken good care of them", made suitable wet nurses since "they know how to take care of a child".[138] Of one particular wet nurse she wrote: "She is diligent and takes great care of the child...and the child, in turn, loves her greatly."[139] The nurse would move to the house where the child lived, and it was considered important for there to be a good relationship with the child and his or her family. One nurse, who was unhappy about being away from her husband, was warned by her mother not to be upset but to "serve the noble lady's child with joy, love and cheerfulness".[140]

Parents also did their best to keep the nurses cheerful. Letters often mention presents being bought for them. Ferkó Csáky's dry nurse, for example, who was then staying at the home of Anna Wesselényi with her little charge, sent word to the boy's mother thanking her for the new-year gift and sending her new-year greetings in return.[141] Ferkó Nádasdy's father wrote to ask his wife what he should bring for Ferkó, the wet nurse and the two dry nurses "who dance attendance on Ferkó more than anyone else". He then adds: "And write and tell me what I should buy for you, too."[142] The fact that Nádasdy writes of buying presents for the nurses at the same time as he mentions buying gifts for his only son and his wife is revealing of the relationship between the child's nurses and his parents.

The child's relationship with his or her nurses did not usually come to an end once the child was grown up, although the nurses naturally moved back home to their own families. János Kemény's nurse continued to visit him as an adult. As he wrote in his autobiography, "my nurse…still lived for many years after I got married and had children and she often visited me…"[143] He was probably more generous than the Pálffy family, who, although immensely rich, gave only a tiny sum of money to "a poor woman called Felicitas Stanglin who is supposed to have been the nurse of Master Istók".[144]

We have no information concerning the possible jealousies felt by noble mothers with respect to nurses, or the impact of this system of child care on the children themselves. It is certain, however, that children were breast-fed for at least one year. In July 1646 the "German barber" suggested to György Rákóczi II that it was time for his son, who had been born in March 1645, to be weaned.[145] By the time one of the daughters of Borbála Thurzó was weaned she had already been taught to eat and drink and was expected to walk any day.[146] Ferkó Nádasdy was breast-fed even when he was over a year and a half, although he was given other things to eat as well. The doctor prescribed boiled sour cherries for him, something he would not have done if the boy had not been used to eating fruit. Had the little boy not already started to eat fruit, the wet nurse would have been put on a stricter diet; as it was, the only things she had to avoid were fish and wine because of the little boy's digestive problems.[147] It was quite common for ailments in young children to be treated by means of the wet nurse's diet. In 1602 Pál Nyáry gave dietary advice to his daughters' two wet nurses.[148]

It is particularly striking that no mention is made in the letters of teething. One reason could be that if a child was biting the nipple it was a problem for the nurse rather than the mother, and was thus overlooked. However, if the children had been particularly restless due to teething trouble the fact would have been mentioned in the letters. It is possible that occasional fevers might have been caused by teething, without the connection being made in the letters. Slight fevers, colds, constipation and diarrhoea were recurrent problems in otherwise healthy children, and slight indigestion is also mentioned in the case of young babies.

Weaning was never forced, although there could be problems even in normal cases. János Telegdy, for example, who seems to have been nearly as much of an expert as the doctor, in spite of being a soldier, diagnosed his baby nephew as "being ill because of having been taken off the breast".[149]

In most cases a child would be weaned just as he or she was beginning to walk. We know practically nothing of the way in which babies learned to walk. Apparently they wore some kind of protection on their heads. Little Mária Erdődy, who was staying with her grandmother when she was old enough to be taking her first steps, was sent a "little pillow" to be tied to her forehead. The absence of any explanation for this implies that such a precaution was quite common.[150] Nor do we have much information regarding the diet of weaned children, although there are many references in the sources suggesting that children in general were given light meals with plenty of fruit and vegetables. Miklós Bethlen, for example, regarded this as quite natural. He says in his autobiography that "Just like other children I also liked fruit, lettuce, radishes, cabbage and any dish made with herbs and fruit."[151]

The letters more often include references to the children's clothing, probably because cloth had to be bought and because certain pieces of clothing could not be made at home. Occasionally, such items of clothing were given as gifts. In 1610

Bódiskó Batthyány asked his father, who was staying in Vienna, to bring him "a pair of trousers and other things".[152] A thoughtful grandmother ordered a cap "lined with white fox" for her grandson, Gyuricskó Radvánszky, from the boy's father, and asked for another one "of some light material" for his brother Janicskó.[153] There are also references to sheepskin coats and shirts. The wife of Kristóf Batthyány asks for shirts for her little son because the old ones are already "in rags".[154] Little Anna Révay must have been given a beautifully embroidered blouse from her grandmother, since she was not allowed to wear it on weekdays. However, the letter that was sent with the gift, written to the little girl's mother, contained the following warning: "If I happen to come to your house, or you happen to come to our place and I find that the blouse has not been worn, I will be very hurt."[155]

It was mainly the parents and grandparents who wrote to each other about the children's clothes and who bought items of clothing for them. All other activities were carried out in the separate children's court within the parents' household. The first member of the child's court was the wet nurse, followed by the dry nurse and the servants. Some children had both a wet nurse and a dry nurse when they were very young. Ferkó Csáky, for example, had two nurses in 1632, and it seems that the two were frequently at odds.[156] Over eighty years earlier Ferkó Nádasdy seems to have had one wet nurse as well as two dry nurses.[157] There is no information to suggest that these little boys were in any way difficult or unmanageable. In contrast, Bódiskó and Gáspárkó Batthyány appear to have terrorised their family. In the 1530s they spent a great deal of time with one of their father's uncles, who often wrote to their parents concerning them, as did his wife, Kata Szvetkovich. It is not always clear which boy is being referred to in these letters, but every now and then one or other of them is reported to have hurt himself falling over. The young boy who was supervising one of them had to be replaced by an adult, since the naughty child was too much for a mere boy to manage.[158] A particularly capable woman was then found to take care of one of the Batthyány boys, then aged between three and five, since "he likes to be outdoors all the time" but he "cannot be entrusted to the boy, and a girl would not be able to take him for a walk".[159]

Little boys were often looked after by older boys or men, and many of them had learned to write by the age of four or five. However, learning to read and write was a kind of game for them, and both the children and the parents regarded it as such. Imriskó Thurzó's father suggested that his son, then aged five, should start "playing with a spelling-book from now on".[160] Ferkó Nádasdy, also at the age of five, asked his father to bring him toys and pomegranates and "a little inkstand so I can learn to write".[161] Little Marianka Erdődy was taught by her mother "to say the Lord's prayer in Hungarian...every evening and every morning".[162] When they were a little older, boys and girls were no longer educated together, since boys usually left their parents' home, while girls stayed with their parents and received no formal education.

At a younger age, however, boys and girls were not educated separately. They played together, were taught elementary skills together, and had the same playmates—children of lower-class families who were brought to the house for that purpose. They must have been accepted into the aristocratic households in just the same way as the aristocratic children were invited to the royal court. The actual circumstances in which a servant child entered the household of his or her young master are not usually described in the letters. However, some cases are better documented. For example, when Ádám Batthyány was seven years old, his mother asked a woman called Eszter to give them her little boy, Adamkó, to be a playmate for him. Adamkó's mother gave up her son "with full confidence in the family", and asked only "to be allowed to see him at times out of maternal affection".[163] In 1560, when Ferkó was five, the Nádasdy family formally "inherited" a little boy, Györkó Őry, who was left to the family as a permanent servant in his father's will. Nádasdy sent him to Sárvár with the message that "Ferenc should receive him" into his court.[164]

Few children had the opportunity to be masters of their own courts. Ferkó Nádasdy, as an only child, was one of the exceptions. In general there were several children of approximately the same age in a household, since children followed one another at short intervals and the marriages of widowed parents often resulted in a child having sisters and brothers of the same age. Little Simon Forgách, for example, who lived less than four and a half years from 14 December 1580 to 13 April 1585, had four younger sisters in his short lifetime, and even the oldest of his six older siblings and half-siblings was only fifteen when he was born. Magdica Esterházy, who lived from 19 July 1625 to 7 May 1627, had a younger brother, two half-sisters who were three and four years older than her, respectively, and who were her mother's children by a previous marriage, plus a half-brother, nine years older than herself, her father's son by a previous marriage.[165] A typical example was that of little Erzsébet Thököly. In the six years after her birth on 19 November 1586, three brothers and a sister were born to her parents. One of the boys, Palika, did not reach his first birthday, but the others survived. An older brother and an older sister had died before she was born. One of her older brothers was five years older than her while the other was exactly one year older. The latter died shortly after her birth. The dates of birth of one younger sister and two younger brothers are not known.[166]

In aristocratic families there was a relatively long gap between the first and last child, although not all children survived into adulthood. The children, especially the girls, often married at a young age, and their own children grew up alongside their younger brothers and sisters. Young uncles and aunts played together with nieces and nephews of the same age. Little Miklós Pálffy, who was born in 1599, often played with Ádám Forgách, born in 1601, as well as his sister Kata's other children. He was probably still at his parents' house in 1611 when his brother-in-law, Zsigmond Forgách, inquired after the health of his own children, Adamkó and Evicska, in a letter written to his mother-in-law. He had heard that the children "busy themselves" about their grandmother.[167]

Family relationships were made still more complicated when the parents married several times and there were several half-sisters and half-brothers. János Zrínyi, the son of Miklós Zrínyi and his second wife, was born after 1564[168] and was about twenty years younger than his oldest half-brother. Several of his half-brothers and half-sisters were already married when he was born. One of his sisters, the wife of Imre Forgách, had a daughter called Anna in 1565, who was followed by several little nieces and nephews for János. He was about ten when some of his sisters and brothers married for a second time and further baby nieces and nephews arrived.[169]

The large number of children born in a family did not necessarily mean that there were many children in the household at the same time. The clearest example of this is the case of Pál Esterházy, who had twenty-seven children. The first-born, Miklós Antal, was thirty-seven years older than the last-born, Zsigmond, who was born in 1692. However, by the time Zsigmond was born, of all his half-sisters and half-brothers born to his father's first wife, only two half-brothers were still living, and he himself was to die as a baby. Thus most of the twenty-seven sisters and brothers did not even know one another.

ILLNESS AND DEATH

There was an enormous disparity in the ways in which families succeeded in caring for their children. Pál Esterházy and his two wives were probably among the worst examples of inability to cope. Miklós Pálffy and Mária Fugger represent the other extreme—seven out of eight of their children grew up safely. Only their first-born, Márk, born in 1584, died as a young child. We know that his sisters and brothers married, some of them several times, so clearly they all survived into adulthood.[170] In an age of disease and war this was rare indeed. The accuracy of the data is borne out by the fact that Miklós Pálffy died in 1600, not quite sixteen years after the birth of his first child. The birth of eight children in sixteen years was quite normal, and it is very unlikely that others died early without being noted down in the family records.

The case of Tamás Nádasdy and his wife, Orsolya Kanizsay, is also exceptional. Their son, Ferkó, was born in the eighteenth year of their marriage when Orsolya was thirty-three and Tamás fifty-eight. The child survived his parents by many years, even his mother who was widowed when the boy was seven years old. Statistically speaking, one hundred per cent of the Nádasdy's offspring survived, a percentage that was most unusual at the time. Wherever there are data on the children in a family, deaths are also recorded.

Miklós Zrínyi had twelve children by his first wife after 1545, and four of them died in early infancy.[171] One of his daughters, Kata Zrínyi, had five children by her first husband. One died within three weeks of birth but the others survived. Three of her seven children born during her second marriage died between the ages of one and four.[172] Sebestyén Thököly and Zsuzsanna Dóczi had twelve children in quick succession, the first born in 1581. Six of them died before they reached the age of ten. The eldest of Sebestyén Thököly's sons, István, had twelve children by two wives, Zsuzsa Hoffmann and Kata Thurzó. Eight of them died before reaching the age of ten, between 1610 and 1633.[173] Krisztina Nyáry had two daughters by her first husband, Imre Thurzó. The younger, Krisztina, died at the age of five, but the other married and had a daughter. With her second husband, Krisztina had nine children, four of whom died before their second birthday. The others survived into adulthood.[174] László Rákóczi lost one of his two daughters in 1656 at the age of seven months.[175] Miklós Zrínyi, the poet and general, had four children, three of whom died in early infancy.[176]

There is no apparent regularity in the death rates and birth rates in a family, and the available data do not allow us to draw any demographic conclusions. The fact that children's deaths were not usually caused by epidemics is indicated by the fact that only small numbers of children died at the same time. Three of Boldizsár Batthyány's children died in 1575, "almost on the same day", according to the letter of condolence written by Bishop János Liszti.[177] The illness which claimed them is not mentioned. Pál Esterházy and Orsolya Esterházy lost two children on the same day in 1664, but again the illness remains unknown. The unfortunate couple lost two more children to smallpox in 1673.[178] It is not surprising that contemporaries did not consider epidemics to be necessarily fatal. A letter written by Tamás Nádasdy is typical. He informs his wife of a view he had recently heard quoted as being that of certain doctors on the subject of epidemics: "Little children easily catch the plague."[179] At the time he himself was calmly staying in plague-stricken Vienna, and he even asked his wife to visit him. She did not hesitate to go, but left Ferkó at home.

The nature of the illnesses from which children suffered is rarely mentioned in the letters. However, besides minor catarrh and digestive problems, which were common in otherwise healthy children, boils were particularly frequent, especially on the face and head. Gáspárkó Batthyány had a boil on his neck in 1545 when still a baby,[180] and Ferkó Csáky had "some big swellings on his head and his face" in 1632 while he was still being breast-fed.[181] Palatine Miklós Esterházy wrote of his granddaughter, Orsika Esterházy: "As far as my little grand-daughter is concerned, I have heard that she has some small red boils under her chin. They are harmless, as far as I know, but the doctor should still be informed about them."[182]

The advice given by Miklós Esterházy is characteristic of the attitude of aristocratic families towards childhood illnesses. The palatine, who was staying in Pozsony at the time, must have been sent news from home about the boils on his granddaugh-ter's chin. Although he considered them harmless he thought it necessary to write home with advice, in spite of all his political preoccupations. His behaviour was by no means unusual. Par-ents, grandparents and other relatives took great care of children when they were ill. They informed each other of the children's condition, gave advice, summoned doctors and sent medica-ments. Such behaviour was considered natural in those days.

Ferenc Batthyány severely reproached his nephew, Kristóf Batthyány, when he found out about the illness of four-year-old Boldiskó. He felt "great anxiety and sympathy": "We have al-ready told you that you are treating him carelessly and improp-erly, but you have not taken our advice", he wrote.[183] Lord Chief Justice István Báthory, who had no children himself, expected his niece, Kata Várday, to inform him regularly about the health of her children. On one occasion he heard from someone else that the little girls were ill and reprimanded their mother at once: "I have heard that the children have fallen seriously ill and you have not told me anything about it. I should like you to let me know when one or the other falls ill." However, he was not deeply offended. He obtained medicine from Transylvania through the barber in Kolozsvár and suggested that the children's mother should "send someone for it if it is needed"[184], leaving Kata Várday free to decide if she wanted the medicine or not.

It was quite common for medicaments to be obtained without a prescription from an expert, simply on the basis of a relative's description of the illness. However, experts were often called to attend sick children, or the children were taken to see experts. The boils on Boldizsár Batthyány's head were cured by Kata Szvetkovich with medicine brought by her husband. On another occasion when the child fell ill at home she sent a doctor to the family.[185] The other little Batthyány, Gáspárkó, was once taken to a famous "herbal doctor" by his father's uncle.[186] When Margit Choron's son Tamás became seriously ill in 1584 his mother took him to a doctor in Pozsony.[187] In contrast, Éva Forgách was not prepared to take her critically ill son, Istók Csáky, to Pozsony, since the journey would have been too exhausting for him. As the Pozsony doctor was unwilling to travel all the way to their home she decided to take the child part of the way to Pozsony and ask the doctor to visit him there.[188] Ferkó Nádasdy was examined by a doctor several times at the age of two.[189] When Ferkó Rákóczi was one and a half years old, three doctors and someone who "anointed with unctions" were summoned to treat him.[190] Borbála Thurzó committed her little daughter to the care of a "woman doctor", but when the treatment proved unsuccessful she cared for the child as she had learned from her mother.[191]

Families made every effort to ensure that their children made a full recovery, aware that their children's lives depended on careful nursing, as those cases in which a couple successfully brought up an only child suggest. There are no data to support the idea that the carelessness of the families concerned contributed to a higher rate of infant mortality. Similarly, there are no data suggesting cases of serious neglect among aristocratic families. It is still bewildering that several of the children born to the first wife of Miklós Zrínyi died in early infancy, while his only son, born to his second wife, survived. The son was brought up by his mother, Éva Rosenberg, who had been left a widow two years after her marriage.[192] Several of the children born to Miklós Esterházy's second wife died in childhood, while his only child by his first wife, a son, István, survived and was brought up first by his widowed father, then with the help of his stepmother, Krisztina Nyáry. Likewise, István Csáky lost several of the children who were born to his first two wives, but his only son, born to Mária Perényi, who died giving birth to him, survived and was brought up by his third wife, Krisztina Mindszenti.[193] These cases are not so obvious, since these children had many half-brothers and half-sisters and lived in big families. The case of Ferenc Nádasdy, mentioned above, who grew up as an only child, is more clear-cut.

Good fortune played an important role in survival, but it is also probable that those who were more valuable in the eyes of their parents, for emotional or financial reasons, were treated with even greater care than their siblings. The parents' struggle to keep their children alive sometimes ended in success, sometimes in tragedy, but all the evidence indicates that everything possible was done to keep children alive.

The fact that families were aware of the importance of treating children with care and attention is proved by the statements of two prominent figures of the day, who belonged to two different denominations. One of them, Éva Poppel Lobkovitz, was the wife of Count Ferenc Batthyány and a devout member of the Lutheran Church. Both her husband and her son converted to the Catholic faith, but she remained a Protestant. Even Péter Pázmány, the most convincing of apologists, failed to convert her.[194] She herself had a profound knowledge of theology. The other figure was Miklós Esterházy, who became a Catholic as a young man and counted as the lay leader of the Catholic aristocracy. He wrote a theological tract and few of his contemporaries would have had a better knowledge of the teachings of the Catholic Church.[195]

These two personalities gave concurring statements in connection with the death of Krisztina, the younger daughter of Imre Thurzó, in 1627. The little girl and her sister Erzsébet were looked after by their mother and her second husband, Miklós Esterházy, for some time. After Krisztina's death Esterházy wrote to his wife concerning Erzsébet: "The little child has to be taken great care of. The wife of my lord Batthyány blames us for the death of the other one, too, as if she had not lost children herself."[196]

Esterházy seems to have agreed with the charges made by Countess Batthyány, since he cautions his wife to take better care of the other child. At the same time he establishes that the Batthyánys were just as careless, for some of their children had also died. So neither the Protestant nor the Catholic spoke in terms of God's will, however well they knew the tenets of their respective religions. They must have been aware that, according to the religions they followed, human life is in God's hands, but here they spoke not of abstract dogmas but about the actual death of a child. Everyday experiences led them to the view that a child's life depended on the care provided by the family. Their views were probably shared by most of their contemporaries of the same social position.

God's will is mentioned only in official statements such as the notification of a child's death. Such letters are reminiscent of the letters we have mentioned announcing the birth of a child. Newborn babies were called "gifts of God", and the death of children was also accounted for with reference to God's will. God gave the child, and He takes the child back.

Bishop Pál Bornemissza wrote concerning the daughter of a relative: "God gave her to us and God has taken her back..."[197] Miklós Bánffy wrote that: "Our elder son was suddenly taken by the Lord out of this world."[198] György Thurzó wrote of "my little daughter taken from me by God" when his daughter Erzsóka died.[199] When one of his grandchildren died he wrote: "No one can oppose God's will..."[200]

There must have been very few who committed to paper their anger at God's will, and no such letters have been found to date. What parents and grandparents really thought and actually said at the deathbeds of small children and babies remains hidden forever. These most intimate feelings were not expressed in writing. The bereaved members of the family could only speak about such feelings personally, if they were articulated at all.

It was very rare for people to write about the state of bereavement. Even when they did, they tended not to express themselves directly. Feelings of grief were alluded to by comparing them to the feelings of others. A letter written by Bishop Bornemissza in 1564 serves as a good example: "I am sorry with all my heart for the death of your younger sister because I know...how great your mother's sorrow is."[201] Over a hundred years later Miklós Bethlen, himself a married man at the time, wrote in response to the death of his three-year-old sister: "God has made us very wretched with the death of our poor sister Sofika, who left us at one o'clock yesterday afternoon to the great sorrow of our dear father, her brothers and their family..."[202] When György Thurzó informed his wife of the death of the child of some distant relatives, he alluded to his own sorrow at the recent death of his son: "Their great bereavement I can judge by my own experience."[203] A few years later the same György Thurzó allowed his brother-in-law, Zsigmond Forgách, to return home from before the Castle of Buda, an important area of operations during the Fifteen Years' War, since "he has received evil news. His little daughter has been taken by God from this world."[204]

Losing a child was a terrible tragedy, a feeling that was expressed in letters of consolation. Pál Pálffy wrote to a friend in 1644 after the death of his infant daughter at the age of six weeks: "Thanks to God, our dear little daughter is very well now, for she is with the Lord God Almighty. However great our grief and sorrow, may His will be done."[205] In simple words he was expressing the consolation he found in the salvation of the child and the fact of her now being with God. Miklós Bethlen also attempted to console one of his best friends in a similar manner after the loss of his son, although his thoughts are expressed in a somewhat more complex manner: God appears "terrible", but He has taken little Boldi "in accordance with his ever merciful attitude towards his followers". By so doing, He is testing the love of the parents towards Him and proving His mercy.[206]

Such attitudes can only be regarded as sincere. There are no sources available to enable us to carry out research into faith in God.

Notes

(For boldface references to Tables, see Genealogical Tables at the end of the book, p. 251).

1 Autobiography of János Kemény: *János Kemény és Miklós Bethlen művei.* Published by Éva V. Windisch. Budapest, 1983 (hereafter: *Kemény*): 19.

2 Autobiography of Miklós Bethlen: Ibid. (hereafter: *M. Bethlen*): 193.

3 Pál Telegdy to Kata Várday, March 1588 (no day given): *Két vitéz nemes úr levelezése.* Published by Sándor Eckhardt. Budapest, 1944 (hereafter: *Két vitéz*): 22.

4 Éva Thököly to Pál Esterházy, 1 May 1691. Hungarian National Archives (Magyar Országos Levéltár, hereafter: MOL) P 125. Documents of Palatine Pál (hereafter: P 125).

5 Documents of the court case: Ervin Roszner, *Régi magyar házassági jog.* Budapest, 1887 (hereafter: Roszner): 379–383.

6 Erzsébet Czobor to György Thurzó, 12 February 1608: In Zsuzsa Bozai, *Nők a 16–17. században.* Unpublished doctoral thesis (hereafter: Bozai). The appendix contains letters without page numbers.

7 György Thurzó to Erzsébet Czobor, 30 September 1603: *Bethlenfalvi gróf Thurzó György levelei nejéhez, Id. gróf Zichy Edmund megbízásából,* I–II. Budapest, 1876 (hereafter: *Thurzó* I; *Thurzó* II), II: 87.

8 Miklós Esterházy to Krisztina Nyáry, 30 November 1626: The letters of Miklós Esterházy to Krisztina Nyáry, 1624–1639. Published by Lajos Merényi. *Történelmi Tár* (hereafter: TT) 1900: 34.

9 Katalin Thurzó to Erzsébet Czobor, 3 March 1622: Bozai.

10 13 January 1623: Ibid.

11 Thurzó family tree with data for the distaff side: Carolus Wagner, *Analecta Scepusii Pars IV. Posoniae et Cassoviae 1778* (hereafter: Wagner): 60–61.

12 Genealogical notes. Published by Samu Barabás. TT 1884: 778–779.

13 Family records of István Csáky, treasurer, and his son István, lord chief justice: *Oklevéltár a gróf Csáky család történetéhez* I. 2. 1500–1818. Budapest, 1919 (hereafter: *Csáky*): 616; data regarding Lord Chief Justice Csáky: Ibid., 612–619.

14 Csáky family tree, **Table II/2.**

15 *M. Bethlen,* 193.

16 György Thurzó to Erzsébet Czobor, 31 May 1608: *Thurzó* II, 231.

17 See note 4.

18 Báthory family tree: Iván Nagy, *Magyarország családai czímerekkel és nemzedékrendi táblákkal* (hereafter: Iván Nagy) I: 221.

19 Rákóczi family tree, **Table V.**

20 Anna Nádasdy to Orsolya Kanizsay, 12 January 1548: *Nádasdy Tamás nádor családi levelezése.* Edited by Árpád Károlyi and József Szalay. Budapest, 1882 (hereafter: *Nádasdy*): 129.

21 Balázs Szikszai Fabricius, *Panegyricus Helenae Orszagh defunctae.* Wittenberg, 1570.

22 Article 26 from the Diet following the coronation of 1608.

23 Since at present we have no information regarding methods of contraception used by the aristocracy, there is little point speculating.

24 The legitimation of the birth of Ferenc Soós, decree of Leopold I: Roszner, 490–491.

25 Biographies of Balassi (e.g. Sándor Eckhardt, *Balassi Bálint*. Budapest, 1941; idem, *Az ismeretlen Balassi Bálint*. Budapest, 1943; idem, *Új fejezetek Balassi Bálint életéből*. Budapest, 1957) do not make any mention of children born to the poet outside marriage.

26 *M. Bethlen*, 619.

27 Anna Wesselényi to István Csáky, 12 October 1630; 24 June 1631: Farkas Deák, *Wesselényi Anna özv. Csáky Istvánné 1584–1649 életrajza és levelezése*. Budapest, 1875 (hereafter: *Wesselényi*): 85–86, 91.

28 Boldizsár Bartha, *Rövid krónika a Debrecenben esett dolgokról*. Vienna, 1819: 17.

29 Records from the trial for witchcraft against Zsuzsanna Jakusich, wife of Miklós Thököly. Published by Antal Áldásy. TT 1896: 171–175.

30 Anna Wesselényi to Anna Balassi, 24 May 1612: *Wesselényi*, 70.

31 *M. Bethlen*, 616.

32 Records of interrogations: Katalin Péter, *A csejtei várúrnő: Báthory Erzsébet*. Budapest, 1985: 49.

33 The correspondence between the doctor and Nádasdy has been published in Nándor Szmollény, *Caspar Traxinus de Zegedinus és Nádasdy Tamás levelezése*. Szeged, 1910.

34 The charge was recorded in a political pamphlet at the time of Bethlen's campaign. István Török, *A Querela Hungariae és az általa támasztott polémia*. Kolozsvár, 1883: 15.

35 *M. Bethlen*, 191.

36 Diary of the Esterházy family. Published by Sándor Szilágyi. TT 1888: 210.

37 György Thurzó to Erzsébet Czobor, 25 September 1610: *Thurzó* II, 283.

38 György Thurzó to Erzsébet Czobor, 26 August 1603: Ibid., 79.

39 Péter Orosz to János Szalay, 11 July 1542: *Négyszáz magyar levél a XVI. századból*. Published by Ágoston Szalay. Pest, 1851 (hereafter: Szalay): 16.

40 Miklós Esterházy to Krisztina Nyáry: TT 1900, 385.

41 Miklós Esterházy to Krisztina Nyáry, 16 July 1628: Later letters from Miklós Eszterházy to Krisztina Nyári. Published by Lajos Merényi. TT 1901, 486.

42 Miklós Esterházy to Krisztina Nyáry, 29 July 1628. Ibid., 488.

43 Orsolya Kanizsay to Tamás Nádasdy, 1 October 1555: *Nádasdy*, 93–94.

44 Anna Bakich to Mihály Révay, 14 October 1560: *Magyar hölgyek levelei 1515–1709*. Published by Farkas Deák. Budapest, 1879 (hereafter: *Magyar hölgyek*): 26.

45 Kata Zrínyi to Imre Forgách, 19 March 1585: Ibid., 68.

46 György Thurzó to Erzsébet Czobor, 31 December 1594: *Thurzó* I, 124.

47 György Thurzó to Erzsébet Czobor, 2 January 1595: Ibid., 124–125.

48 György Thurzó to Erzsébet Czobor, 26 February 1598: Ibid., 137; and 1 March 1598: Ibid., 240.

49 Quoted by Sándor Takáts, *Magyar nagyasszonyok*. Budapest, 1926 (hereafter: Takáts): 235.

50 Miklós Esterházy to Krisztina Nyáry, 19 February 1625: TT 1900, 23.

51 Kata Szvetkovich to Kristóf Batthyány, 24 January 1542: MOL P 1314. Batthyány family archive. Missiles (hereafter: P 1314), No. 3782.

52 Anna Wesselényi to István Csáky, 27 February 1649: *Wesselényi*, 215.

53 Records of the family of Prince Palatine Pál Esterházy: *Az Eszterházy család és oldalágainak leírásához oklevéltár*. Compiled by Count János Eszterházy (hereafter: Eszterházy). Budapest, 1901: 213–215.

54 Family records of Ferenc Esterházy: Eszterházy, 178–179.

55 Wagner, 185–186.

56 Erzsébet Czobor to György Thurzó, 18 August 1616: Bozai.

57 Thurzó family tree: Wagner, 60–61.

58 Kata Savetkovich to Kristóf Batthyány, 30 May 1542: P 1314, No. 3790.

59 István Ecsedi Báthory to Kata Várday, 13 January 1590: *Két vitéz*, 155.

60 János Telegdy to Miklós Telegdy, April 1591 (no day given): Ibid., 110.

61 From the court case against Anna Rozina Liszti, the sister-in-law. Quoted by Bozai.

62 *Csáky*, 610.

63 György Thurzó to Erzsébet Czobor, 26 February 1598: *Thurzó* I, 237.

64 Miklós Bánffy to Boldizsár Batthyány, 22 September 1571: P 1314, No. 1593. Miklós Bánffy to Boldizsárné Batthyány, 21 September 1571: Ibid., 2006.

65 Erzsébet Czobor to György Thurzó, 28 August 1615: Bozai.

66 Anna Wesselényi to Gábor Vadas, 4 November 1635: *Wesselényi*, 125.

67 István Gyulai to Kristóf Batthyány, 19 April 1541: P 1314. No. 17532.

68 György Thurzó to Erzsébet Czobor, 31 May 1608: *Thurzó* II, 231.

69 Pálné Czobor to Péter Révay, 11 July 1609: *Magyar hölgyek*, 207.

70 Pál Pálffy to Ádám Batthyány, 3 September 1644: *Pállfy Pál nádor levelei 1644–1653*. Published by Éva S. Lauter. Budapest, 1989 (hereafter: Lauter): 49.

71 *Rákóczi László naplója*. Published by Ildikó Horn. (Hereafter: *Rákóczi László*.) Budapest: 228. (In German, "Frauenzimmerchen" means, jocularly, "little woman".)

72 See note 46.

73 György Thurzó to Erzsébet Czobor, 1 January 1593: *Thurzó* I, 21.

74 Miklós Esterházy to Krisztina Nyáry, 5 February 1625: TT 1901, 363.

75 György Thurzó to Erzsébet Czobor, 16 October 1597: *Thurzó* I, 233.

76 Mária Thurzó (?)to Erzsébet Czobor, not dated: Bozai.

77 Wagner, 60–61.

78 Rákóczi family tree, **Table V**.

79 Iván Nagy, III: 298–299.

80 The family of István Csáky, **Table II/2**.

81 Esterházy family tree, **Table III/1**.

82 Quoted in Takáts, 94.

83 Ferenc Batthyány to Kristóf Batthyány, 21 October 1537: P 1314, No. 3494.

84 Quoted by Takáts, 263.

85 Anna Nádasdy to Tamás Nádasdy, 24 October 1561: *Nádasdy*, 171.

86 István Csáky to Zsigmond Kornis, 31 December 1629: Deák Farkas, *Egy magyar főúr a XVII. században*. Budapest, 1888: 232.

87 Borbála Thurzó to Erzsébet Czobor, 12 October 1620: Bozai.

88 Quoted by Takáts, 525.

89 Quoted by Takáts, 525.

90 Miklós Esterházy to Krisztina Nyáry, 4 November 1625 and 2 December 1625: TT 1901, 376, 377.

91 *Esterházy Pál*, 113.

92 The letters of Zsuzsanna Lórántffy and György Rákóczi I. In: *A két Rákóczi György fejedelem családi levelezése*. Edited by Sándor Szilágyi. Budapest, 1875 (hereafter: *Rákóczi*).

93 Kata Szvetkovich to János Sztorocsay, 24 April 1558: P 1314, No. 3876.

94 György Thurzó to Erzsébet Czobor, 28 August 1599: *Thurzó* I, 288.

95 György Rákóczi II to Zsuzsanna Lórántffy, 12 April 1649: *Rákóczi*, 401.

96 For a description of the incident and a collection of sources relating to it, see Mihály Sztárai, *História Perényi Ferenc kiszabadulásáról*. Edited by Imre Téglásy. Budapest, 1985.

97 Testimonies of Miklós Styllnowyth: Ibid., 180.

98 Account by Sztárai: Ibid., 36.

99 Idem: Ibid., 36.

100 Zsófia Báthory to György Rákóczi II, 29 September 1645: *Rákóczi*, 369.

101 Quoted by Takáts, 286.

102 Tamás Nádasdy to Orsolya Kanizsay, 19 December 1560; Orsolya Kanizsay to Tamás Nádasdy, 23 and 26 December 1560: *Nádasdy*, 63, 111–112.

103 Mária Forgách to Péter Révay, 28 October 1621. *Magyar hölgyek*, 135.

104 Anna Bakich to Mihály Révay, 13 June 1565: Ibid., 33.

105 Quoted by Takáts, 126.

106 MOL P 707. Zichy family archive. Missiles (hereafter: P 707), No. 544.

107 János Telegdy to Pál Telegdy, 1595 (no month, no day): *Két vitéz*, 147.

108 Anna Wesselényi to István Csáky, 19 February 1643: *Wesselényi*, 158.

109 Borbála Thurzó to Erzsébet Czobor, 14 July 1625: Bozai.

110 György Thurzó to Erzsébet Czobor, 4 January 1596: *Thurzó* I, 162–163.

111 György Thurzó to Erzsébet Czobor, 6 January 1596: Ibid., 164.

112 Tamás Nádasdy to Orsolya Kanizsay, 14 December 1560: *Nádasdy*, 62.

113 György Thurzó to Erzsébet Czobor, 4 October 1608: *Thurzó* II, 240.

114 Zsuzsanna Lorántffy to György Rákóczi I, 21 September 1638: *Rákóczi*, 60.

115 Ferencné Batthány to Kristóf Batthyány, 11 October 1543 and 1 June 1549: P 1314, No. 3799 and 3825.

116 Borbála Thurzó to Erzsébet Czobor, 4 June 1625: Bozai.

117 Kristóf Batthyány to Sister Anna, 18 April 1554. *A körmendi Batthyány-levéltár reformációra vonatkozó oklevelei 1527–1625*. Collected by Béla Iványi. Szeged, 1990 (hereafter: Iványi): 25.

118 Tamás Nádasdy to Orsolya Kanizsay, 6 May 1560: *Nádasdy*, 56.

119 19 December 1560: Ibid., 63.

120 Pál Esterházy's memories of his youth. *Esterházy Pál Mars Hungaricus*. Published by Emma Iványi. Budapest, 1989 (hereafter: *Esterházy Pál*): 314.

121 György Szerémi: *Magyarország romlásáról*. Published by László Kardos. Budapest, 1961: 53. The chronicler erroneously reported that the gift given to the children was poisoned.

122 *Esterházy Pál*, 142.

123 Boldizsár Batthyány to Kristóf Batthyány, 11 April 1554: P 1314, No. 3089.

124 Tamás Nádasdy to Orsolya Kanizsay, 25 June 1558: *Nádasdy*, 24.

125 Ibid.

126 Tamás Nádasdy to Orsolya Kanizsay, 10 November 1557: *Nádasdy*, 20.

127 Tamás Nádasdy to Orsolya Kanizsay, 10 October 1558: *Nádasdy*, 27.

128 Borbála Thurzó to Erzsébet Czobor, 19 November 1625: Bozai.

129 *Balassy Bálint Összes versei és Szép magyar comoediája.* Edited by Béla Varjas. Budapest, no date: 248.

130 *Rákóczi László,* 315.

131 Tamás Nádasdy to Orsolya Kanizsay, 26 February 1559: *Nádasdy,* 36.

132 Quoted by Takáts, 247.

133 *M. Bethlen,* 501.

134 *Rákóczi László,* 96–186.

135 *Nádasdy,* 70–114.

136 Erzsébet Czobor to György Thurzó, 25 September 1613: Bozai.

137 János Telegdy to Pál Telegdy, April 1591 (no day given): *Két vitéz,* 110–111.

138 20 June 1542. Damaged letter on Xerox: P 1314, No. 3792.

139 Ferencné Batthyány to Kristóf Batthyány, 1 November 1547: Ibid., No. 3832.

140 Damaged letter to Katus, after 29 September 1556: Szalay, 201.

141 Anna Wesselényi to Erzsébet Forgách, 21 January 1632: *Wesselényi,* 135.

142 Tamás Nádasdy to Orsolya Kanizsay, 16 May 1559: *Nádasdy,* 41.

143 *Kemény,* 36.

144 Expenses of the sons of Miklós Pálffy in Vienna, 1598–1601. In Pál Jedlicska, *Eredeti részletekek a gr. Pálffy család okmánytárához 1401–1653.* Budapest, 1910 (hereafter: *Pálffy*): 13.

145 György Rákóczi II to Zsuzsanna Lórántffy, 20 July 1646: *Rákóczi,* 363.

146 Borbála Thurzó to Erzsébet Czobor, 3 August 1620: Bozai.

147 Orsolya Kanizsay to Tamás Nádasdy, 29 March 1557: *Nádasdy,* 98.

148 Pál Nyáry to Kata Várday, 31 October 1602: *Nyáry Pál és Várday Kata levelezése.* Published by Kálmán Benda. Debrecen, 1975: 25.

149 János Telegdy to Pál Telegdy, November 1593: *Két vitéz,* 48.

150 Borbála Thurzó to Erzsébet Czobor, 2 August 1620: Bozai.

151 *M Bethlen,* 513.

152 Quoted by Takáts, 475–476.

153 Kata Johanna Máriássy to János Radvánszky, 6 October 1690: *Magyar hölgyek,* 361.

154 Erzsébet Szvetkovich to András Török, 16 August 1552: P 1314, No. 4741.

155 Magdolna Guti Ország to Jánosné Révay, 6 December 1563: *Magyar hölgyek,* 63

156 Anna Wesselényi to Éva Forgách, 25 January 1632: *Wesselényi,* 110–111.

157 Tamás Nádasdy to Orsolya Kanizsay, 16 May 1559: *Nádasdy*, 41.

158 Ferenc Batthyány to Kristóf Batthyány, 31 August 1547: P 1314, No. 3649.

159 Kata Szvetkovich to Kristóf Batthyány, 10 July 1548: P 1314, No. 3837.

160 György Thurzó to Erzsébet Czobor, 3 January 1604: *Thurzó* II, 107.

161 Ferenc Nádasdy to Tamás Nádasdy, 28 May 1560: *Nádasdy*, 235.

162 Borbála Thurzó to Erzsébet Czobor, 4 July 1619: Bozai.

163 Szabina Lobkovitz Poppel to Ferencné Batthyány, 10 February 1617: Iványi, 208–209.

164 Tamás Nádasdy to Orsolya Kanizsay, 5 December 1560: *Nádasdy*, 58–59.

165 Family records of Krisztina Nyáry: *Eszterházy*, 207–208.

166 The children of Sebestyén Thököly and Zsuzsa Dóczi: Iván Nagy XI, 288.

167 Zsigmond Forgách to Maria Fugger, 13 July 1611: *Pálffy*, 20–21.

168 Invitation of Miklós Zrínyi to his marriage to his second wife, to be held on 3 September 1564: TT 1907, 75.

169 Iván Nagy XII, 436.

170 Iván Nagy IX, 73.

171 Iván Nagy XII, 436.

172 TT 1884, 778–779.

173 Iván Nagy XI, 288.

174 TT 1888, 210–212.

175 *Rákóczi László*, 260.

176 Tibor Klaniczay: *Zrínyi Miklós*. Budapest, 1964: 615.

177 János Liszti to Boldizsár Batthyány, 8 May 1575: Iványi, 75–76.

178 Eszterházy, 215.

179 Tamás Nádasdy to Orsolya Kanizsay, 19 December 1560: *Nádasdy*, 93.

180 Kata Szvetkovich to Kristóf Batthyány, 27 December 1545: P 1314, No. 3826.

181 Anna Wesselényi to Éva Forgách, 25 January 1632: *Wesselényi*, 110.

182 Miklós Esterházy to Erzsébet Thurzó, 7 September 1641: TT 1907.

183 4 April 1548: P 1314, No. 3660.

184 19 November 1598, according to the old calendar: P 707, Missiles, No. 10209.

185 Kata Szvetkovich to Kristóf Batthyány. 15 August 1549: P 1314, No. 3845.

186 Ferencné Batthyány to Kristóf Batthyány, 1561 (no month, no day): Ibid., No. 3882.

187 Anna Franciska Csáky to István Csáky, 26 (no month) 1657: *Magyar hölgyek*, 286.

188 Éva Forgách to István Csáky, 18 December 1630: *Wesselényi*, 123.

189 Orsolya Kanizsay to Tamás Nádasdy, 29 March 1557: *Nádasdy*, 98.

190 György Rákóczi II to Zsuzsanna Lórántffy, 20 July 1646: *Rákóczi*, 363.

191 Borbála Thurzó to Erzsébet Czobor, 15 June 1625: Bozai.

192 The wedding took place on 3 September 1564 (TT 1907: 75) and Zrínyi died on 8 September 1566 in Szigetvár.

193 *Csáky*, 612–619.

194 Péter Pázmány, *Bizonyos okok...* Pozsony, 1631.

195 Data relating to Miklós Esterházy: Esterházy, 191.

196 20 June 1627: TT 1900, 36.

197 Pál Bornemissza to István Várday, 13 February 1564: P 707, No. 10048.

198 Miklós Bánffy to Boldizsár Batthyány, 10 February 1575: P 1314, No. 1997.

199 György Thurzó to Erzsébet Czobor, 17 May 1597: *Thurzó* I, 222.

200 György Thurzó to Erzsébet Czobor, 31 August 1611: *Thurzó* II, 290.

201 20 June 1627: TT 1900, 36.

202 Miklós Bethlen to Mihály Teleki, 20 May 1668: *Bethlen Miklós levelei* 1–2. Published by József Jankovics. Budapest, 1987 (hereafter: Jankovics): 213.

203 György Thurzó to Erzsébet Czobor, 24 May 1594: *Thurzó* I, 82–83.

204 György Thurzó to Erzsébet Czobor, 23 October 1603: *Thurzó* II, 96.

205 Pál Pálffy to Ádám Batthyány, 15 November 1644: Lauter, 57.

206 Miklós Bethlen to Mihály Teleki, 7 March 1689: Jankovics, 399–400.

CHAPTER 2

ORPHANS OF NOBLE BIRTH

"HAD MY GOD allowed me to be raised by my own parents like you, I truly believe that I would have been blessed. But God deprived me of this blessing."[1] The words of Pál Béldi could probably have been echoed by many of his contemporaries. It is generally accepted that there were large numbers of orphans in early modern times. Mothers often died giving birth, and wars, epidemics and poor hygiene also took their toll in this period. The lack of accurate demographic data means that we cannot be certain of the proportion of orphans within the population. However, there are several examples which can serve to illustrate the situation.

Between 1600 and 1650, forty-three children were born to the Esterházy family. Fifteen of them died as infants. Twenty-eight survived into adulthood, or at least long enough to be married. Eighteen of this latter group grew up without one or both of their parents: five had lost their father, four their mother, and nine both parents. Four of this latter category had lost both their parents by the age of ten.[2] In the Rákóczi family of Felsővadász, only seventeen children were born during the entire century, and only twelve lived long enough to be married. Ten of them were orphans, six losing both parents. Three grew up without their father, and one girl was raised by a stepmother.[3] Of the ten children born to the Zrínyi family, one lost a father and five lost both parents.[4]

The raising of orphaned children was therefore a problem of general concern. What happened when a family suffered the loss of one parent, or was completely broken up as a result of the deaths of both parents? How did society manage this problem? How were orphans cared for? Were orphaned children able to retain their fathers' social status? What kind of legal support did they receive, and what was the actual legal practice of the day in this area? Could one actually benefit from being an orphan?

This investigation into the lives of seventeenth-century orphans can be little more than impressionistic. The discussion of the various phenomena connected with the problems of orphaned children in early modern times would demand extremely complex and wide-ranging research. There are substantial differences between the various fates that awaited orphans of equally noble birth during the sixteenth to eighteenth centuries. The lives of orphaned children of the lesser nobility were dramatically changed by the legal regulation of guardianship in 1715 and 1723, which led to the institutionalisation of care for orphans. A thorough and complete survey would also have to include a discussion of the fate of orphans in middle-class or lower-class families. However, since the present study is a pioneering work in this field in Hungary I have had to be content with the limited scope that is possible at present.

THE CONSEQUENCES OF BEING ORPHANED

The fate of orphans depended on several factors, but above all on whether the children in question had lost one or both of their parents. The lives of children who had lost both parents differed greatly from the lives of those who had a mother or father still living. The situation also differed according to whether children had lost their mother or their father. Legally there was hardly any difference between the status of orphans who had lost both parents and those who were left with only their mother. Owing to family structures and the existing law of inheritance, orphans in early modern times were not necessarily ruined financially by the deaths of their parents. Everything depended on the number, social standing, and character of their relatives. An orphan's safety was assured if he or she had at least one uncle, a married aunt, an older married brother or sister, or a grandparent. Even more distant relatives could sometimes provide support, although it often proved to be the case that the more distant the family ties, the greater the relative's greed.

Another important factor was the orphan's age. According to contemporary legal regulations, a child reached his or her majority, or "came of age", at twenty-four in the case of boys, and sixteen in the case of girls. This marked difference was partly due to the fact that most girls at that time were married, or at least engaged, by the time they were sixteen. According to István Werbőczy, one of the most influential lawyers of the period, women could never legally be fully independent. They were obliged to remain under the care or supervision of their fathers, older brothers, husbands or guardians. Otherwise they "could easily be misled or cheated owing to the simplicity of their thinking".[5]

Below the age of twenty-four and sixteen respectively, boys and girls were not regarded as being "of legal age".[6] However, the life of a minor was divided by the law into sub-periods, according to the child's level of development.

The first sub-period lasted twelve years, and during this time the child was "not of legal age". The child had no right to make decisions and was under the authority of his or her parents or guardian, and represented by them. If a child lost his or her fa-

ther before the age of twelve, he or she was left completely defenceless. Such orphans had no say in the identity or actions of
their guardians; they were not free to dispose of their inherited
property, nor could they be involved in lawsuits. However, their
material interests were largely defended by the law. Because
they could not be involved in lawsuits, any legal actions initiated during the father's lifetime, as well as lengthy legal cases
regarding their estate, had to be postponed until the child had
reached the age of twelve.[7]

The second sub-period began at the age of twelve, at which
stage the child was regarded as an adolescent and was considered to have reached a legal age. This meant that orphans over
the age of twelve could, through their guardians, bring actions
against people and be involved in lawsuits.[8] Attaining their
legal majority was a turning point for all children, and particularly so for orphans. Once an orphan reached the age of
twelve, the legal status of his or her guardian also changed.
While still called guardians in the majority of cases, they were
entitled to act only as administrators. If a father made a will
when his son was already over the age of twelve, he could not
appoint a guardian without the child's consent or against the
child's will. On reaching his majority, a boy could have the
appointment of his guardian revoked and could make his own
choice of guardian. Pál Révay, for example, after losing both
his parents, asked his brother-in-law, Pál Nádasdy, to be his
guardian in 1624, ignoring his relatives on his father's side
who should, theoretically, have enjoyed priority. Nádasdy and
Révay even consulted together and set down in writing the
guardian's duties.[9] Miklós Zrínyi was over thirteen and his
younger brother, Péter, had just reached the age of twelve
when they ordered a pay rise for Tamás Mikulich, their only
remaining guardian.[10] A boy over the age of twelve was also
entitled to sue his guardian for the careless administration of

his estate.[11] However, girls over the age of twelve had no say in choosing their guardians.

Boys over the age of sixteen were entitled to have some say regarding their debts and pawns; over the age of eighteen they were able to dispose of their wealth in gold, silver, and other movable property; and at twenty-four they gained full power over their estates. The same rights were granted to girls at fourteen and sixteen, respectively, thus in theory they were free to dispose of their own property after reaching the age of sixteen.[12] In the case of children orphaned after their sixteenth birthday, relatives would often try to arrange things as quickly as possible. Girls were usually married off, while boys were often declared to have reached their majority and were put in possession of their property, installed in their inherited offices, and wives found for them. László Esterházy, for example, was eighteen when his father died. The king emancipated him within a year and appointed him lord lieutenant of Sopron county and guardian of his younger siblings.[13]

Since there was a considerable difference between the legal status of boys and girls, one might assume that greater care was taken of boys, who would have been regarded as more valuable. As far as girls were concerned, it might be supposed that the burden of bringing them up was avoided by marrying them off or, in the case of Catholic girls even as young as five or six, by sending them to a convent, the latter option being better financially. However, this simply did not happen.

The available examples suggest that orphans in this period, girls as well as boys, were given the kind of education befitting their age, social status and sex. Furthermore, the biggest legal cases involving the care of orphans were for the guardianships of girls. When János and Erzsébet Homonnai Drugeth lost both their parents the king himself provided for their care and education. There was no dispute as far as the boy was concerned, but rights to the guardianship of Erzsébet were also claimed by Prince Gábor Bethlen.[14] The lawsuit for the guardianship of Erzsébet and Krisztina Thurzó, between their mother's second husband and their grandmother, lasted four years.[15] The Esterházy family also had to turn to the king to claim the guardianship of Orsika Esterházy, which had been granted to their brother-in-law, Ferenc Nádasdy.[16] Several more examples could be cited. The desirability of being the guardian of a girl was due to the legal standing of female orphans. While boys gained an increasing degree of independence as the years passed, and gained increasing rights vis-à-vis their guardians, the guardians of female orphans were in a different situation. They were required to administer the property of their charges for a much longer time, practically unrestricted, and were in a position to enjoy any benefits. Together with their wives, the guardians of female orphans could decide whom the girls were to marry, thus giving them the opportunity to make a favourable match for their own family.

Apart from factors such as whether the children had lost one or both parents, the extent of their property and their gender, the age at which children became orphans was also decisive. The younger they were when their parent or parents died, the more defenceless they were. All parents could do for their children was to try to secure their future, and the fulfilment of their own intentions as the children's parents, by including provisions in their wills, thus defending their children against being thrown on the mercy of others.

LAST WILLS AND TESTAMENTS

It was very important for parents to ensure that after their deaths the family would not lose the social status it had acquired. The lifestyle, education and rights of their orphaned children also had to be secured. It was for these reasons that parents set down their intentions in a will. It was common for several wills to be written over the years or for amendments to be added to existing wills in response to changing circumstances and the growth of the family's material assets. The extent of the family property and the order of succession were precisely defined in the will, and all possible changes within the family were taken into consideration. This was very important since dramatic changes could take place within a very short time: Pál Esterházy, for example, lost two children unexpectedly through smallpox at the very time he was making his will in 1664.[17]

Parents made every effort to appoint guardians who would be ready and able to put their intentions into practice and defend the rights of their orphaned children. However, some fathers were well aware that a will alone might not be sufficient. Orphans were easy prey for anyone, not so much for their property, since this was safeguarded by law, but in themselves. Orphans might well be left without their parents at their most impressionable age and before they had developed the faculty of sound judgement. Adolescents in search of an identity might easily choose a role model for themselves and be easily influenced by others. Seeking someone to replace a lost father they would readily give their trust.

On this point it is interesting to look at the famous circle of young politicians from noble families whom Palatine Miklós Esterházy attracted around him and whom he organised in support of his own political ideas.[18] Those who belonged to this circle were nearly all orphans. István and László Csáky were orphaned before the age of four, while György and Gábor Erdődy were both younger than seven when they lost their father. Miklós Zrínyi was six when he lost both his parents; Ferenc Nádasdy lost his father at the age of thirteen, and Ádám Batthyány's father died when Ádám was about sixteen. Ádám

Forgách, Ferenc Wesselényi and László Bercsényi had almost reached their majority when they were orphaned. Many young members of the lesser nobility who gathered around the palatine were also orphans, although several of them were relatives of the Esterházy family. Other members of the aristocracy besides Esterházy also became role models for orphans and for young people throughout the country. Pál Esterházy's idols were his own deceased father and Miklós Zrínyi, and, as an art collector, his taste was greatly influenced by Ferenc Nádasdy.

Many wills included provisions that attempted to control the external influences affecting orphaned children. Parents often gave precise instructions as to the education and future environment of their child. The change most dreaded by all parents, whatever their denomination, was their orphaned child's forced conversion to another faith. Lord Chief Justice István Báthory, a Calvanist, forbade his heirs even to appear at "papist courts".[19] In the case of the Catholic Count, Ferenc Nádasdy, as in the wills of many other parents, adherence to the parents' faith was made a precondition of inheritance.[20] Count István Illésházy, a Lutheran, disinherited one of his nephews on learning of his conversion to Catholicism.[21]

It was generally stipulated that boys were to study until the age of twenty or twenty-two, as in, for example, the will of Ferenc Dobó made in 1602. He left instructions that his son "shall not live at home before the age of twenty", but should study or live at the royal court until his twentieth birthday, spending his time in useful and praiseworthy pursuits in preparation for his future.[22] As far as actual studies are concerned, the picture is varied although there is no significant difference between the education of orphans and that of children living with their parents. What is important is to establish how far the guardians and tutors were ready and able to fulfil the wishes of the parents as expressed in the parents' wills. Miklós Esterházy dealt in detail with these problems in the two wills that he made. There are major differences between the will written in 1623 when he had only one son, István, and the will that he made in 1641, by which time he had had several more sons. In the first, Esterházy expressed the desire that his son should study until the age of at least twenty, but not after he had reached twenty-two. He was to attend the Jesuit grammar school at Nagyszombat until the age of sixteen, then spend between three and six years in Vienna. At the age of twenty-two, he was to complete his studies with a short tour in Germany and Italy. In the second will, the number of years to be spent at Nagyszombat was radically reduced. His sons were to leave the grammar school at the age of twelve, then go to Vienna. Furthermore, there is no mention whatsoever of tours in Germany and Italy.[23] However, the wishes of the palatine were not carried out to the latter. Pál studied at Nagyszombat and Graz until the age of eighteen and spent only one year in Vienna. All three boys completed their studies at the age of eighteen since it was in their interests to be emancipated as soon as possible and, assume their full rights as adults.

Farkas Kovacsóczy, the chancellor of Transylvania, wanted his children to attend Transylvanian German schools to learn German at the age of ten, and to study at foreign universities from the age of sixteen.[24] However, he fell victim to the struggle for power among the Transylvanian elite in 1594 and his family lost much of their social prestige and material wealth. Kovacsóczy's sons were saved by conversion, and attended Jesuit schools in opposition to their father's will.[25]

In addition to stipulating the type and length of their children's education, fathers usually gave instructions as to the kind of people who were to surround their sons. Ferenc Rédey even listed the names of the tutors and the servant, who were to attend his son.[26] The two wills written by Miklós Esterházy differ greatly on this point, also. In the first he gave instructions for István to be surrounded by an extraordinarily large retinue and great luxury. Eight youths of noble birth, possibly relatives, were to accompany him. He was to have a priest of his own, a steward of the household was to take charge of the whole company, and there were to be a tutor and two servants in addition. This type of ostentatious power is absent in the second version, in which the boys are to be accompanied only by two or three cousins of the same age during their school years. The cost of their education was reduced to one-third of the sum originally envisaged. In the 1624 will the palatine intended that István should spend two years in Vienna, but in the version drafted in 1641 he wrote that he did not wish László "to be at the court at a young age. Not because of the court, but because of the company there."[27]

Despite being eminent patrons of the Catholic Church, both Esterházy and Nádasdy wanted to guard their children against its excessive influence. "It is well known", Nádasdy wrote concerning the friars, "that there are some superiors who persuade the young to anything they want." In his will he therefore forbade his children from giving to the church anything beyond the wealth he himself had donated. Nor did he have a very high opinion of the recruiting principles and methods used by the religious orders: "I wish, and expressly command, that no one who still has only the discretion of a child should be allowed to opt for that state. They should wait until they are able to understand just what it means to be a friar or a nun...I have seen and experienced, in the short time I have lived so far, that the monastic orders often need these young persons not for themselves but for their wealth."[28] Esterházy, too, warned his daughter, Marianka, not to join the Poor Clares "as a consequence of some childish persuasion".

In most wills boys were permitted to take possession of the property they had inherited at the age of twenty or twenty-one. However, Nádasdy was fearful that even at this age his sons would be subject to harmful influences. He forbade his sons to mortgage their property before they came of age. Young men were free to get married at the age of twenty-one or twenty-two in order to prevent their being "diverted from other duties by the flesh and the outer world". Brides were usually supposed to be of equal social and financial standing, and also of the same denomination. Furthermore, in contrast to the Pálffys, Zrínyis and Batthyánys, Palatine Esterházy wanted his sons to marry Hungarian girls, "not out of any aversion to foreign peoples but to avoid collision with foreign morals, the introduction of which into a family rarely brings any good".[29] Lord Chief Justice István Báthory forbade Anna Báthory to marry a Pole.[30]

All the evidence we have indicates that parents tried to defend their children's interests, especially the interests of their sons, and to eradicate any potential harmful influences on them even after their own deaths. However, the fate of an orphan depended largely on his or her guardian.

GUARDIANS

Werbőczy's *Tripartitum*, a collection of customary law, stipulated that all minors were to be placed in the care of guardians. However, in reality—as can be seen in wills made in this period—guardianship continued until the orphan reached the age of twenty or twenty-four or until he or she married. Three types of guardianship were defined by law: a) that stipulated in the last will and testament of the parents; b) natural and legal guardianship based on kinship; and c) that exercised by guardians appointed by the ruler in the absence of a will and in the event of there being no living relatives.[31]

If the father had expressed his wishes concerning the identity and actions of the guardian or guardians, guardianship was usually unproblematic. By long-established custom it was the king or the prince of Transylvania who was asked to support orphans as their primary guardian. In Royal Hungary it was deemed proper to win the support of the palatine and of the chancellor or other magnate also. The archbishops of Esztergom and Kalocsa, who often also bore the title of chancellor, were frequently asked by Protestants to act as guardians should their children be left as orphans. Even Zsigmond Rákóczi, a leading patron of the Reformed Church, committed his three sons and one stepdaughter to the care of the chancellor and the bishop of Eger not long after he had been elected prince of Transylvania.[32] In the case of rulers and high dignitaries, the title of guardian was usually only a formality. Their only function was to settle possible disputes among guardians or to find a replacement should a guardian die.

The initial formalities in a will were followed by an enumeration of the executors of the will. Several names were included here, since, as members of the parents' generation or of the previous generation, it was probable that at least some of them would have died by the time the will came into force. The four or five guardians, sometimes even more, took care of the orphans either in turn or as a body. If a parent named only one guardian, for example his or her younger brother, the latter would name a further guardian or guardians in his own will. If the estates inherited by orphans were some distance apart—in different counties, for example—it was again practical to appoint several guardians. In the event that significant property was inherited on the mother's side, a relative from the mother's family had to be included among the guardians. Thus guardians were recruited from among the child's relatives and from among the country's highest dignitaries. These guardians decided on all important questions relating to the person and property of orphans and administered the orphans' estates, although the everyday duties were naturally performed by administrators appointed in the will from among the administrative officials of the estates.

Natural and legal guardianship served the interests of orphaned children and secured the order of succession. A surviving mother therefore played a very delicate role. Although Werbőczy recognised the right of mothers and grandmothers to be guardians, and especially their right to administer property inherited on the mother's side, this right remained only as long as the mother did not remarry. The administration of the paternal inheritance was usually claimed by relatives on the father's side.[33] In most cases relatives on the father's side did their best to enforce their rights in opposition to the mother, since guardianship exercised by the mother might endanger the right of inheritance through the male line. If orphans died young, without heirs of their own, the father's property was inherited by the father's relatives. However, if the mother was acting as guardian, she and her relatives would be in possession of this inheritance when the child died. If she remarried and had further children she might try to keep the paternal inheritance of her deceased child unlawfully for her new family.

In spite of this, mothers were often appointed as the natural and legal guardians of their orphaned children. It was only reasonable that mothers should not be excluded from bringing up children under the age of twelve merely on the basis of legal considerations. Lawsuits could be avoided with some foresight. Husbands could empower their wives to remain guardians of their own children even after a second marriage. It was practical to make these provisions in a will, since an appointed guardian usually had primacy over a blood relative. Widows and stepmothers sometimes requested confirmation of their rights as guardians from the ruler or the palatine. The most straightforward solution was, of course, for members of the father's family to be included among the guardians.

In the absence of the first two types of guardian the king or palatine would appoint guardians for orphaned children. The ruler concerned himself only in cases of children from families of the highest rank, while the palatine appointed guardians for orphans belonging to families of the lesser nobility. He exercised unlimited power in this area, and even the archbishops of Esztergom could only put forward proposals in cases of importance to them. In most cases the palatine appointed the guardian or guardians and sent their mandate to the general assembly of the county in question. There it was either acknowledged or opposed by those who could prove their right to be guardians. It often happened that the palatine transferred to the general assembly his right to appoint guardians.

Anyone, who was requested to act as a guardian, was obliged to do so, although an exemption could sometimes be obtained in the event that the nominated guardian had many children of his own, that his estates were scattered, that he lived at a great distance from the estates of the orphan, or that he was engaged in diplomatic, military or other public duties. He could also be exempted if he was able to prove himself unfit for the role. This meant being illiterate, suffering from a serious illness, being on bad terms with the orphan's family, or being of an unsuitable age. People under twenty-four could claim to be too young, while those above sixty could claim to be too old for the responsibilities of guardianship.[34] This left open the possibility that a nominated guardian could be excused from fulfilling his duty. On the other hand, for the same reasons individuals could find themselves deprived of the possibility of becoming a guardian. However, none of the obstacles worked automatically.

One relevant example is that of Tamás Erdődy. After the death of his son, Kristóf, his widow and the mother of his children, Borbála Thurzó, became the children's guardian. She administered their inheritance without a problem for years, but in

1619 she came into conflict with her sisters-in-law over the division of certain estates. At that point the grandfather of the orphans, Tamás Erdődy, asked the king to appoint him guardian of his grandchildren. Borbála Thurzó argued against this request, saying that Erdődy lived a long way from the inherited estates, that he was over sixty and seriously ill, and that he had many children of his own. However, her arguments proved ineffective and the case remained open until the death of Tamás Erdődy in 1624.[35]

People who had been condemned for a capital offence or who were regarded by others as "suspicious guardians" for the careless administration of their own property, as well as those who treated their wards cruelly, were of dubious morals, or poor, could not be appointed guardians. Imre Majthényi, for example, wanted to become the guardian of his nephews. In 1599 he had been denounced on charges of bigamy and his own children had been taken from him and were being brought up by his younger brothers. However, because no cases had been initiated by anyone against him for twenty years the charge was withdrawn in 1618. In theory, Majthényi was therefore eligible to be a guardian. However, in a bitter letter his younger brother reminded him of all his wrongdoing as noted in the family records. The accusations included the murders of three women—two of noble birth and one servant—and the murder of Majthényi's own illegitimate child. We do not know for sure whether or not these charges were justified, although we do know that after receiving this letter Majthényi abandoned his attempt to win the guardianship for which he had sued.[36]

The majority of those who were asked to act as guardians accepted, since the responsibility could be highly profitable. The administration of an orphan's estates was a paying concern, although there were some legal safeguards to protect the interests of the orphans—for example, guardians had to draw up an inventory of the property in the presence of county officials when they took over the administration. They could be removed in the event of incorrect administration or fraudulent misuse, or be obliged to pay very high damages. However, such precautions were rarely effective. The inventories were often inaccurate or were never drawn up at all, and cash was often returned only in part, and even that only in instalments. The annual income from the orphan's estates was often invested by the guardian to make a profit for himself. According to some wills, a regular salary was to be given to the guardians in order to prevent them simply granting themselves any allowance they chose. However, some wills invested them with full powers. Only a few guardians were as careful as the Majthényi brothers or Zsigmond Bánchy, deputy lieutenant of Zemplén county, who had detailed accounts prepared including the sums spent on supporting their wards. The Majthényis even entered in their accounts the two forints per year paid for nurses and the twelve forints paid annually for tutors.[37]

HALF-ORPHANS

The appointing of guardians and administrators did not resolve the question of whose family the orphan was to live in. Orphans did not necessarily grow up in the household of one of their guardians. Their new home was determined by certain social rules. A widowed father, for example, could not bring up his daughters, nor even sons under the age of eight or ten, without the help of a woman of appropriate rank, even if the whole female household of the deceased mother, often comprising many members of staff, remained at his disposal. It was also not considered suitable for a very young widow—for example a woman under the age of twenty-four—to live alone with her children, although this was not without precedent.

Here again, the age of the orphans was a crucial factor. Boys of school age were sent to colleges, leaving only their accommodation during the holidays to be arranged. Girls of about the same age were usually sent to the households of distinguished ladies who generally tried to find husbands for them. Orphaned boys over the age of sixteen could, theoretically, live alone in their own households on their own estates, but in practice this usually happened only once they had reached eighteen or twenty. Girls legally came of age at sixteen but were not allowed to live alone before their marriage. As Erzsébet Czobor wrote, "…a girl is a weak creature and however sound her morals, however pious her life, there will inevitably be bad things said of her. There are examples of girls living alone who have been obliged to suffer unjust slander."[38]

Orphans, who had lost both their parents, were cared for by their closest relatives, usually by their grandparents. Grandmothers, in particular, were often eager to bring up their grandchildren, either as guardians or without official authorisation. The children of Ferenc Illésházy, for example, lost first their mother, then their father. Their stepmother married again but did not take the children with her into her new family. They were brought up by their grandmother who received 150 forints a year for their maintenance.[39] Gyurkó Haller was also brought up by his grandmother, Borbála Segnyey, the wife of Mihály Károlyi.[40] If the orphans had older married brothers or sisters they were automatically given a home by them. Boys usually went to live with their older brothers, and girls with their older sisters. If they had no older brother, young boys could also be raised by their married sisters. Pál Révay, for example, was brought up by his brother-in-law, Pál Nádasdy.[41] The solution adopted by Szerafin Daróczy was rather unusual and doubtless very problematic for his wife. Not wanting to leave to the care of his second wife the children born to his first wife, he stipulated that his first wife's mother and his second wife should live together and take care of the children between them.[42]

The situation of orphans, who had lost both parents and who had no living relatives, or none with whom they could live for one reason or another, was the most problematic of all. Each case was unique, and they will be discussed separately.

From the legal point of view, the least problematic situation was that of children whose mother had died. However, it was often the loss of a mother that was the most difficult for the family to bear. Since childbirth was a major cause of death among women, children were often bereaved of their mothers. In the event that a father died, a good guardian, helpful relatives and careful administrators could make the loss less painful for the children. The higher the social rank of the widow, the less dramatic was the change for the children. They continued to live in the familiar environment and in familiar surroundings, and had to cope "only" with the emotional aspect of their loss.

In contrast, a mother's death changed everything. The father had to decide where his small children were to live, even if only for the duration of the year of mourning. They were often sent to another family and had to get used to new faces and a new life-style. Sisters and brothers might be separated and might see very little of their father. Zsigmond Forgách's second marriage solved none of these problems since his new wife, Katalin Pálffy, disliked her stepdaughter. In order to keep the child away from home she had her brought up by her own mother, Mária Fugger, at Vöröskő.[43] On his wife's death, László Károlyi took his seven children to the Dowager Princess Zsófia Báthory at Munkács. His two eldest daughters even found husbands there— the Perényi brothers, János and Pál.[44]

An ideal solution in terms of the care of children bereaved of their mother, although one that was resorted to only rarely, was that adopted by Imre Forgách. Forgách had five daughters with his first wife,who were aged between one and eight when their mother died. His second wife also died after a few months. Not wanting to get married for a third time, but obliged to find someone to care for his daughters, Forgách persuaded one of his relatives, an elderly widow, to become part of his household at his castle in Komjáti, and entrusted her with the task of bringing up his children. This was an ideal solution for all concerned. The widow had been living in difficult circumstances and had no living child of her own. She proved to be an excellent lady of the house and was so good with the girls that they came to love her like a mother.[45]

In contrast, families belonging to the lesser nobility, who were living in much worse financial circumstances were often devastated by a mother's death. If the father chose not to re-marry, and if there was no reliable widow in the family, the children had to be sent to live with relatives. If the parents had brothers or sisters, or other married children, these relatives usually brought up the orphans out of love, either without any compensation or in return for services previously performed by the parents. If the family that undertook to bring up the children was not wealthy or was only distantly related to the orphans' family, the father had to pay for their maintenance. The sum to be paid was between 100 and 300 forints a year per child. Most fathers could not pay for four, five, or even more children, while relatives who offered to look after the orphans out of love could usually take in only one or two of them. This meant that broth-ers and sisters were often separated.

The Révay children, for example, were separated in this way. Márton Révay's wife, Zsófia Esterházy, died in 1620 leaving seven young children. Their father immediately sent fourteen-year-old Ilona to the household of Gáspár Illésházy's wife. Two of the children were sent to their cousin, Erzsébet Révay, who, herself an orphan, had been brought up by Márton Révay. She was thus able to repay the kindness done by her foster-father by bringing up some of his own children. Erzsébet and her husband had no children of their own, so the little orphaned relatives were most welcome. Révay's sons were already of school age and therefore presented no problem. Only the youngest of them, Miklós, had to be entrusted to the care of his eldest brother.[46]

While the death of a father brought about a tragic situation from the legal point of view, it usually presented no problems in relation to the accommodation of the orphans. The children remained with their mother even if she was not their official guardian. It was the guardians, however, who determined the question of the children's education and the sum the widow could spend on her own and her children's maintenance. Conflicts arose usually only in the event of the mother's second marriage. Szerafin Daróczy, for example, wrote in his will that if his wife were to remarry their child was to be taken away from her so as "not to be harassed by a stepfather".[47] This was a cruel but fairly common procedure; mothers who remarried were compelled to renounce their children.

At the same time, people were aware of the importance of the relationship between a child and his or her mother, especially during the child's first ten years. Ferenc Nádasdy tried to resolve the difficult situation, and to safeguard both his property and his grandchildren's interests, by stipulating in his will that if his daughters-in-law were widowed and then remarried, their daughters should remain with them until their own marriages. The mothers, however, were not to administer their inherited properties but were to be given a sum for the maintenance of their daughters: 200 forints until the children reached the age of ten, and a maximum of 500 forints thereafter. Boys were to remain with their mothers only until the age of eight, and were to be given maintenance of 200 forints a year. After this they were to be sent to school and were to be brought up by male relatives.[48]

Mothers naturally made every effort to keep their children. The best-known case is that of Krisztina Nyáry who sued her mother-in-law, Erzsébet Czobor, for the guardianship of her two daughters. When her son, Imre Thurzó, died, Erzsébet Czobor extracted a statement from her daughter-in-law to the effect that the daughter-in-law left the maintenance, education and custody of the children to her. Krisztina Nyáry was subsequently forced to return to her mother and leave not only her daughters, but also her dowry, wedding presents and personal belongings with Erzsébet Czobor. In 1624 she married Miklós Esterházy and her husband supported her in her fight to reclaim her children. King Ferdinand II ordered Erzsébet Czobor to give the children back but the countess refused to obey. She presented the young mother's letter of renunciation and, using arguments based on customary law, was not willing to accept even a reasonable compromise. When Esterházy was elected palatine by the Diet in 1625 he at once succeeded in having a decree passed against Erzsébet Czobor. However, the grandmother still refused to give up; this time it was she who urged for a compromise. She wished to retain the guardianship of her son's daughters and the administration of their property but was willing to allow one of the little girls to live with her mother on condition that she should be allowed to continue to live according to her faith and should be able to visit her grandmother regularly. Erzsébet Czobor promised the huge sum of one thousand forints a year for her maintenance. She argued that "it would be advisable to consider that the custody of the children themselves is more important than the administration of their estates". However, her efforts proved futile and she was forced to return the children to their mother.[49]

THE CARE OF ORPHANS AFTER THE DEATHS
OF BOTH PARENTS

Orphans of aristocratic families who lost both parents, while still minors, and who had no close relatives, or no relatives who, for whatever reason, were eligible to act as their guardians, were handed over to the care of the king as their primary guardian. This happened, for example, to several generations of the Homonnai family; to Miklós and Péter, the sons of György Zrínyi; and to the children of Pál Rákóczi.

Where the orphans were to live, the identity of their tutors and teachers, and their lifestyle was determined by the palatine and by the archbishop of Esztergom. The most famous of the archbishops, Péter Pázmány, entrusted orphan girls and all orphan boys under the age of ten to the custody of distinguished widows with large households. His own nephew was an orphan and was brought up by Margit Bakits, the widow of Menyhért Balassa.[50] At the age of five Erzsébet Homonnai Drugeth was taken in by Zsuzsanna Erdődy, the widow of Kristóf Thurzó. When she reached eight years of age she was sent to Vöröskő, to Mária Fugger, the widow of Miklós Pálffy. Finally, she spent the five years before her marriage in the court of the palatine, in the care of Krisztina Nyáry.[51]

The wishes of the parents were also taken into consideration when a home was chosen for an orphan. Anna Rákóczi, the daughter of Lord Chief Justice Pál Rákóczi, was given a home in the Convent of St. Jacob in Vienna, which was in the same street as her family's palace. According to her mother's will she had the right to decide whether or not to remain at the convent,[52] and in 1642, at the age of thirteen, she decided that she would become a nun. The fate of her younger brother, László Rákóczi, was determined by political factors. His uncle, György Rákóczi I, naturally agreed to become his guardian and to bring him up when the boy was left an orphan at the age of four. However, the king decided to have him brought up at the royal court in Vienna. Due to the tension that existed between Vienna and Transylvania he was regarded almost as a hostage. It was also feared that the prince might force the boy to convert to the Calvinist faith. In order to counter the protests of György Rákóczi I, the young child was treated with special care and was brought up in the imperial court as the playmate and fellow-student of the future Ferdinand IV. He spent almost fifteen years, nearly half his life, at the court.[53]

The education of children at court followed the classical Catholic pattern, even if the children themselves belonged to a different denomination. The Calvinist Pál Rákóczi studied at the Jesuit College in Graz for five years. He subsequently converted to the Catholic faith.[54] The Zrínyi orphans had only one Catholic lay teacher and spent much time at the court of the Protestant Batthyánys, therefore the king ordered them to attend the Jesuit College in Graz when they were seven and eight years old.[55] László Rákóczi was educated mostly in Vienna and spent only one year, 1645, in Nagyszombat. György Homonnai Drugeth studied in Nagyszombat and spent the year 1647 at the University of Vienna.[56] Children not brought up in the court of the palatine or the archbishop, nor at a place near enough for regular meetings with these dignitaries to take place, were summoned for audiences in order to ensure that they were making suitable progress.

The archbishop of Esztergom, Péter Pázmány, was also in charge of the administration of the orphans' estates and other property. In 1622 he had the movable property and treasures inherited by János and Erzsébet Homonnai taken temporarily to the chapter of Esztergom for safekeeping. He also made arrangements in connection with the orphans' estates in Poland, and even appealed successfully to King Ferdinand II to intervene on their behalf with the king of Poland.[57] Guardians often tried to secure for the orphans the non-hereditary titles that had belonged to their fathers. In 1628 the king appointed eight-year-old Miklós Zrínyi as Master of the Horse, and three-year-old László Rákóczi also received one of his father's counties, becoming lord lieutenant of Sáros.[58]

Guardians could instruct, or allow, orphans to travel within the country or abroad with the consent of the ruler. Pál Rákóczi and the Zrínyi brothers travelled in Italy. László Rákóczi was allowed to make a long journey in the western part of Royal Hungary, in the course of which he visited the most important castles along the border. After this he accompanied Ferdinand IV to Spain. Miklós Pázmány went first to Rome, and then spent three years in Paris. As befitted their rank, the orphaned sons of noble families were thus given the same kind of education as boys whose fathers were still living. Their guardians regularly informed the king of the children's activities.

Guardians also played a part in arranging the marriages of their highborn wards. There was, for example, a difference of opinion between Esterházy and Pázmány on whether twelve-year-old Erzsébet Homonnai Drugeth should marry her twenty-eight-year-old cousin, László Révay. Pázmány was against the idea and wrote in a letter to the king that Révay was only a simple, uneducated nobleman, much older than Erzsébet and unworthy of the hand of a countess. Pázmány asked the king to let the orphan be brought up at his court. The case was settled two years later, in 1630, when Erzsébet Homonnai did in fact marry László Révay.[59] Fifteen years later her nephew, György Homonnai Drugeth, was also entrusted to the guardianship of the king. He was later attracted by Esterházy's court, although by that time the palatine was no longer living, and in 1651 he married Mária Esterházy.

This system for the care of orphans belonging to aristocratic families was perpetuated not only through solidarity towards the

caste or by the principle of reciprocity among the families belonging to it. Young highborn orphans were especially important
to the royal court. However young they were, they were owners
of huge estates and treasures, and inherited important titles and
offices. If the father had been a faithful supporter of the king, it
was important to ensure that his children followed his example.
If the father had belonged to an opposing faction, everything had
to be done to prevent the child from doing so. If the orphan's
estates were situated along the Polish, Transylvanian or Turkish
border, they were vitally important in terms of the defence of the
realm. If his family had recently been converted to Catholicism,
the representatives of the Catholic Church did their best to protect the child or the young man from the influence of other denominations. Orphans could be brought up under the authority
of the royal court along such lines as were considered proper by
the king. They could also be linked to those political trends
thought appropriate by the king with regard to his own interests.

By acting as guardian to orphans from aristocratic families
the king was able to consolidate his influence among the Hungarian elite. The royal court sometimes proved successful in its
strategy, as in the case of the Homonnai brothers, György Zrínyi
and Pál Rákóczi. In other cases success was only partial. The
intentions of the court were sometimes frustrated by the palatine
and the archbishop, who were also trying to exploit the orphans'
defenceless state to their own advantage, both politically and
economically.

In the principality of Transylvania, orphans who had lost
both parents were likewise taken into the care of the rulers, the
princes of Transylvania. However, there were no specific officials in Transylvania charged with the care of orphans. Orphans
were far more often supported by their own relatives, something
which was facilitated in the principality by the close relationships within the narrower circle of the elite.

WIDOWED MOTHERS AND THEIR CHILDREN

A comparison between the circumstances of widows and widowers suggests that many more women than men remained alone. One particular group of women, who were members of the elite in their own right, were able to survive on their own as a result of their financial standing, strong will, prestige, political connections and influential relatives. Some female members of the aristocracy, like Dorottya Zrínyi, the widow of Boldizsár Batthyány; Anna Wesselényi, the widow of István Csáky; Éva Poppel, the widow of Ferenc Batthyány; Borbála Segnyey, the widow of Mihály Károlyi; Anna Thurzó, the widow of János Szunyogh; Erzsébet Czobor, the widow of György Thurzó; and Zsuzsanna Lórántffy and Zsófia Báthory, the two dowager princesses Rákóczi, were among those belonging to this privileged group. They all had children and had all lost their first husbands. They were all either young or middle-aged, but were of high standing and certainly wealthy enough to attract several suitors. However, they all refused to remarry. While each may have had her own individual reasons, as a group they benefited from the many opportunities for power enjoyed by widows of high rank.

Often widows of lesser standing also preferred not to remarry. This could have advantages both legally and socially, since customary law recognised a mother's right to be the guardian of her own children only as long as "she bears the title and name of her deceased husband and does not remarry".[60] A husband's will often contained the stipulation that his widow was only able to enjoy her inheritance as long as she bore his name. Mothers who remarried could even lose the right to care for their own children. This was due not to the selfishness of the deceased father but to the need to defend the family's property and to safeguard the children's interests. A mother's second husband could easily become guardian of her children and administrator of their property, and as such he would have ample opportunity to misuse his powers in the interests of his own family. If a mother had further children by her second husband, those, made orphans by the death of her first husband, could be at a disadvantage. As Ferenc Nádasdy wrote, "it is often the case that a widow of this kind supports her second husband with income from the property inherited by the children born to her by her first husband…"[61]

It was therefore natural that women who remained widows were highly respected. However strange it sounds to modern ears, contemporaries would have found nothing surprising in the words used by Anna Wesselényi, herself a widow of forty-four years, when she recommended her son's future wife to him: "She is not one to put aside her black clothes after your death."[62] It should be noted, however, that while the state of widowhood was held in high esteem, the sources tell us very little about the actual morals of widows. In this respect, the funeral sermon for Borbála Apor, the widow of Ferenc Torday, invites reflection. The priest quoted the words of St. Paul in his funeral address for this woman who had worn black "with great honour" for fifty-one years: "Honour widows that are widows indeed."[63]

Women who could afford to remain widows were supported in the bringing up of their children by their relatives and acquaintances in high positions. If their financial status remained unchanged the bringing up and education of daughters was not affected by the death of their father. Mothers of young boys were apparently in an easier position, since they had to keep and support their sons only until the age of ten, when they were sent to colleges and to the court of the ruler, the palatine, or some distinguished magnate. The only say a mother had in her son's development thereafter was in the decision as to which college he should attend, in whose court he should live, and where he should spend his holidays. The everyday care and actual education of the child were provided by the schools. Mihály Károlyi, for example, was ten years old when he lost his father. In his will, written in 1626, he mentions his gratitude to his mother, who had sent him away first to study and later to the court of Matthias II.[64] His own son, László Károlyi, was left an orphan at the age of only four, and it was owing to his mother that he received a good education and was able to spend four years at the court of György Rákóczi I.[65] Protestants often entrusted the education of their sons to carefully selected teachers rather than sending them to a college. This was what happened, for example, in the case of Ádám Batthyány, Ferenc Nádasdy and Ferenc Rédey. Nevertheless, despite all the help they received and despite the well-established system of care for orphans, a widowed mother's relationship with her son or sons was often extremely delicate.

Some mothers found it impossible to get on with their sons at all. Judit Imecs, the wife of Lázár Apor, was widowed while pregnant. She already had five sons and two daughters and the child she was carrying, a son, Zsigmond, died when he was one year old. The mother sent her eldest son, Lázár, to study in Nagyszombat. When he had completed his studies he went to the court of György Rákóczi II and became famous, both for his excellent knowledge of Latin and for his courage. Péter became a valet of the prince and died during the latter's campaign in Poland. The careers of János and Farkas also started promisingly. It was only István whom Judit was unable to manage. He badly needed a father's strictness, and was therefore sent to a relative, István Pettki, captain-general of the Szeklers and lord steward of the prince. Pettki imposed a rigid discipline on the boy and tried to break him both physically and mentally. István was stripped and whipped in front of the whole household and was made to follow Pettki's carriage barefoot. Pettki did go as far as to have a carpet laid down on that particular occasion, saying that the boy was a relative after all. István escaped and ran home more than once. The first time this happened, his mother also gave him a beating, but when he arrived home in rags she took pity on him. She let him stay for a few days, gave him good food and bought him new clothes, but eventually sent him back. Pettki wrote the mother an angry letter asking her not to interfere if she wanted him to bring up her son. It took three years to break the boy but Pettki's methods proved highly effective: István became the most successful of all the Apor brothers.[66]

Even without problems such as these, a mother could come into conflict with her son once he began to regard himself as an adult and to take an interest in the division of the estate. Although, law gave male heirs the power to dispose of their own estates only when they came of age, parents had the right to share their property with their children during their lifetime. Boys growing up without a father found it difficult to wait until the legal age for inheritance, something which was quite natural, considering that in many cases they already bore their fathers' titles, were accepted as adults by their contemporaries, and had to fulfil their duties in the Diet or even on the battlefield, but were still not in a position to dispose of their estate and become the head of their family. They were often prevented from doing so by their mothers, women of strong will who had managed to live on their own and keep the family together for many years. These strong and determined women were used to being independent and powerful. They rarely resigned the headship of the family voluntarily. Many widows refused to divide the property before their sons came of age, even though this inevitably led to tensions within the family. Such tensions often had an impact on the relationship between mother and son for the rest of their lives.

Problems also arose between mothers and sons who lived together after the estate had been divided; and similar difficulties arose in relationships between mothers-in-law and daughters-in-law. A number of serious conflicts between mothers and sons are known from this period. One such case was that of Anna Wesselényi and István Csáky. Despite their love for one another, these two strong-willed and obstinate individuals quarrelled incessantly for thirty-one years.[67] The relationship between Ádám Batthyány and Éva Poppel was similar, but in their case it was the mother who soon found herself on the losing side. She was forced to retreat to the estate she had inherited from her mother's family, from where she tried to defend the interests of her daughters once it became clear that her son had designs even on their property. "You are a constant cause of distress to me", she wrote to her son. "Do not kill me with sadness, let me live...You have quite ruined me and have turned me into a living corpse...I do not think anyone else in the world would have treated their mother as you have treated me since your father's death."[68]

The relationship between a mother and her son who had come of age could also be made difficult if the mother chose to remarry. Such conflicts were generally caused by material, rather than emotional, concerns. One typical case was that of Ferenc Nádasdy. His father died in October 1633 and the king appointed his mother, Judit Révay, to act as guardian to him and to his two siblings.[69] She had the full support of her relative, Miklós Esterházy. The smooth and rapid settlement of the question of guardianship was due to the palatine's intervention, as was the appointment of ten-year-old Ferenc to the vacant post of lord lieutenant of Vas County. It was common to appoint hereditary lord lieutenants nominally, even if the child appointed was a minor. However, it was by no means common for a young man actually to perform the duties of his office at the age of thirteen, which is what happened in the case of Ferenc Nádasdy, who was a particularly precocious child. His teachers were highly educated men of letters and ministers in his parents' court—men such as István Zvonarich, Bertalan Kis, György Letenyei and Gergely Muzsai—whose influence was a decisive factor in his development. At the age of ten or twelve he was studying theology and literature, and at the age of thirteen—encouraged by his mother—he published a translation from Latin into Hungarian, prepared with the help of his teachers. He had little time for his teenage contemporaries: "Many of them…are more interested in tales and games than in serious and useful pursuits. They leave the serious discussion of the Scriptures and other holy things to their fathers and to churchmen."[70] All the evidence indicates that the young Nádasdy was able to manage his affairs as lord lieutenant properly, even if with a certain amount of help and that he was treated as an adult by his contemporaries. His relationship with his mother was still unproblematic at this stage and Judit Révay supported her son in his ambitions.

Difficulties began to emerge in 1638. Ferenc Nádasdy's sixteenth birthday was approaching, and with it a new era in the life of this ambitious boy. At the same time, however, his mother decided to remarry. Her powerful relative, Miklós Esterházy, wanted her to marry Ádám Forgách. The existence of a stepfather would have resulted in certain limitations for Nádasdy, even if the boy could not be forced to accept his mother's new husband as his guardian. Furthermore, Forgách was a Catholic and Nádasdy's Lutheran supporters turned the boy against him, fearing an attempt to convert the boy to the Catholic faith. Nádasdy, on his part, was afraid that the estates that he had inherited from his father and that were administered by his mother as his guardian would be transferred to the hands of his stepfather.

His fears were well founded; half of the Csejte estate was mortgaged by Judit Révay to Forgách at the very beginning of their relationship. Later, when Nádasdy wanted to redeem the estates, Forgách demanded the very high sum of forty thousand forints. The relationship between mother and son was poisoned as Nádasdy argued in a letter to Esterházy, due to the former's unhappy disposition. In the same letter he informed the palatine that he intended to take his mother under his own authority and to pay her a wage.[71]

The boy had supporters; the Révay family, and even the prince of Transylvania, stood behind him in his protest against the planned marriage. Meanwhile, Esterházy had no time to waste. He summoned Forgách and Judit Révay to Keresztúr where she was converted to the Catholic faith before the betrothal took place. Things happened so quickly that the engagement ring had to be borrowed from the palatine's wife. Forgách had not counted upon such a quick decision and had no ring with him. After the betrothal Nádasdy simply locked the gates against his mother on her return home.

Even the king intervened in this conflict between mother and son. He and the palatine tactfully asked Ádám Batthyány to explain to Nádasdy the importance of filial love, obedience and duty. Although Batthyány did not have a great deal to say to Nádasdy with respect to these qualities, he still managed to include a valuable piece of advice in his letter: "You should not make your prince heavy of heart and alienate him from you while you are so young. You have hardly entered the world and should live long by the grace of God. If you start setting up obstacles for yourself so early in life and disobey His Majesty, what do you hope to achieve in the world in your remaining years?"[72] Nádasdy and his mother finally reached a compromise and made peace with one another, but neither of them forgot the conflict. When Nádasdy took leave of his mother before his journey to Italy in 1642, she answered him with bitter words: "…you ask for my maternal blessing, so God bless you. But as a rule maternal blessings are only of help to obedient sons."[73]

There were doubtless many instances of deteriorating relationships between mothers and sons. Thus fathers often tried to give advice and to secure adequate maintenance for their widows in their wills. Ferenc Rédey warned his son to be obedient and to love and serve his mother, while the latter was asked to be patient and gentle with the boy. In the event of a disagreement the mother was to take possession of sufficient property to allow her to live comfortably, independent of her son. However, she was requested not to let things "reach such a state but to teach the boy as loving mothers are wont to do".[74]

STEPMOTHERS

There were few men who continued to live as widowers after bereavement. Zsigmond Kornis survived his wife by eleven years. Ferenc Nádasdy was widowed at the age of forty-four and it was probably only his political ambitions and his ill health that prevented him from marrying again. Miklós Esterházy decided to remain alone at the age of fifty-nine when his second wife died. However, Ádám Forgách remarried at the age of about fifty for the third time after nearly twenty years as a widower, since he had had no children in his previous marriages.

Men were not forced to remarry out of defencelessness or insecurity. However, there were three common reasons for them to remarry when the year of mourning was over. The first, in István Csáky's words, was to enable them to find "physical and mental peace".[75] The second reason was in connection with their children's interests: the presence of a second or third wife solved the problem of caring for children born to a previous marriage or marriages. Last, but not least, remarriage was a way to increase their wealth.

The arrival of a stepmother usually had a positive impact on family life. It was regarded as natural for her to take care of her husband's children and we know of many instances where this was the case. Erzsébet Czobor, for example, brought up the two daughters of György Thurzó. Ferenc Gyulai describes in his will how his second wife "...loves my dear son, Ferenc Gyulai, as her own...".[76] It was also common for a second wife to bring children of her own into the marriage.

However, it was also possible for the arrival of a stepmother to disrupt the domestic peace. It was mainly the boys who suffered from the arrival of a new mother. The new wife might have an excessive influence over their father and prefer her own offspring. Many children of fathers who remarried experienced such situations, and the older the children, the greater the problems that arose.

Miklós Bethlen, for example, who was twenty when his father married for a second time, actually wrote an indictment against his stepmother, Klára Fricsi Fekete, in his autobiography and in his letters. He argued that she deliberately turned his younger brother and himself against their father, alienating them from him. She even contributed towards the breaking off of his brother's engagement by underhand means, forced their chief servants to leave them, and cheated them of tens of thousands of forints to the benefit of her own son, Sámuel, when the family property was divided. Miklós Bethlen summed up his opinion of her by quoting Ovid's words: *Lurida terribiles miscent aconita novercae* (*Stepmothers mix terrible black poison*). He was still seething with anger even forty years after the events: "...she made my father take Kamarás away from me, since Samuka needed it to keep cattle there. There is pasture enough at Szent-Miklós, too, as God is my judge! And is there not grazing land, hay and straw at Pagocsa, Teremi, Bonyha, Keresd or Szent-Pál?"[77]

The case of Palatine Zsigmond Forgách was similar. When he was left a widower for the second time his little daughter, Éva, had to be taken care of.[78] He therefore married for a third time, taking Katalin, daughter of Miklós Pálffy and Mária Fugger, as his wife. After the birth of a child of her own Katalin was embarrassed by the presence of the little girl from her husband's former marriage and tried to have her sent away. Thus little Éva Forgách lived between 1611 and 1617 mostly with Katalin Pálffy's mother at Vöröskő. She was not properly educated and could hardly write. "I am bad at writing", she confessed to her husband later, when it became clear that she needed help in composing a letter.[79]

Zsigmond Forgách died in 1621, and the distribution of the property led to serious disputes within the family. Éva Forgách was in the most unfavourable position, since her fate depended entirely on her stepmother. She reached marriageable age just at the time of her father's death and the ideal solution for her would have been immediate marriage. Her family background was excellent. Both her father and one of her uncles, Szaniszló Thurzó, had been palatines, and her other uncle, Ferenc Forgách, was archbishop of Esztergom. She also owned considerable property. Her dowry comprised 36,000 forints in cash and other property.[80] A woman with such a background would normally have had no difficulty finding a husband, but four years later, at the age of eighteen, Éva Forgách was still unmarried. Her stepmother was clearly preventing her from marrying, since she herself wanted to administer Éva's property for as long as possible.

Thus Éva Forgách decided to take a bold step; she met with István Csáky in secret, without her stepmother's knowledge. The young couple decided to get married. Kata Pálffy was furious and did everything she could to prevent the marriage. She charged Csáky with seduction, while the latter accused his future mother-in-law of misappropriating her stepdaughter's

dowry and giving the money to the Pálffy family. The scandal
continued for half a year until finally Péter Pázmány, archbishop
of Esztergom, was obliged to intervene. With his mediation the
family was eventually able to settle the matter and the betrothal
took place in the spring of 1625. Éva Forgách left home immediately and moved in with her future mother-in-law, Anna Wesselényi. However, her dowry was only recovered in total after
years of litigation.[81]

All the existing evidence points towards the conclusion that
the death of a father was often a turning point in the relationship
between his widow and her stepchildren. It might even lead to
their being separated for good, as children were only rarely entrusted to the care of their stepmother. Lord Chief Justice István
Báthory took Gábor and Anna, the children of István Báthory of
Somlyó and his first wife, into his protection when their father
died, removing them from the care of their Polish stepmother
and leaving her with just her own son, András Báthory. In other
families stepmothers and their husbands' children continued to
live together, but with the connecting thread between them broken there was nobody to suppress the tensions that emerged. The
inevitable division of the property often gave rise to protracted
lawsuits. The younger the orphans, the more defenceless they
were. If the orphans were minors they were at a distinct disadvantage, as illustrated by the case of Éva Forgách. If they were
nearer legal age it was the position of the stepmother's own
children that proved to be more vulnerable.

In the late sixteenth century, Gábor Kendy's widow, Anna
Révay, was concerned for her two little daughters as she lay on
her sickbed. The prince of Transylvania, Zsigmond Báthory, had
had her husband beheaded and his property confiscated. Only
the widow's own property was left to the family. Anna Révay
was anxious that her stepsons, deprived of their land by
Báthory, would do her daughters out of their inheritance in the

event of her death.[82] The example of Anna Héderváry is more typical. In order to force her to divide the property so that they could set up separate households, her stepsons attacked her in every possible way after the death of their father. She complained to her sons-in-law that they had heaped insults on her and had treated her as a servant. Her maidservants had been beaten and threatened with death and had all left her. The boys had also terrorised Anna Héderváry's two daughters and had stolen her wine and everything she had.[83]

Bearing in mind these and other similar cases, it seems to have been very wise of Judit Imecs to accept Lázár Apor's proposal of marriage on condition, that before the wedding, he assign to András and Ferenc, his two sons by his late wife, the portion of his property due to them.[84]

The death of a father did not necessarily result in the deterioration of the relationship between his children and their stepmother. Borbála Telegdy, the widow of Zsigmond Rákóczi, had four children to take care of—Zsuzsanna Csapy, her daughter by her first husband, and György, Zsigmond and Pál, then in their teens, who were Rákóczi's sons by his former wife. The boys had been with her from their early childhood and, as indicated by the letters she wrote to their guardian, Lajos Rákóczi, she cared for them as lovingly as a mother. In a letter to Lajos Rákóczi she wrote: "Our son, György, is in very poor health. He has been suffering from severe headaches and we have even had to cut his hair short because of them. He is now beginning to walk about again slowly, but for a time he was confined to bed."[85] The family remained united and fought as one for their estates against the Homonnai, Mágócsy and Szunyogh families. The decision as to where the two eldest boys should continue their studies was made in common, and it was the boys' stepmother who most keenly insisted that Pál should go to Nagyszombat and Graz.

However, this ideal relationship was spoilt when István Kendy became a member of the family after his marriage to Zsuzsanna Csapy, Borbála Telegdy's daughter from her first marriage. As chancellor of Transylvania and councillor of the prince he was an extremely rich man and seemed a good match for Zsuzsanna. However, hardly a year after the wedding he organised an attempt on the life of the ruler and subsequently lost everything he had. Borbála Telegdy was staying with her daughter at the time to help her with her newborn baby, and Kendy exploited his mother-in-law's kindness in order to re-establish himself. The plan was to seize the Rákóczi estates and to make use of the family's political influence. Kendy was unsuccessful in the latter of these two aims, but he was able to persuade Borbála, after some hesitation, to initiate a dispute regarding the division of property between herself and her stepsons from her marriage to Zsigmond Rákóczi. The acrimonious dispute lasted for five years. However, Borbála was unhappy about the whole process. While the dispute continued through intermediaries, she repeatedly assured the Rákóczi boys of her continuing motherly love for them: "…my dear sons, you will be aware that my deep motherly love towards you has remained unbroken and I do not spare myself on your behalf or refuse you my money. Whatever God has given me I shall share with you as with my own children."[86]

STEPFATHERS

In our discussion of guardians and widows, mention has already been made of the fact that, in Hungary, just as in other parts of Europe, noble families were often suspicious of second or third husbands. It was generally feared that newcomers would insist on assuming a leading role in the family. Those not affected personally usually had moral objections, regarding second marriages as bigamous. This was the attitude among the English aristocracy, for example. It is said that William Harvey believed marrying a widow meant being cuckolded by her first husband. Such views may sound strange coming from a scientist of his stature, but he maintained that children born to a widow by her second husband would take after her first husband.[87] However, the relatives of orphans were anxious lest the second husband might ignore the rights of his wife's children and use their property for the benefit of his own children.

Nor was this fear entirely unfounded. The Diet of 1659 referred the case of Miklós Pázmány to a special court. He was charged with having sold and spent the entire inheritance of his stepson, Imre Jakusith, totalling 250,000 forints in estates, jewels, furniture and cash.[88] István Listius, stepfather of Borbála Balassa, financed the Italian studies of his son, János, using the property of his stepdaughter. Furthermore, he relied on this same source when reorganising the finances of his married daughter by his first wife, Anna Rozália, when her estates were about to be confiscated as a result of debt. Although he regarded these transactions as loans, they were still referred to as unsettled matters in Borbála Balassa's will, made twenty-one years later.[89] The will made by Péter Szirmay reveals a similar situation: "...my dear father left me an orphan at the age of three and...my stepfather made my mother sell my father's house at Szendrő and he spent the little money she got for it, together with my dear father's beautiful *res mobilis*...".[90]

Relatives on the father's side did their best to prevent the stepfather from becoming the guardian of the orphans but were successful generally only after the death of the mother. Examples of such situations are typical among the lesser nobility. Kata Kürti's mother, Anna Által, married István Péchy after the death of her first husband. Anna and her second husband were granted guardianship of her daughter. However, when Anna died shortly afterwards, the father's relatives were successful in defending Kata's interests. The palatine took the guardianship away from the stepfather and granted it to her uncle, István Kürti.[91]

An interesting difference existed between the kingdom of Hungary and the principality of Transylvania, as regards the position of stepfathers. In the kingdom, fewer widows with children remarried. Those who remained widows and who had daughters were in a more favourable situation. Boys could choose to be independent of the guardianship of their stepfathers when as young as twelve.

In the principality, the presence of a stepfather in a family presented fewer problems. The chances of a widow remarrying were the same, regardless of whether she had sons or daughters. Women in the principality remained alone as widows far less often than their counterparts in the kingdom.[92]

The reasons for this are to be found in the differences between the two elites. The Transylvanian elite was much narrower and more limited in scope. It therefore had much stricter policies with respect to marriage. Some families were traditionally linked by marriage on the basis of either religion or territory. Such families had intermarried in almost every generation. Brothers and sisters of one family would often marry brothers and sisters of another. A widower would often marry another member of his deceased wife's family, usually her younger sister. Of course, such things also happened in Royal Hungary, but in Transylvania they occurred more often and were more conspicuous in the smaller community. As a result, the network of kinship became very complex and stepfathers usually came from within the wider circle of relatives.

In addition, the Transylvanian elite accumulated smaller properties and very few widows had the necessary financial means to remain independent. Even if they were able to support themselves, they frequently fell victim to greedy princes. No doubt there were also political considerations behind these ma-noeuvres. Ruining the widows of high-ranking politicians was an excellent means of intimidating the opposition. Under Prince Gábor Bethlen legal cases of this kind, as well as the actual for-feiture of property, took place largely in the years 1614 to 1618 and were directed against the supporters of his predecessor, Gábor Báthory. Lawsuits were initiated against the widows of János Imrefi, Mihály Dengeleghy and Dénes Bánffy, who was born a Báthory. As a result of the case against the widow of Boldizsár Kornis, the prince forced her to leave Transylvania and take refuge with the Poor Clares in Pozsony.[93] György Rákóczi I got rid of the circle of followers of Gábor Bethlen's brother, István, in the same manner. All widows and children of his followers, and even those, on whom the slightest shadow of suspicion had fallen, were in danger. Many highborn widows ceded their property rights to György Rákóczi in the hope of escaping accusations.[94] Thus their strained financial circum-stances and their legal vulnerability encouraged widows in Transylvania to remarry.

It was quite common for a woman to marry three, or even four times. However, remarriage was far from being a secure haven. Borbála Füzy's first husband, Pál Gyulay, was killed in December 1592 during the internal struggles of the Báthory family. Without even waiting to complete the one year of mourning, Borbála married István Jósika in February and they had two children during their six years of marriage. Her second husband was executed on the order of Zsigmond Báthory in September 1598. Her third and last husband was Zsigmond Sarmaséghy, who, although neither killed nor executed, spent several months in prison in 1604. In 1610 and 1612 his property was confiscated and he was forced to leave Transylvania. He was sent to prison once again between 1616 and 1622.[95]

As regards remarriage, the differences between the principality and the kingdom were not as noticeable among the lesser nobility. Below a certain age widows in both regions, whether they had children or not, had a fairly good chance of a further marriage offering them financial and legal security.

Despite general fears and the existence of certain negative examples, the majority of stepfathers did fulfil their tasks, ensuring proper financial and legal stability for their family. If the father and the stepfather had the same social and financial status, and if the latter also had children, it was just as important to augment the two incomplete families as to increase their property by marriage. Zsuzsanna Kovacsóczy was married first to János Mikola, the prince's chancellor. When her husband died she married the widower István Lázár. Both of them had children, and seven-year-old Zsigmond Mikola, István Lázár and Erzsébet Lázár were brought up as sister and brothers. Even distant relatives treated them as such. Zsuzsanna Kovacsóczy's sister-in-law even remembered the new members of her family in her will. In 1633 the prince granted Zsigmond Mikola the estate of Szász-Lóna and allowed him to leave it to the children or heirs of his stepfather, should his own line die out earlier. As the social status and religion of the father and the stepfather were identical, Zsigmond's education was uninterrupted. István Lázár sent him to the Jesuits in Kolozsmonostor, then to the court of György Rákóczi I. The boy was soon granted high honours.[96]

The influence of stepfathers on the lives of their stepchildren can best be observed in cases where the children changed religious denomination, and in the children's marriages. Where a child's parents had been of different denominations, the widow usually chose a man belonging to her own denomination when she remarried. As a result, most boys were obliged to abandon the denomination to which their fathers had belonged. Farkas

Bethlen, for example, was a Unitarian, and his wife, Anna Kemény, a Calvinist. When Bethlen died Anna Kemény married the Calvinist Ferenc Macskási. Her son, János Bethlen, who had originally been a Unitarian like his father, soon converted to the Calvinist faith.[97] There were also cases in which parents were of the same denomination but the new stepfather, who became a member of the family after the father's death, converted his wife and her children to his own faith. The Catholic Church made conversion to Catholicism a condition of marriage whenever it had the opportunity to intervene. This was the case in marriages between the Czobor and Thurzó families. Since the couples to be married were second cousins, they had to obtain a dispensation from the pope. In 1613 the Catholic Mihály Czobor was only permitted to marry the Lutheran Zsuzsanna Thurzó on condition that she and her son became Catholic. Czobor Imre wanted to marry Borbála Thurzó, the widow of Kristóf Erdődy. In his case, the condition was that his future wife should convert and the two stepsons be sent to be educated at a Jesuit college.[98]

The stepfather, as the children's guardian, was of course also responsible for the marriages of his stepchildren. In order to keep the family property intact, he usually selected a partner from his own family. Half-brothers and sisters were often united by marriage if they were of a similar age. There are several examples of such marriages. The marriages of Ferenc Rédey and Druzsina Bethlen, István Esterházy and Erzsébet Thurzó, István Nyáry and Anna Telegdy, and of many other couples, were arranged by their parents in this manner. It was not uncommon for the denomination and marriage of an orphan to be influenced in this way, even if the orphan had no stepfather and the guardianship had been entrusted to a relative.

Stepfathers sometimes had an undeniably harmful influence over the fate of their stepchildren. The best-known and most extreme example of this is the relationship between Imre

Thököly and the orphaned children of Ferenc Rákóczi I. Not only did the orphans lose most of their estates, as a result of the political ambitions of their stepfather, but even the life of little Ferenc Rákóczi II was threatened. He was seven years old when his stepfather exposed him to the dangers of war and nine when his stepfather planned to send him to the Ottoman Porte as a hostage. There were even rumours within the household about attempts against his life. The orphans and their mother, Ilona Zrínyi, survived three sieges of their castle in Munkács. Finally, after the collapse of their stepfather's campaign against the House of Habsburg, the children were sent abroad under the guardianship of the king and were separated from their mother for good. The six years they spent with their stepfather had completely ruined their lives and were to have a decisive influence on their future. In his *Confessions,* written thirty years later, Ferenc Rákóczi II tells of how one day, at a time when Ilona Zrínyi was sharing a bed with her children, a snake had been found among the bedclothes. The story may well have been true, but it may also be understood symbolically: the snake that had taken the children's place in their mother's bed was in fact Imre Thököly.[99]

Zsigmond Sarmasághy, a politician in the principality, had started out as a good stepfather, but his political career eventually ruined the life of his stepson, Zsigmond Jósika. At first sight he appears to have been the saviour of the Jósika family. The head of the family had been executed and his estates confiscated, leaving the mother and her sons defenceless. It was quite common for such families to be socially isolated; people were unwilling to risk bringing the prince's wrath down on their own heads and doubtless wished to avoid being suspected of sympathising with those who had been executed, or of sharing their political ideals. However, Sarmasághy married the widow without any such risk, since he was regarded as not particularly wealthy and as a respected follower of the ruling prince. It was obvious that his eagerness to help Borbála Füzy in this tragic period of her life had financial rather than political motives. She had remained fairly wealthy even after the confiscation of her husband's estates. Having witnessed the fall of too many of his contemporaries during his short career, István Jósika had been very prudent and had had much of the property that had been granted to him registered in his wife's and mother-in-law's names. As a result, these estates were not confiscated after his execution. In exchange for wealth, Sarmasághy offered safety for the family through his good relationship with the prince. Thus the sons of Jósika, a man who had risen from humble circumstances, were not forced out of the Transylvanian elite. In 1610 and 1612, however, their stepfather was forced to flee the principality after taking part in a conspiracy against Prince Gábor Báthory. He also implicated one of his stepsons, Zsigmond, in the political debacle. After the death of Gábor Báthory, Sarmasághy attempted to change sides and arranged for the marriage of Zsigmond to the sister of the late prince, Anna Báthory. However, this proved to be a gross miscalculation; the whole family, stepfather and stepsons, were forced to flee the wrath of the new ruler, Gábor Bethlen.[100]

LIFE AS AN ORPHAN

Becoming an orphan meant suffering both emotional and material loss. How did children cope with this dramatic change in their lives? Reactions were usually recorded much later, mostly in wills. The decades that had passed since their bereavement had probably attenuated their bitterness, and they express their feelings objectively or simply make commonplace remarks. "I was not yet even one and a half years old when I was made an orphan. Fate got the better of me, for which I do not bless it, though nor do I blame it either", wrote Péter Apor.[101] Funeral sermons and farewell poems written to commemorate the deceased and to give consolation to the family talk only of the shock of loss: "Your leaving us and your burial in the earth are so painful for us, beloved Mother, not because you are now in Heaven, but because we are left here alone as orphans, oh, my dearest Mother. You have filled with bitterness the heart of my respected Father, he who lived with you so kindly. You have left your faithful companion as a widower, and all of us who remain alone now weep."[102]

There were many poems expressing similar thoughts and even using the same lines. Orators had stylebooks for all occasions—for the funerals of old men and women, young people or children. All that had to be done was to change the names.[103]

The plight of orphans was such a central problem, especially during and after the Thirty Years' War, that a version of the "Prayer for Widows and Orphans" was included in all European prayer books. The prayer was so popular that it was published separately in illustrated form in German-speaking territories.[104] In Hungary the prayer for widows and orphans was composed by Péter Pázmány. The prayer offered consolation and comfort in time of loss: "Although you have taken from me my support in this world you have taken me into your care and have taught me that I should trust in no man, but only in You, for You live forever and care for all things."[105]

It is extremely difficult to judge how far the death of a child's parents influenced that child's emotional or spiritual development. Our only information is in the form of words written in the hope of finding some relief from distress. Pál Esterházy, for example, wrote of bereavements that had befallen his family during his childhood. Describing his father's terrible grief and mourning for his wife helped him in his own mourning for his mother. He lost thirteen close relatives—his father, his mother, an uncle, two half-brothers and eight cousins—between the ages of six and ten, when he was already old enough to have an understanding of death. He was not yet seven when he had to witness the death of his own sister. "My sister, Countess Erzsébet Thurzó...died before my very eyes at about two o'clock in the afternoon, resigning herself to the will of God in the little room at Lakompak. I wept bitterly for her, being already old enough to understand what had happened."[106] Despite being an orphan and facing bereavement so often, the young Esterházy was lively and loving as a little boy. At the same time he was particularly sensitive to the supernatural and was visited by his deceased relatives, both when he was awake and in his dreams. He wrote that he was surprised at first but not frightened, and that he regarded such "visits" as natural.

Contemporaries spoke more often of financial loss than of emotional loss. There is an interesting story, told by generations of the Apor family, regarding Lázár Apor, who was orphaned at the age of fourteen. His father, András Apor, had died in war in 1603, and his mother subsequently left him, her only son, taking all their possessions with her in the form of ready cash. When a faithful servant of the family asked the boy why he was weeping so bitterly, his response was somewhat unexpected: "I have every right to cry...since my mother has left me with only two bushels of wheat flour. How shall I be able to eat wheat bread in the future?" Lázár Apor became a kind of role model, giving strength to orphans in his family for generations to come. Although he had been orphaned and had lost all his property he managed to survive. He regained most of his lost estates and was able to leave significant wealth to his own sons when he died.[107]

As this story indicates, it was generally their material loss that was considered hardest for orphans to bear. Guardians often took over large portions of their property, selling their estates or at least enjoying the income from them. Guardians often spent the orphans' ready cash and sold their movable property. How much of the original inheritance remained by the time the orphan came of age was a matter of luck. Even the orphans' lives might be threatened if their relatives or guardians were not satisfied with the income from their estates only. The administration of the orphans' estates and the care of the children themselves were entrusted by law to the person who was to inherit them should the orphans die. Since infant mortality was high anyway, some guardians might well have contributed to the untimely death of the young heirs. Some orphans were indeed rumoured to have died in suspicious circumstances. The diary of the eminent Reformed Church minister, Sepsi Máté Lackó, records the story of little István Homonnai, the last member in the senior line of the Homonnai family. He died suddenly in 1612 after a visit from his only uncle. On the third day after his funeral the uncle took over his entire property and moved into the ancestral castle where the boy had lived. At the end of an account, hinting at accusation in every line, Sepsi Lackó refers to the "ancients" who, in similar cases, would ask *Cui bono fuit mors?* (Who profited by the death?)[108] However, despite the fact that the minister was obviously not the only person to have had suspicions, no investigation was ever carried out into the matter.

Questioning the legitimacy of an orphan's descent was also a well-established means of depriving orphaned heirs of their rights and property. This was exactly what happened in the case of György Homonnai, mentioned above as a suspected murderer. His mother, Fruzsina Dóczy, was accused of bringing up someone else's child in the place of her own. It was rumoured that the nurse had dropped the baby boy born to her and her deceased husband. According to the rumour the child had died and the mother had hidden its body, spreading news of a serious illness. She had then had a boy of similar age and appearance found in one of her villages and had brought him up as her own son. The real son had been buried in secret. The story was used to prove that György Homonnai was not entitled to his inheritance.

Although contemporaries regarded this story as a foolish lie, an investigation was carried out. One of the people who was accusing the mother was a close relative who wished to get hold of the inheritance himself. Even the king was in favour of there being a trial. In 1601 the widow and her son were condemned to be beheaded and their property was confiscated. Fruzsina Dóczy and her daughter managed to escape to Poland, and the boy soon followed them. The mother never returned to Hungary but György Homonnai was eventually pardoned after sacrificing large estates.[109]

Another way of questioning the legitimacy of a child was to attack the marriage of his or her parents. It was possible to demand that a marriage be annulled if a blood tie between the partners could be proved. According to marriage laws in early modern times children born to such marriages were to be regarded as illegitimate and could not inherit their parents' property, which passed as a result to their closest relatives.

There were many ways of avoiding or preventing such an outcome. If a blood tie was undeniable, dispensation had to be obtained prior to the marriage. If the partners were relatives to the third or fourth remove it was the archbishop of Esztergom who had to give his consent. If there was an even closer relationship between the couple, consent had to be obtained from the pope and the king. The consent of the king was the more important since in lay courts incestuous marriages were regarded as high treason and were punished even more severely than in the ecclesiastical courts. Close relatives who married without obtaining the required consent risked their lives and their property.[110]

However, there was only a real danger when the amount of money needed by the treasury was so great as to overshadow any rational considerations. The trial for high treason against Tamás Nádasdy and Zsuzsanna Pethő in 1601, on the pretext of their incestuous relationship, was a typical case in the wave of property confiscation during the Fifteen Years' War.[111] In more peaceful times, permission could be obtained after the marriage had taken place if it was argued that the couple had been unaware of their blood relationship and had married in good faith. This process was much quicker, simpler and cheaper than obtaining permission before the marriage. If the couple already had a child they also had to ask that she or he be made legitimate.

Even after the death of her husband it was worthwhile for a widow to apply for this permission if the legitimacy of her marriage was open to question, since her relatives would be motivated by financial rather than moral considerations. Most lawsuits for incest were initiated against defenceless widows. In 1642 Bálint Czobor managed to have the marriage of his late father and his stepmother annulled. He even demanded that she give back everything inherited from her husband, including all presents and jewels.[112] Even after her marriage to her second husband, Miklós Pázmány, Rozina Pethe, the widow of Imre Jakusith, tried to avoid a similar ordeal by having her marriage with her first husband authorised after Jakusith's death. At the same time she had her infant son by her first husband made legitimate. By so doing she prevented any possible attack against the orphan on the part of her relatives.[113]

One of the biggest hardships for an orphan was that he or she was utterly defenceless and might end up being passed from one guardian to another. This is exactly what happened to Ferenc

Rákóczi II and Judit Kendy. The fate of the young Rákóczi has already been described in connection with his stepfather, an ambitious and unscrupulous politician. Judit was the daughter of István Kendy, whose erratic political manoeuvring affected the life of his own child as well as the lives of his stepsons. The little girl was sent from guardian to guardian, since nobody was willing to care for the unfortunate child of this impoverished family. Finally, she went to live in the household of Menyhért Bogáti's wife "at whose hard stepmotherly hand she suffered greatly". Her future husband, István Haller, saved her from her predicament against the will of her guardians.[114]

One consequence of becoming an orphan that was not necessarily negative was that a child might be educated in a way that did not totally conform to his or her father's intentions. Orphans were only put at a disadvantage if that education was limited. In the preface to his volume of history, János Bethlen, who undoubtedly received a good education by Transylvanian standards, described the setbacks he had endured as a result of being an orphan: "I am fully aware of my shortcomings. Having lost my father at the age of two and having been brought up by a stepfather not versed in literature, I had no acquaintance with the Muses outside the borders of Transylvania."[115]

The education of György Bánffy, the son of Dénes Bánffy, who had been executed on a charge of conspiracy against the prince, was restricted for political reasons. He was deprived by the Diet of Transylvania of all his property, except for his ancestral property and property inherited on his mother's side. As to his education, the following resolution was passed: "1. His mother has the right to decide if she wishes to have him educated at home or at the Kolozsvár school, but she is not allowed to send him to study elsewhere. 2. He is not permitted to be educated at court."[116] However, further restrictions were also added. Although, according to the Diet's ruling, his mother had a free hand in the matter of her son's upbringing at home, the prince interfered in the choice of György's private tutors.[117]

The education of children who had lost both parents usually ended earlier than prescribed in the parents' will. Pál and Miklós Esterházy, the son and the nephew of Palatine Miklós, finished their studies at the age of seventeen; Miklós Zrínyi, Miklós Pázmány and György Homonnai at the age of fifteen; and Péter Zrínyi, László Rákóczi and Sándor Esterházy at the age of fourteen. This did not necessarily mean that the time spent on their education was shorter, since those orphaned at a very young age were usually sent to school earlier than others. However, in most cases there was no grand tour abroad as would otherwise have been usual. Only the Zrínyi brothers were able to do the standard tour in Italy. Pál Esterházy made only a short trip to southern Germany when he attended the election of Ferdinand IV as Holy Roman Emperor, while László Rákóczi visited Spain as a member of Ferdinand's retinue. Miklós Pázmány spent three years in Paris where he became familiar not so much with the university as with the more frivolous aspects of the metropolis. There are as yet no further data regarding the foreign tours undertaken by other orphans as young men.

During this period marriages were contracted according to the will of parents, relatives and guardians. As a result, the couple's happiness did not depend on whether or not they were orphans. The choice of spouse for an orphan was determined according to the interests of guardians and step-parents. This choice sometimes coincided with the wishes of the orphan, but could also be disadvantageous for them. When Erzsébet Homonnai Drugeth married László Révay at the instigation of Miklós Esterházy, it was an undeniable misalliance. Such a situation was not uncommon in families, in which there were many girls to marry off, but in the case of Countess Homonnai there was no such pressure of circumstances. She was an only daughter and had a large dowry. Her marriage proved to be a happy one, but she certainly lost social prestige by marrying a man from the lesser nobility. Since she no longer belonged to the aristocracy she was not supposed to correspond with aristocratic ladies as a partner of equal rank, nor could she have a household like theirs. Her children were not counts or countesses by birth, nor could her sons expect hereditary positions in political life. Her position improved when her husband was given a title as a consequence of her property and the support of her relatives and the palatine.[118]

There are far fewer examples supporting the claim that being an orphan could also have advantages. Although this was far from typical, there were children, such as Miklós Pázmány, for example, whose standard of living significantly improved after the death of their parents. Miklós Pázmány was the nephew of Péter Pázmány, archbishop of Esztergom, and lost both parents at the age of four. The archbishop, who had earlier neglected his relatives, then realised that the little boy was the only one who could perpetuate the family name and he started to support the child generously. In 1630 he obtained for him the title of baron, and in 1636 that of count. He bought substantial estates in Moravia for him and had them naturalised. He also found a distinguished benefactor in the person of Zsigmond Kornis, a relative on the mother's side, to defend the family's Transylvanian estates. The education that Miklós Pázmány received was also much better than that which his father could have given him.[119]

It would therefore be no exaggeration to say that the life of Miklós Pázmány took a favourable turn after the death of his parents. However, he was still not entirely content. Having estates in Moravia excluded him from the Hungarian nobility, although the archbishop's intentions were precisely to defend him from attacks at home. Péter Pázmány was afraid that his political and religious opponents would take revenge on his nephew after his death. However, it is not certain whether the wealth he had acquired so suddenly and easily, and the advance in his social life due neither to a long line of ancestors nor to his own merits, had a positive impact on Miklós Pázmány. He tried his hand at several things but never proved sufficiently committed. When his uncle died he decided to become a Jesuit. He went to Rome, but wrote afterwards from Faubourg Saint Germain: "I seem to be in Heaven while you are in Purgatory, since Paris and the whole of Gaul are a paradise full of gaieties. Those who have not seen it would never believe it. There are more things in France than in the whole of the rest of Europe."[120] He returned home after three years in France and joined the army, without any preliminary training or experience. Although Ádám Bat-thyány and others voted against him, he still managed to become captain of Pápa and Veszprém. His aim was "to make a name and reputation" for himself, but realising that it was not an easy job he resigned after a few years of service. He also tried his hand at literature, and two novels and a poem by him sur-vived.[121] His political, military and literary careers were never fully developed and were overshadowed by his less laudable behaviour, that is, his interception of a draft of his uncle's will and his misappropriation of his stepson's property. Qualities of firmness and resoluteness, seen in orphans such as István Kovacsóczy, István Kendy and György Bánffy, whose fathers perished at the scaffold or in prison but who still managed to regain their positions within the Hungarian elite, were missing in Miklós Pázmány.

Several orphans converted to another denomination as a re-sult of the influence of their guardians or step-parents. It is diffi-cult to judge the impact of this step on their future lives. In the case of those, who changed denomination soon after they were orphaned, such a step may have helped them adjust to their new environment and may have led to their being more readily accepted. Efforts to force people to return to Catholicism, supported by the king in Royal Hungary, also affected orphans during this period. Although the pressure began while they were at school, mainly at the Jesuit colleges, as in the case of Pál Rákóczi, for example, the actual conversion would take place at around the time of the orphan's coming of age. The advantages of conversion soon manifested themselves in the careers of these young aristocrats. Twenty-four-year-old György Zrínyi was made governor of Croatia in 1622, taking priority over his elder brother who had adhered to his Lutheran faith. Following his conversion Ferenc Nádasdy was able to marry into the family of Palatine Esterházy, and he soon became royal councillor and lord steward. Other converts experienced similar advantages. Pál Rákóczi became lord lieutenant of Sáros and Torna counties; Ádám Batthyány was granted the title of count; and György Homonnai Drugeth was awarded the Order of the Golden Fleece in 1614.

Comparing the careers of young men growing up in complete families or those whose fathers were still living, with those growing up without their fathers or those who had lost both parents, one can conclude that the latter group advanced more rapidly in their careers. Their childhood years were shorter, which was experienced as a positive advantage. They came of age at between sixteen and twenty and were subsequently entitled to have control over their own estates. They even assumed the hereditary offices held by their fathers. Ferenc Nádasdy, for example, was actively working as lord lieutenant at the age of thirteen; László Esterházy became lord lieutenant of Sopron County at the age of nineteen and captain of Pápa at the age of twenty-one. When he died his younger brother, Pál, was appointed to both posts at the age of seventeen. As a result, these young men were able to acquire political, military and administrative experience at a much earlier stage and could obtain offices other than hereditary ones sooner than their contemporaries. They were also helped in this by the important connections established during their years in the royal court or while growing up under the guidance of the palatine or the archbishop.

In contrast, fathers usually postponed the division of their estates until their sons reached the age of twenty-four or until they got married. The eldest son could naturally assume the hereditary offices held by his father only after his death.

It is worth comparing the career of the orphan György Homonnai Drugeth with those of Ferenc and István Csáky who were brought up by their father. Their social background was similar: both fathers were aristocrats—János Drugeth was lord chief justice and István Csáky senior was lord treasurer. The boys were roughly of the same age: Ferenc Csáky was born in 1630, György Drugeth in 1633 or 1634, and István Csáky in 1635. György lost his father when he was two. Officially his guardian was the king, but he and his sister were brought up by their widowed mother. The mother of the two Csáky boys died in 1639 and the orphans were sent to their grandmother, Anna Wesselényi.

The three young men attended the same schools. They studied in Pozsony at the Nagyszombat Jesuit college, and at the university of Vienna. However, while Homonnai's school years were spent quietly under the guidance of Archbishop Lippay, at one stage the Csáky boys' father was on the verge of summoning his sons home owing to the high cost of their education. Due to their father's miserliness the young Csákys went to school together despite the difference in their ages. This meant they had to pay less for their accommodation and only had to have one tutor to teach them reading and philosophy. In 1643 Archbishop György Lippay was obliged to intervene and persuade the boys' father to let them continue their studies. "The archbishop says it would be unfortunate to force the boys to abandon their studies.

He praises them and says that Istók behaved well, even when acting." At the time Ferenc was thirteen and István only eight. Eventually the two Csáky boys studied until the age of nineteen, while György Homonnai Drugeth continued with his studies only until the age of fifteen.

All of them married between 1651 and 1654, but there was a great difference between the weddings. György married thirteen-year-old Mária Esterházy in the summer of 1651. The extravagance of the festivities amazed the whole country, and the couple moved into a luxurious household. At the time Ferenc Csáky was being held in the prison of Szepes castle by his father because of his refusal to marry Homonnai's sister, Katalin. He managed to escape to Vienna where he secretly married Imre Czobor's daughter, Erzsébet, and he subsequently demanded that his father give him his share of the property. His father disinherited him, accusing his son of hiring assassins to kill him. Finally Archbishop Lippay persuaded them to make peace. Young István, his father's favourite, caused no problems in the family. At the age of nineteen, in 1654, he married a widow, Margit Lónyai, as his father had intended. However, the family property was not divided and, in their twenties, the married Csáky sons received only one thousand forints per year with which to support themselves.

Even the political careers of the Csáky brothers had to be postponed. The hereditary post of lord lieutenant of Szepes was still held by their father, and he even obtained a similar post for himself in Bereg County in 1660. Homonnai, in contrast, had taken over his inheritance and the lord lieutenancy of Ung County at the age of fifteen. He was about twenty-five when he was appointed captain-general of Upper Hungary in 1659. His impressive career was cut short by his death in 1661. The father of the Csáky brothers died a year later, in 1662. After his death his sons divided the property and started to build careers for themselves. Ferenc became lord lieutenant of Szepes at the age of thirty-three and died in this post seven years later. István Csáky was thirty-five when he inherited the lord lieutenancy from his brother. At the age of fifty-four, he became lord chief justice.[122]

In the course of this chapter we have explored many different examples of the experience of life as an orphan. Despite the differences, there are obvious similarities as regards where the orphans lived, their education, the administration of their estates and other family matters. These illustrate the responses of the seventeenth-century nobility to the challenge of bringing up orphans. However careful the parents had been and however conscientious their guardians, children inevitably suffered as a result of being orphaned. Orphans were vulnerable and their lives were dictated by the interests of others. Whether their vulnerability resulted in disadvantages or did not fundamentally affect their lives depended on their individual circumstances and fortunes. In spite of the tragedy suffered, in some cases it could eventually lead to advantages in the world. Contemporary society's responsibilities with respect to orphans were generally fulfilled. Their lifestyles, and partly also the property and positions inherited from their parents, were preserved for them. The opportunity to survive and to start a new life remained open to them.

Notes

1 The will of Pál Béldi, not dated [1678]: *Történelmi Tár* (hereafter: TT) 1899:348.
2 Esterházy family tree, Table III.
3 Rákóczi family tree, Table V.
4 Zrínyi family tree, Table VI.
5 István Werbőczy, *Tripartitum opus juris consuetudinarii inclyti regni Hungariae*. Several editions. (Hereafter: *Tripart.*) I, 112, § 1. See also I, 11, § 8; I, 113, §1.
6 *Tripart*. I, 111, § 1–2.

7 *Tripart.* I, 111, § 3; I, 126–130.

8 *Tripart.* I, 111, § 5.

9 Pál Nádasdy to Pál Révay, 2 April 1625: Štatni Archyv v Bratislave. Archyv rodu Révay; documents relating to the guardianship case of Pál Révay: Hungarian National Archive (Magyar Országos Levéltár, hereafter: MOL) P 508. Nádasdy family archive (hereafter: P 508.) Documents I, Fasc. 99, No. 387.

10 Károly Széchy, *Gróf Zrínyi Miklós* I-II. Budapest, 1896, I: 60–61.

11 *Tripart.* I, 115, § 5; I, 124, § 1–3.

12 *Tripart.* I, 111, § 4; § 6–8.

13 Zsigmond Bubics and Lajos Merényi: *Herczeg Esterházy Pál nádor, 1635–1713.* Budapest, 1895 (hereafter: Bubics-Merényi): 79–83.

14 Péter Pázmány to Ferdinánd II, 22 April 1623: *Pázmány Péter összegyűjtött levelei* I. Published by Ferenc Hanuy. Budapest, 1910 (hereafter: Hanuy): 336–337.

15 Arnold Ipolyi, *Bedegi Nyáry Krisztina 1604–1641.* Budapest, 1887: 73–81.

16 Bubics-Merényi, 79–84.

17 The will: MOL P 108. Esterházy family archive. Repositorium (hereafter: P 108) 4, 22, Fasc. G. No. 53. Six-year-old Palkó and five-year-old Katica died on 6 April 1664.

18 Katalin Péter, *Esterházy Miklós.* Budapest, 1985: 164–178.

19 The will of István Báthory: MOL A 148. Neo-regestrata acta (hereafter: NRA), Fasc. 57, No. 7.

20 The will of Ferenc Nádasdy, 10 July 1663: TT 1888, 381.

21 Istán Fazekas, *Az Illésházy család XVII. századi leszármazása.* Turul, 1992: 13–17.

22 The will of Ferenc Dobó, 28 January 1602: Béla Radvánszky, *Magyar családélet és háztartás a XVI. és XVII. században.* Budapest, 1879 (hereafter: Radvánszky), III: 214.

23 The 1624 will of Miklós Esterházy: MOL P 108. Esterházy family archive. Representationes (hereafter: P 108) 4, Fasc. E, No. 33. The 1641 will: Bubics-Merényi, 268–271.

24 The will of Farkas Kovacsóczy, 22 October 1591: Radvánszky III, 140–141.

25 *Die Matrikeln der Universität Graz.* Edited by Johann Andritsch. I. 1586–1630. Graz, 1977: 1597/3; *Giovanni Argentini jelentései magyar ügyekről.* Published by Endre Veress. Szeged, 1983: 173.

26 The will of Ferenc Rédey, captain of Várad, 25 March 1621: TT 1884, 130–134.

27 The 1641 will of Miklós Esterházy. See note 23.

28 The will of Ferenc Nádasdy. See note 20.

29 The 1641 will of Miklós Esterházy. See note 23.

30 The will of István Báthory: See note 19.

31 *Tripart.* I, 112–120.

32 The will of Zsigmond Rákóczi, 19 July 1607: TT 1884, 562.

33 *Tripart.* I, 113, § 4, 5.

34 *Tripart.* I, 122.

35 Documents relating to the guardianship of the Erdődy children: MOL E 200, Fasc. 14, 13/b. Erdődy documents, Fasc. 1–3. f. 11–44. Photocopies of the documents

were kindly supplied by Zsuzsa Bozai. I would like to express my gratitude to her for this and for all her help in relation to this study.

36 György Majthényi to Imre Majthényi, 25 September 1624: TT 1897, 95. In relation to Imre Majthényi it should be mentioned that in certain cases a father could lose his right to make decisions concerning his children—for instance due to criminal offences, imprisonment or insanity. Such children would be brought up as if they had no father, under the care of a guardian. Cases of this type are not dealt with in the present study. Nor do I discuss the children of divorced parents, or the rare cases in which children were dispossessed before reaching adulthood.

37 Accounts: TT 1897, 62–66, 70.

38 Erzsébet Czobor to Zsófia Révay, 4 April 1624: Farkas Deák, *Magyar hölgyek levelei 1515–1700*. Budapest, 1879 (hereafter: *Magyar hölgyek*): 198.

39 *Magyar hölgyek*, 311–312.

40 Lajos Szádeczky and Ödön Boncz: *A gróf Haller-család nemzetségkönyve*. Budapest, 1886: 26.

41 The diary of the Révay family, 1555–1661: *Új Magyar Múzeum* 1857 (hereafter: *Révay*): 445–448.

42 The will of Szerafin Daróczy, 4 February 1586: Radvánszky III, 133.

43 Pál Jedlicska, Eredeti részletek gróf Pálffy család okmánytárához. Budapest, 1910. Introduction: 20–22.

44 The will of László Károlyi, 11 December 1688: *Nagykárolyi gróf Károlyi család oklevéltára*. Published by Tibor Károlyi and Kálmán Géresi. Budapest, 1887 (hereafter: *Károlyi*), IV: 562–564.

45 Farkas Deák, *Forgách Zsuzsanna 1582–1632*. Budapest, 1885: 11–16.

46 *Révay*, 445–448.

47 The will of Daróczy Szerafin. See note 42.

48 The will of Ferenc Nádasdy. See note 20.

49 Documents of the case, the petitions and will of Erzsébet Czobor: P 108, Repositorium 29, Fasc. B, No. 26–34.

50 Pázmány Péter to Ferdinánd II, 22 April 1623: Hunuy I, 336–337.

51 Esterházy Miklós to Krisztina Nyáry, 4 November 1628: TT 1901, 490.

52 Sándor Szilágyi: *Egy apáca a Rákóczy-házból*. Budapest, 1875: 229–235.

53 Ildikó Horn, "Rákóczi László pályája, 1633–1664". *Hadtörténelmi Közlemények* 1990/2: 63–65.

54 Baron Fülöp Skrebenszky, "Rákóczi Pál tanulókori levelei a gráczi egyetemből 1611–1616." TT 1887, 259–268.

55 On the upbringing of Miklós and Péter Zrínyi, see Tibor Klaniczay, *Zrínyi Miklós*. Budapest, 1964 (hereafter: Klaniczay): 26–36.

56 *Die Matrikel der Universität Wien. IV. 1579/II.-1658/59*. Edited by Franz Gall. Graz-Köln, 1961: 122, 125, 186, 188, 202, 205.

57 Letters of Pázmány, 31 October 1622 and 8 August 1626: Hanuy I, 309, 527; Ferdinánd II to Pázmány, 28 June 1624: *Pázmány Péter levelezése 1605–1625*. Edited by Vilmos Frankl (Fraknói). Budapest, 1873 (hereafter: *Pázmány levelezése*): 388–389.

58 Klaniczay, 26; Péter Pázmány to Ferdinand II, 17 March 1636: Hanuy II, 640.

59 Pázmány Péter to Ferdinand II, 10 March 1628: Hanuy I, 683; *Révay*, 448.

60 *Tripart*. I, 113.

61 The will of Ferenc Nádasdy. See note 20.

62 Anna Wesselényi to István Csáky: Farkas Deák: *Wesselényi Anna özv. Csáky Istvánné 1584–1649 életrajza és levelezése*. Budapest, 1875 (hereafter: *Wesselényi*), letter 57, 150–151.

63 Péter Apor: *Lusus mundi*. Kolozsvár, 1912 (hereafter: Apor): 25–26.

64 The will of Mihály Károlyi, 29 June 1626. Károlyi IV, 204.

65 The will of László Károlyi, 11 December 1688. Károlyi IV, 651.

66 Vencel Bíró: *Altorjai gróf Apor István és kora*. Kolozsvár, 1935: 10–16.

67 Farkas Deák, *Egy magyar főúr a XVII. században. Gróf Csáky István életrajza*. Budapest, 1883 (hereafter: *Gróf Csáky*); Ildikó Horn, "Csáky Anna Franciska és a pozsonyi klarisszák." *Aetas* 1992/3: 28–43.

68 Éva Lobkovitz Poppel to Ádám Batthyány, 29 May 1633. Quoted by Sándor Takáts, *Magyar nagyasszonyok*. Budapest, 1934 (hereafter: Takáts): 487.

69 Edict of Ferdinand II, 16 January 1634. MOL P 507. Nádasdy archive (hereafter: P 507). Documents III, Fasc. 143. No. 535.

70 Ferenc Nádasdy to Bertalan Kis, 9 March 1636. *Régi Magyar levelestár XVI-XVII. század*. Edited by Emil Hargittay. II, 60.

71 Ferenc Nádasdy to Miklós Esterházy, 6 August 1638. MOL E 174, Fasc. 2.

72 Draft letters of Ádám Batthány, no year, c. 1639–1640. MOL P 1313. Writings of Ádám Batthyány. Fasc. 3. Draft letters.

73 Judit Révay to Ferenc Nádasdy, 24 March 1642. *Magyar hölgyek*, 236–237.

74 The will of Ferenc Rédey. TT 1884: 131–132.

75 Family records of István Csáky, treasurer, and his son István, lord chief justice. *A "Zöld könyv": Oklevéltár a gróf Csáky család történetéhez*. Published by László Bártfai Szabó. Budapest, 1919 (hereafter: Csáky okmánytár) I, 2, 612.

76 The will of Ferenc Gyulai, 24 September 1691. TT 1884: 138–139.

77 The autobiography of Miklós Bethlen: *Kemény János és Bethlen Miklós művei*. Published by Éva V. Windisch. Budapest, 1983: 237.

78 There are contradictory data regarding the birth of Éva Forgách. Most probably she was born in around 1609.

79 Quoted in *Wesselényi*, 55.

80 The will of Zsigmond Forgách, 1 September 1620. NRA, Fasc. 250, No. 45.

81 *Wesselényi*, 8–16; László Bártfai Szabó, *A Forgách család története*. Esztergom, 1910: 479, 489, 500–501.

82 The will of Anna Révay, widow of Gábor Kendy, 22 February 1595. Radvánszky III, 154–163.

83 Anna Héderváry to Ferenc Lessenyei Nagy, 24 June 1668. *Magyar hölgyek*, 322–323.

84 Apor, 19.

85 Borbála Telegdy to Lajos Rákóczi, 13 May 1609. *Magyar hölgyek*, 200

86 Sándor Szilágyi, *I. Rákóczi György 1593–1648*, 30–38.

87 Antonia. Frazer, The Weaker Vessel. London 1993, 90.

88 Corpus Juris Hungarici, 1659: 110.

90 The will of Balassa Borbála, 27 January 1637. P 108, 4, No. 7.

91 The will of Péter Szirmay, 29 February 1656. TT 1902: 149.

92 Mandate of Miklós Esterházy, 10 October 1632: MOL N 4. *Archivum Palatini Comitis Nicolai Esterházy.* See Fol. 58, 310. Microfilm: No. 17558.

93 I have restricted myself here to an examination of those families where the data—on remarriage, the birth of children, and the time spent in widowhood—can be traced back to primary sources.

94 Court cases initiated by Gábor Bethlen: the case of János Szendrei and Katalin Török, 1614, TT 1891: 317; András Komáromy, "A 'bűbájos Báthory Anna'". *Századok* 1894: 298–314; copies from the archives of the Kornis family: the manuscript archive of the library of the Hungarian Academy of Science. Endre Veress collection. MS. 425/II, Fol. 966–995.

95 On the court cases initiated by György Rákóczi I, see László Makkai, *I. Rákóczi György birtokainak gazdasági iratai.* Budapest, 1954: 18–30.

96 György Szabó, *Abafáji Gyulay Pál.* Budapest, 1974: 65; for the will of Jósika, see Endre Veress, *Documente privitoare la istoria Ardealului, Moldovei si Ţării-Romaneşti.* Bucharest, 1932: 184–186; On Sarmasághy, see Miklós Lázár, *Erdély főispánjai 1540–1711.* Budapest, 1989: 109–112.

97 The will of Zsófia Telegdy, widow of István Kovaczóczy, 25 June 1637. Radvánszky III, 272–276; Miklós Lázár, *A gróf Lázár család.* Kolozsvár, 1858: 140–142.

98 The autobiography of Kozma Petrityvity-Horváth 1634–1660: *Történelmi kalászok. 1603–1711.* Edited by Kálmán Thaly. Pest, 1862: 6.

99 Roszner, 283–289; Hanuy I, 232.

100 Kálmán Thaly, *II. Rákóczi Ferenc ifjúsága.* Pozsony, 1881: 7–115; Ágnes R. Várkonyi: *A fejedelem gyermekkora.* Budapest, 1989.

101 See note 95.

102 Apor, 26.

103 Farewell poem by Péter Szathmári Baka: *Régi Magyar Költők Tára XVII. század* (hereafter: RMKT): 9. Edited by Imre Varga. Budapest, 1977: 164.

104 See the introductory study by Gábor Kecskeméti and Hajnalka Nováky: *Magyar nyelvű halotti beszédek a XVII. századból.* Budapest, 1988: 9–37.

105 *"Aller Verlaßnen Wittiben und Vatterlosen Waysen / zu Gott im Himmel abgeschicktes Seuffzen und erhörtes Gebett": Deutsche Illustrierte Flugblätter des 16. und 17. Jhs.* Published by Wolfgang Hamsr. Vol. III. Wolfenbüttel, 157, III/180. My thanks go to Nóra G. Etényi who called my attention to this publication.

106 Péter Pázmány, *Özvegyek és árvák könyörgése.* In *Pázmány Péter. Válogatás műveiből.* Selected by Miklós Őry, Ferenc Szabó, Péter Vass. Budapest, 1983: 168.

107 Pál Esterházy's recollections of his youth. In: *Esterházy Pál Mars Hungaricusa.* Published by Emma Iványi. Budapest, 1989: 309.

108 Apor, 13–14.

109 "Sepsi Laczkó Máté Lorándfi Mihály udvari concionatora Krónikája és emlékezetre méltó hazai dolgoknak rövid megjegyzései. 1521–1624." *Erdélyi Történelmi Adatok*, III. Edited by Count Imre Mikó. Kolozsvár, 1858: 135.

110 Takáts, 369–409.

111 Roszner, 195.

112 *Magyar Országgyűlési Emlékek* IX. Edited by Vilmos Fraknói. Budapest, 1885: 545.

113 Judgement of the commissary court of Esztergom regarding the case of Bálint Czobor against Zsuzsanna Bánffy, widow of Imre Czobor, 26 April 1642. Roszner, 376–379.

114 Legitimation of the birth of Imre Jakusith, 14 August 1648. Roszner, 489–490.

115 Family records of István Haller. Published by Imre Lukinich. *Erdélyi Múzeum,* 1903: 535.

116 János Bethlen. *Erdély története 1629–1673.* Edited by József Jankovics. Budapest, 1993: 10.

117 Laws of the Diet of 1674 in Gyulafehérvár. Articulus XXIX: *Erdélyi Országgyűlési Emlékek.* XV, 471.

118 Order of Mihály Apafi to György Gyerőffy, 24 December 1674. Ibid., 476.

119 See note 59.

120 Ferenc Jenei, *Pázmány Miklós veszprémi főkapitány.* Veszprém, 1963 (hereafter: Jenei): 161–169; Vilmos Fraknói, *Pázmány Péter és kora.* Budapest, 1868–72, II, 446–449; III, 270–277.

121 Miklós Pázmány to István Kolosvári, no date. *Jenei Függelék,* 165–166.

122 *Praxis et Usus Schedae Menstruae.* Cologne, 1639; "Arbor scienti boni et mali": undiscovered manuscript; poem about Mikló Zrínyi: RMKT, 10, XVIIth century, 567.

123 *Gróf Csáky,* 166–174, 181–184, 201; Csáky archive, 610–612.

CHAPTER 3

COUNT ÁDÁM BATTHYÁNY I AND HIS CHILDREN

THE ARCHIVES of the Batthyány family, housed originally in Körmend and currently forming part of the Hungarian national archives, represent one of the largest private archives in the country. The archives have been accessible to the public since the nineteenth century, and although serious losses were suffered during the Second World War and again in 1956, interest in the material has never diminished. However, there are very few publications that deal with the history of the family and the careers of the Batthyánys, although the rich collection of letters provides ample opportunity for such a study. The life of one of the most interesting characters in the family, Ádám Batthyány I, is particularly well documented. He left an enormous quantity of notes and letters, bordering on graphomania. He loved his family dearly, and there are several letters in the collection on the subject of his children. Some of the almost 350 letters, instructions, notes and other documents have been published, and the diary kept by Kristóf Batthyány during the foreign tour undertaken to complete his studies has also appeared in print.

LIFE IN THE NOBLE HOUSEHOLD

Ádám Batthyány was born in 1609, the second of seven children born to Ferenc Batthyány II and Éva Poppel. He was the only one of their three sons to survive into adulthood. Very little is known about his education. In 1625 his father was looking for a Calvinist teacher for him,[1] a post that was later filled by György Zvonarich who came from a family of famous preachers.[2] Batthyány's rather dull writing style and his somewhat limited mastery of the language indicate that he may not have attended an ordinary school. Nevertheless, he was highly intellectual, as shown, among other documents, by the letter he wrote to explain his conversion to the Catholic faith. He showed great interest in matters of faith throughout his life. The provost of Vasvár, his former chaplain Mihály Lónyi, reminded him in a letter in 1641 of his promise to find in the Bible proofs "that the gates of Heaven had been closed" when Jesus died, as stated in a Passion sermon by Pázmány.[3] In a letter written on 20 July 1648, Ádám Batthyány wrote that he intended to expose a mistake by the Lutherans published in the Lőcse almanac.[4] He was also a patron of literature and financed the translation of Seneca by Sámuel Kéry. He wrote, or at least compiled, a prayer book, *Lelki Kard* (The Sword of the Soul), which was published in Vienna along with the funeral addresses preached at his wife's funeral.[5] Batthyány frequently bought books, his favourite subjects being religion, history, warfare and practical topics. A strange habit, and one that betrayed his somewhat amateur approach, was occasionally to buy several copies of the same work.

The administration of his estates also gave Batthyány ample opportunity for writing and note making. He kept a journal of his expenditures, prepared yearly inventories, and made notes concerning his guests and what they consumed. These documents reveal that he made every effort to keep his estates and his finances in order. In spite of his thriftiness he was aware of his duties as an aristocrat and did his best to enhance the family's prestige by extending and decorating his castles at Rohonc and elsewhere.[6] At the same time he was also famous for his excessive love of wine and gambling. He played both dice and cards and even had a "playing table" in his bedchamber.[7] He was a forceful character and was not afraid of confrontation. He came into conflict with his equally strong-minded mother very early in his life. A disagreement arose between them in 1629, on matters of religion. This conflict, which later came to include the question of their estates, lasted until his mother's death.

As a child Ádám Batthyány adhered to the Calvinist faith of his father. When the latter died in 1625 it was probably his mother who urged him to convert to Lutheranism. However, in 1629 he decided to become a Catholic, having come under the influence of Péter Pázmány, Miklós Esterházy, and his brother-in-law, László Csáky.[8] His conversion put an end to his plans to marry Katalin Illésházy, the daughter of Gáspár Illésházy and Ilona Thurzó. However, he found consolation in the arms of Aurora Formentini, a lady-in-waiting at the Vienna court.[9] They were married in 1632 and their marriage proved to be a happy one right up until Aurora's death in 1653. However happy they may have been, his wife never learnt Hungarian and the letters they sent one another were written in German. They had at least ten children—four sons and six daughters.[10] The first-born son, Ferenc, as well as four of their daughters, died in infancy. Only two girls and two boys reached adulthood. One of the countesses, Mária Eleonóra, the wife, and later widow, of Count László Esterházy, died at the age of only twenty-one in 1654.

THE BIRTH OF THE CHILDREN

The birth of Batthyány's first son was keenly awaited. Letters written by the Jesuit Johan Wiltheim, who was staying with the Batthyánys at the time, convey something of the tension and excitement. Ádám Batthyány himself was then in Vienna and Father Wiltheim wrote to him every day. On 11 November 1635 he confided that the baby was expected to be a boy and that the midwife had already arrived.[11] Batthyány's wife felt the first signs of labour at ten o'clock on 13 November, but still had breakfast alone in her room. She received a letter from her husband and occupied herself in reading it. At three in the afternoon the midwife suggested a game of cards. The actual confinement began at half past six and the child was born at ten.[12] In his next letter Wiltheim proudly informed the father that his child looked like a real Batthyány: *vultu verus Batthjanus*.[13] Unfortunately, the child did not live long. In a letter written on 23 July 1636, Father Wiltheim expressed his sorrow at the child's death.[14]

The next child was awaited with possibly even greater anticipation in 1637. The Dominican friars then staying at Németújvár in order to discuss the foundation of a monastery there offered to pray for the child to their patron saint.[15] Their prayers were apparently answered since the countess gave birth to a son on 1 March 1637. The midwife was given a princely reward of fifty gold coins by the delighted father. She was apparently a well-known midwife who had come some distance to attend the birth, since her journey home cost Batthyány eight forints.[16] By the time the couple's third child, Pál, was born, there was less tension and anticipation.

Very little is known about the first years of the children's lives, which they spent mainly with their mother. From various records it appears that they were nursed by wet nurses and were later attended by a dry nurse. When Batthyány listed the members of his household in June 1634 he mentioned a wet nurse, a dry nurse and two children belonging to them. In the list for 1638/39 there were two dry nurses, one wet nurse, and several *Frauenzimmer*, as domestic woman servants were called. In the list for 1639/40, one dry nurse and two other nurses were mentioned. The nurses had a cook and a kitchen of their own and received seven pounds of beef, five chickens, and half a calf a week, with two extra chickens on Saturdays.[17]

It is interesting to note that Ádám Batthyány had no permanent family seat but stayed at each of his castles in turn. In the early years of his marriage the family spent more time at Németújvár than elsewhere, and later on his wife and children preferred Rohonc.

Little is known about the everyday life of the children. Their education began very early, as was customary in those days. A teacher, György Poletincz, was engaged as their preceptor as early as 27 December 1641 when Kristóf, the elder of the two boys, was only four and a half years old.[18] Poletincz taught the children to read and write as well as some basic Latin. In 1647 the demands on the little counts became still greater. On 30 March their father made a contract with Ulrich Neumayr, a highly trained lawyer from Erding, Bavaria, in which it was agreed that the latter would act as steward of the boys' household and inspector of their education. He received the considerable sum of 200 forints and some payment in kind, which suggests that his sphere of authority and his tasks were the same as those of the prefects we know of later in the family.[19] However, we have no further information regarding the activities of Neumayr. At that time the children were probably still at home and had their own room as a study.[20] They occasionally visited their father in Pozsony, where he often stayed during the sessions of the Diet.

The development of the two children was greatly influenced by the aristocratic household in which they lived. Ádám Bat-

thyány had a very large household. Besides menservants, purveyors, scribes, jailers, soldiers, artisans and priests, there were
frequently visitors staying in the castles of the captain-general of
the Transdanubian region. Thus the children were accustomed to
living amid bustle and commotion. It must have been an enormous change for them when they were sent to a boarding school
in July 1649.

AT THE JESUIT SCHOOL IN SOPRON

The Jesuits established themselves in Sopron in 1636 after a
long-drawn-out struggle. Their monastery was granted the title
of college only in 1650, although their school was open to boys
from the very beginning. It is not clear exactly why Batthyány
sent his sons to Sopron. Pál and Zsigmond Csáky, the sons of
his brother-in-law László Csáky, studied in Győr. Pál, the
younger son of Miklós Esterházy, began his studies in Graz and
completed them in Nagyszombat. This suggests that there was a
personal motive behind Batthyány's choice.

The children completed the long journey to Sopron with a
large retinue headed by Mátyás Pongrácz, an old servant of
Batthyány and the steward of the young gentlemen's household,
who was responsible for the boys' behaviour, accommodation
and upkeep.[21] Their education was entrusted to their former
teacher, György Poletincz. Besides the steward of the household
and the preceptor there were several servants, including a cook,
in the retinue.[22] A total of thirteen people had to be fed, housed
and looked after. At first they were accommodated in the house
of an acquaintance. However, Batthyány was dissatisfied with
the rent of 130 forints and the fact that the cellar could not be
used, so he decided to buy a house. The company moved to the
new house in August 1651.[23] Meat and bread were bought on

credit and the accounts were settled every four or six weeks.[24] Veal and lamb were purchased on the spot, but most of the poultry and wine was brought from home, together with fodder for the horses.

The steward of the household, Mátyás Pongrácz, was to ensure that the boys attended Mass and said their prayers every day. It is indicative of his relationship with Count Batthyány that he, although a Lutheran, was entrusted to supervise the boys in matters of religion as well. According to the instructions he received from Batthyány, who by that time had been a Catholic for about twenty years, Pongrácz was to guard them from the "corruption" of other religions. He doubtless had little trouble fulfilling this particular task. In the Jesuit surroundings the young counts were not exposed to any Protestant influence. Mátyás Pongrácz himself, however, had to resist several attempts to convert him.[25]

Pongrácz was to see that the boys were escorted to and from school, and another of his duties was to prevent them from mixing with undesirable company—the children of peasants or of middle-class parents—during their recreation periods. Nor were such children permitted to enter the little counts' home. The only visits the Batthyány boys were allowed to make were to Count László Esterházy at Czindorf, to Count Ferenc Nádasdy, or to other noblemen and friars, should they be honoured with an invitation. Count Batthyány, who was very fond of drinking wine himself, did not allow any member of the household to drink heavily at home since, he maintained, his son Palkó was afraid of people who were drunk.

The healthy rivalry that existed between the two boys, a rivalry typical of young brothers, did not begin in Sopron—there are documents proving that they were already fighting in Pozsony.

Their father wished to protect them from harm in every possible way. In order to appease the powers of the supernatural he strictly ordered them never to let their "Agnus Dei and other relics" be taken away from them. They were to wear them day and night and were to cross themselves with holy water every evening and morning and whenever they entered a church.

Taking care of the children and organising their everyday life seems to have been too great a burden for Pongrácz. Count Batthyány decided to reorganise the system after about six months. The children were not easy to manage and needed an experienced pedagogue. One such candidate was found in the person of Canon János Magnovith from Győr. It was customary among aristocratic families to employ a clergyman to take charge of the children's education. Magnovith had had previous experience of similar responsibilities in Győr where he had supervised the children of László Csáky. However, since Kristóf and Pál were not easy to manage, before accepting the position Magnovith wisely asked their father to give him full powers "concerning their upbringing, education, and all methods to improve their manners". In his letter of application he inquired about the clothing of the young masters and the servants. At the same time he expressed his wish to receive decent payment in ready cash as well as full board for himself, his servant and two horses.[26]

The skills that the boys had acquired at home proved insufficient. In a letter written on 31 March 1650, Magnovith informed their parents that, for various reasons but "primarily in order to preserve their good health", he found it advisable for a change to be made in the boys' classes. The elder boy would be able to resume his present studies "on his own merit in a year's time, as he is very much below the standard now".[27] Kristóf, and perhaps also Pál, were attending the grammar class at the time. In the absence of any records, however, it is very hard to tell which class the boys attended in a particular year. The Jesuits were aware of the usefulness of repetition, and presumably on at least one occasion at the beginning of their studies the young counts were forced to remain in their class for a second year.

The letters sent by the prefect Magnovith reveal that Kristóf and Pál were not particularly keen students. Their tutor was overjoyed at even the smallest sign of willingness on their part: "They are not as averse to learning now as they used to be. It is a great consolation to me that they have recently shown some inclination to study."[28] However, this situation did not last long. As the weather improved the boys' enthusiasm for their studies quickly dwindled. As early as May the prefect wrote that "their minds are wandering, and, being little disposed to study, they are making very slow progress".[29] Besides these problems, the prefect also faced financial difficulties. On various occasions he was obliged to remind the boys' father to send him the promised payment in kind, fodder for his second horse, or a better type of wine.

Batthyány was likewise dissatisfied with the activities of his prefect and took steps towards finding a replacement when the year agreed on in the contract was completed on 1 March 1651. As Magnovith's successor he chose György Borsiczky, a man who had been recommended to him by György Lippay, archbishop of Esztergom.[30] Borsiczky stood up to the boys for two years, from 25 May 1651 to 25 May 1653. Sixty letters written during these two years survive, and reveal something of the new prefect's many and diverse hardships. There was never sufficient money; in August 1651, for example, he received fifty forints in cash but had a debt of forty-four forints at the baker, twenty-six forints at the butcher, ten forints for hay from the parson of Hidegkút, plus a further debt of twenty-four forints elsewhere.[31] In spite of their high birth, the children's clothing seems to have been neglected. The clothes worn by the valets who were studying with the young aristocrats certainly put theirs to shame.[32]

In addition to being a pedagogue and having practical skills, a prefect also had to know a little about medicine. In less problematic cases Borsiczky was able to make a diagnosis himself and prescribe a treatment. On other occasions it was the countess who ordered medicines for the boys. Doctors were called only in more serious cases. One particular episode, in 1651, serves as a good illustration. Borsiczky reported that Pál had had an upset stomach but that "fortunately" he had vomited everything. The next day his mother ordered purgatives for both boys. Finally, only after some days had passed, a well-known doctor was sent for.[33] One interesting detail that emerges from the letters is the fact that the prefect asked permission from the countess to take the boys to the local barber to have their hair washed.[34]

Another difficulty for the prefect was the fact that the relationship between the two brothers was increasingly problematic. According to Borsiczky, Magnovith, while still in Batthyány's service, had warned his successor that the boys were "predisposed to discord and frequently possessed by a spirit of hostility", although he admitted that brothers rarely live in harmony: *rara concordia fratrum*. Borsiczky observed that it was not Palkó, but rather his elder brother Kristóf, who was of a more evil disposition "having stabbed his brother's hand with the iron point of the inkstand". Borsiczky wrote with some satisfaction that they had fought only once during his two years of service, but they were not treated leniently even so.[35] The mutual hostility between the brothers continued throughout their studies.

Unfortunately, the prefect's letters give much less information about the boys' intellectual progress. On one occasion he asked the boys' father not to take them for a holiday in Rohonc at a time when they appeared to be settled and were making good progress with their studies.[36] Further information can be gathered from the accounts prepared mainly in the autumn of 1652. At that time Kristóf was attending the syntax class and Pál was studying grammar. As the books bought for the boys testify, the Jesuits in Sopron strictly adhered to the *Ratio* in their teaching methods. They considered a perfect knowledge of Latin grammar and syntax to be the primary aim. The textbooks used were the grammar of Emmanuel Alvarez, Smetius's prosody, Gretser's Greek grammar, and a collection of phrases by Aldus Manutius. The boys had to read Cicero's *Epistolae familiares, De senectute* and *Somnium Scipionis*, as well as works by Virgil, Ovid, Catullus, Livy and Curtius Rufus.[37] That the *Ratio* was strictly adhered to is shown in a letter written by Kristóf Batthyány, in which he asked his father to send him a book by Virgil that was needed as compulsory reading. In the syntax class either the *Eclogues* or Book V of the *Aeneid* were studied.[38]

The young counts continued to show a great aversion to study—in January 1653 the prefect reported that twelve-year-old Kristóf had stomachache and was spending all day in bed. The real problem was that "he had not done the homework he had been given for the Christmas holidays and was afraid of his teachers and the punishment he would receive". Nor was he alone: "Several of his classmates feel like this. I too suffered a great deal from a similar kind of school-sickness when I was young."[39]

György Borsiczky was typical of the clergymen of the day, in that he considered his activities as a prefect to be a means towards obtaining a paying benefice. Borsiczky came from a family of ancient lineage in Nyitra County and offered his services whenever a good benefice became vacant. In early 1652 he mentioned the living at Nagyhöflány, under the patronage of the Esterházy family, although it was very likely that György Esterházy would be appointed to it. Nevertheless, Borsiczky considered that he had a fair chance of becoming abbot of Zalavár,

although he was forced to put up with being a parson meanwhile.[40]

When György Borsiczky left his service, Batthyány tried to
find another prefect to replace him but soon gave up the search.
Finally, unable to find another prefect, he appointed a preceptor,
István Pathay, and György Kelcz, "a servant of good will", giving them the task of supervising the boys' education. Although
Pathay and Kelcz were considered suitable for the post as they
"were past childhood", they were warned not to take it to heart
if the two boys became angry with them.[41]

In terms of the boys' education, day to day work was in the
hands of their preceptors. It was their task to cram the lessons into
the boys' heads, and it was therefore just as important to have a
good preceptor as a good prefect. The two previous prefects had
recommended at least a dozen young men for the post. In one of
his letters Magnovith wrote of the then preceptor, probably
György Poletincz: "His presence will never make the young men
good students. They cannot learn brave and pious behaviour from
him but only drunkenness and the bad morals that result from it.
No one will ever be able to drive such bad morals out of their
heads, yet they are exceedingly slow in accepting what is good."
This was why it was so important, he continued, to find a person
who would set them a good example.[42]

Although János Magnovith was dissatisfied with György
Poletincz as a preceptor and did his best to find a replacement in
the autumn of 1651, Poletincz remained. In the autumn of 1651
he had completed almost ten years in this post. He was eventually replaced by István Pathay, who stayed with the boys from
early 1652 to the middle of 1655. In one of his letters Borsiczky
spoke of him as an experienced teacher who was able to do his
work well, having been employed in that capacity for four years.
However, he was unable to explain syntax and the more obscure
parts of the texts without Borsiczky's instructions.[43]

The names of those who were suggested as possible preceptors before the appointment of Pathay are not without interest here. In a letter written on 29 January 1651, Magnovith mentioned several candidates.[44] The first of these was Pál Selyei, a student in the syntax class. He was "a good, lively boy, the same age as Lackó…He is a Catholic, a good student, and has beautiful handwriting. He has an adequate knowledge of Latin, Hungarian, German and Croatian." Another candidate was János Balogh, the son of a nobleman from Alsólendva, who was then working as preceptor for the son of Péter Káldy, attended the same class as the Batthyány brothers, and was also a Catholic. The third candidate was a boy from Moravia who knew both Hungarian and German and attended the same class, but he had already been engaged as preceptor by a family from Sopron. As his letter of 12 April 1651 testifies, Magnovith decided to appoint Selyei, but he is mentioned only as a valet.[45]

György Borsiczky was also preoccupied with the problem of finding a good preceptor. On 3 June 1651 he wrote of a possible candidate by the name of Pető, whom he had discussed with Father Dombai.[46] On 17 October he wrote that Father Ferenc Lippai had recommended a young Hungarian man by the name of Szentmihályi, who had already studied philosophy for three years, had become a *philosophus absolutus* and was currently studying theology. He did not want to abandon his studies, so would be able to accept the job only if the boys went to Vienna by the following Easter.[47] On 14 November Borsiczky reported that two preceptors had arrived but that both were too young for the post.[48]

The question of a new preceptor was still undecided on 4 January 1652. The prefect was ready to appoint András Pozsgai, the twenty-one-year-old son of a wealthy citizen of Cenk, a clever and pious young man.[49] However, three weeks later he reported that Pozsgai had gone to teach the son of Count Cziráki. A young Hungarian by the name of Némethi, who was at tending the rhetoric class, was also considered suitable for the job but was already employed. There were no others suitable for the post among the students, so Borsiczky suggested that Selyei should be promoted from valet to preceptor. At the same time he recommended his own younger brother, Ferenc Borsiczky, to act as valet to the boys. On 6 February he wrote resignedly that for want of a better candidate he was willing to accept György Poletincz.[50] It was only later that he succeeded in finding a more suitable applicant in the person of István Pathay, who had been recommended by the Jesuits in Nagyszombat.

Besides serving their young masters, valets also had to attend school with them. Not all of them were enthusiastic about doing so. One valet, by the name of Csongrádi, escaped home in early 1652. Borsiczky suggested making him return to Sopron but exempting him from school attendance since he was unwilling to study. He wrote of another valet, Mihók Simoncsics, whom he calls proud and obstinate, that the boy would have run away if only he had had sufficient warm clothing. Later, a boy by the name of Herics, a former serf of Batthyány and a schoolmate of his sons, was taken on to act as valet for Palkó.[51] There was also a stable boy in the retinue to look after the Batthyány boys' horses. However, horse riding was only allowed during the holidays. The wife of Mátyás Pongrácz was in charge of the kitchen and the cook.

Congregations of the Blessed Virgin Mary were important institutions for deepening the religious attitudes of children attending Jesuit colleges. János Magnovith asked permission to have the boys enrolled, which he considered would be "useful both for acquiring knowledge of the classics and a pious disposition".[52] The boys joined the Congregation and presented their gifts on Lady Day, 25 March 1651.[53]

Kristóf and Pál also participated in the school's drama group. On 6 June 1651 Borsiczky wrote that they had roles in both the

Hungarian and the German plays to be performed during the procession the following day.[54]

Kristóf and Pál Batthyány acquired more secular knowledge and skills as well. They had to learn proper forms of behaviour, as well as to ride a horse and handle a sword, although we have little information on this. Most of the information we have refers to their later schooling in Graz. Physical exercise was possible only during periods of recreation. These were times when the boys could ride the horses kept in Sopron and could visit families living in the vicinity of the town—for example their brother-in-law László Esterházy and sister Mária Eleonóra at Cinfalva.[55] An invitation from them could not easily be refused since they always sent a carriage for the boys.[56] They also visited János Püsky, archbishop of Győr, at his nearby summer residence in Rákos.[57] These recreation periods, as the Jesuits called the breaks in the day or during the week in the course of the school year, thus allowed opportunity not only for horse riding but also for establishing social connections and learning proper behaviour.

Recreation periods did indeed serve as a relief from the monotony of study. However, travelling home proved less beneficial. The boys ceased to be students and once again became lordlings—and highly unmanageable with it. In March 1650 János Magnovith complained that although the students had returned in good health "I greatly regret that while this long period of recreation has made them stronger in body, it has made them weaker in classical learning." He subsequently asked the boys' parents not to have their sons at home so often. Apparently their mother already found her sons' absence hard to bear, since Magnovith added: "My dear Lady should not worry about them, for I was not born to be cruel to anyone. Such high-born young masters have to be taken great care of for the sake of your own greater honour."[58]

The boys were still at school in Sopron when their mother died. György Széchényi, bishop of Veszprém, said in his funeral address that "she had suffered from serious maladies, a long-drawn-out and terrible ailment, and from unbearable pain—not just for a day or two, not even for a week or two, but for a year or even longer." Her husband found himself alone after twenty years of marriage. Wishing to immortalise his wife's memory, Batthyány published three of the five funeral sermons preached for her.[59]

SECONDARY SCHOOL IN GRAZ

The death of their mother might have contributed to Batthyány's decision to send his sons to a new school. However, he may also have been prompted to make this move by the widow of Mátyás Pongrácz, who warned him not to send the boys back to Sopron because of an epidemic. "Many people are dying here", she wrote, adding that she herself was considering leaving the town.[60] The boys stayed in Szalónak until the beginning of February 1654, after which they were sent to the Jesuit school in Graz. The register in Graz contains only Pál's name, although his brother must also have been present. Count Pál studied in the poetry class, the penultimate class in the grammar school. György Hericz, Pál Selyi and Ádám Kelcz, all members of his retinue, were also there as his classmates.[61]

In a letter written on 23 February 1654 to István Pathay and György Kelcz, Ádám Batthyány issued new instructions regarding the education of his sons.[62] Kristóf was then seventeen and Pál fifteen. Although they were still not allowed to go wherever they pleased they were given greater freedom than they had had before. They were permitted to leave the town but had to be back home by evening. Nobody was allowed to leave the house at night, since it lay in a neighbourhood where "insolent behaviour and mischief" was common. Only aristocratic families could be visited, or the Jesuits if they invited the boys for lunch. Among the great men whose company Count Batthyány approved of was Prince Eggenberg, one of his close acquaintances.[63] He expressed his wish that Eggenberg's sons, "being of princely birth", be treated with great respect. However, there were also a number of relatives—such as the sons of László Csáky, the cousins of Kristóf and Pál—whom the boys were allowed to visit freely. As Palkó was of an age to be disobedient he was to be taken special care of. In the event of any disobedience on the part of the young men, their father was to be informed at once. A letter was to be written every week, as a matter of routine. In the event of illness, Batthyány's advice was that the doctors in Graz were to be consulted.

István Pathay and György Kelcz soon needed support in their work. In March the household was extended by the arrival of Balázs Vasdinnyei, Batthyány's manservant, who acted as a steward and supervised the boys' education as Mátyás Pongrácz had done. His duty was not so much to supervise their everyday studies, but rather to take care of them. Later events were to prove Ádám Batthyány's apprehensions to be quite justified.

Kristóf and Pál had a large retinue in Graz. Besides István Pathay and György Kelcz they had six valets in the summer of 1654, even before the arrival of Balázs Vasdinnyei who naturally brought a servant with him.[64] There was also Mátyás Pongrácz's wife and the kitchen staff. One of the registers mentions a girl by the name of Baberli, as well as a laundry girl.[65]

Such a large household required plenty of space. In 1655 the rent on the house was 100 forints.[66] As the boys grew up their personal expenditure also rose significantly. Pál in particular was often short of money. Referring to the leaking boots of a certain Hőgyészi, one of his servants, he remarks with bitterness in one of his letters that "nothing is done in the glorious town of Graz without money".[67] Clothes were a permanent problem. When the year of mourning for their mother was over and the boys could set aside their black clothes in the April of 1654, it became immediately apparent that they had no other decent clothing. The widowed father was either inexperienced in such matters or was trying to save money. The boots that had been sent from home were suitable for Kristóf but too small for Pál.[68] A week later the question of hats arose.[69] The preceptor, István Pathay, then asked the count to send some trousers since some of the valets had none and were unable to go to school without them.[70]

As the boys grew older they were less and less interested in their studies, having discovered several other things they wanted to do instead. Kristóf wanted to learn rifle shooting, so he asked his father in the autumn of 1654 for permission to engage a young man who was skilled with a rifle, recommended by the general of Varasd. He had previously taught the son of an acquaintance in Sopron.[71] Pál was more interested in horses and music. On 26 March 1655 he wrote to tell his father that he was learning to play the virginals in his spare time. He wrote later that he wished he could buy his own instrument but that he did not have enough money. The instrument would have cost twenty-one or twenty-two forints.[72]

Social life in the town of Graz, situated as it was in Inner Austria, was far livelier than in Sopron. The boys' visits were prepared for them by contacts of their father. Count Batthyány himself entertained good relations with a number of aristocrats in Styria. On one occasion, during a visit to his sons, he was invited to a meal by Prince Eggenberg, as well as by counts Kinski, Tattenbach, Trautmannsdorff and Saurau.[73] The names of similar great families often appeared in registers of the two boys' classmates. During the holidays new relationships could be established and old ones cultivated. In a letter written on 21

April 1654, István Pathay mentions that the young counts had gone to the castle of Prince Eggenberg.[74] On another occasion they visited a certain Colonel Hoff in the company of the Csáky brothers.[75] The two young Batthyánys formed a particular friendship with the two Trautmansdorff brothers who invited them to a bathing resort about a mile from the town. Balázs Vasdinnyei suggested that the Batthyánys should return the invitation by including them in the approaching name-day celebrations for Kristóf.[76] Kristóf even gave the younger Trautmansdorff brother one of his watches as a gift. On seeing the watch the elder brother also expressed his wish for one, so Kristóf asked his father to send him another.[77]

The cultivation of social relationships was also extended by Kristóf to representatives of the fair sex. A scandal emerged in early 1655 when Count Kristóf fell in love with a young lady of the Stumberger family. His father was against the relationship even when Kristóf promised him that he would study diligently in spite of it. By late March Balázs Vasdinnyei wrote to Batthyány that Kristóf "has told the preceptor that he has come here not to study but to enjoy himself". The young count had been very angry with him for siding with his father, and Vasdinnyei adds bitterly that "he does not say a word to me now that the Stumberger brothers have suggested to him that he should not talk to me at all". He then asks Batthyány to relieve him of his responsibilities: "I am getting on in years and I cannot bear the insults any longer. You have always treated me with respect, but the young master does not do so, which causes me great sorrow."[78] A few days later Kristóf was promising to study diligently once again.[79] In the following April he reported to his father that he and his brother had become prefects of the Congregation and as such he had had a present prepared that had cost him twelve golden coins, so he was asking his father to send him money.[80]

Eventually Batthyány realised that his elder son's promises were in vain and he excused him from continuing his studies. In the autumn of 1655 Kristóf was not made to return to Graz.

The Diet in Pozsony offered a good pretext for them to leave the town. Batthyány took both his sons to the Diet in June. The great attraction was the coronation of the third queen of Ferdinand III. Ádám Batthyány had the task of organising the coronation banquet as Royal Purveyor, and his sons served during the ceremony together with twenty other young squires acting as purveyors.[81] Kristóf took part in a similar ceremony after the coronation of King Leopold on 27 June 1655.[82] The Diet brought Kristóf his first office; on 19 March 1655 he was appointed chamberlain by the king. He took the oath on 13 June.[83]

KRISTÓF BATTHYÁNY'S JOURNEYS ABROAD

After their stay in Pozsony the brothers parted. Kristóf remained at home for some time and in the autumn of 1655 went to Máriacell at the invitation of Pál Esterházy. During the summer of 1656 he undertook his first duty as an individual when his father gave him leave to travel to Prague to the coronation of Leopold as king of Bohemia. The trip lasted about two months. His companions were Márton Nagyfalussy, a scribe of Ádám Batthyány, and János Rácz, one of his trusted servants. Batthyány ensured that the boy also had a patron in the person of Count Hans Christoph Pucheim, captain-general of Komárom, a man close to the king. Before joining the count, however, Kristóf visited Ferenc Nádasdy in his castle in Saibersdorf. Nádasdy raised serious objections regarding the young man's equipage. He expressed his opinion as to what Kristóf would need in Prague to his father: "Since you are known there and even have several relatives there it would be unworthy of your family and of Hungarians in general to let your son go there so ill-equipped…He will have to behave as is becoming for the son of a dignitary like you, and for that he will need more money. I have a fair idea how much it costs to stay at the court, since I have been to Prague myself. To support seventeen persons and eight horses requires a large sum of money and it would be highly ignominious to run short of cash there. You know better than I do how much German friendship is worth. Your son can stay here until noon tomorrow and wait for your command concerning the above comments, that is, to be told whether he should set off or remain at home."[84]

Unfortunately, we do not have Batthyány's reply to this letter. Some of Nádasdy's remarks must have been heeded since the journey was successful. Kristóf was under the supervision of Count Pucheim throughout the journey, which lasted from 7 July to 4 October 1656. He spent six weeks in Prague and then returned to Vienna along with the staff of the imperial court. During this time, prior to the coronation, Pucheim sent him to stay for a week with a Saxon prince who was also in Bohemia for the festivities.[85]

Kristóf's letters are highly enthusiastic, but those written by Márton Nagyfalussy are less so. His reservations concerning Count Pucheim seem to have been justified. The count himself was kind to them but his officials acted quite differently. He remarks that the Germans did not like people who were dependent on others. Nagyfalussy found fault with everything and was very anxious if the young master was invited to families with daughters of marriageable age. He was afraid of a repeat of the Graz episode. He hated the beer, which he called "thick, red water from boiled barley" and which he claimed had "tortured" him twice.

The company returned to Göllersdorf, the seat of the Pucheims in Austria, on 4 October 1656. Pucheim urged Kristóf to stay at the Vienna court for the winter. The young count wrote to his father saying that not only he himself, but also the country would benefit from his stay. Batthyány apparently gave his consent. Kristóf's next letters, written in October 1656, describe his experiences in Vienna. In the middle of October he had to serve the king himself, probably as a chamberlain. However, his service at the court did not last long as he and Pucheim were soon invited by Archbishop Lippay first to Pozsony, then to his estate. Kristóf wrote that Pucheim had promised to obtain the lord steward's permission to leave.

Márton Nagyfalussy was with Kristóf in Vienna but they soon parted company. Nevertheless, his relatively long relationship with the Batthyány family merits attention. His deep involvement in the fate of the family resulted in a famous work of literature. During his service as preceptor he wrote a paraphrase of King St. Stephen's *Admonitiones* to his son Imre, later St. Imre. Nagyfalussy interpreted the relationship between the holy king and the crown prince as being like that between any father and son.

Unfortunately, the letter to which this valuable piece of writing was attached is not dated.[86] The contents, however, give us some idea of the year in which it was written. Nagyfalussy discusses the uselessness of a grand tour in Germany and the benefits of a tour in Transylvania. This indicates that it must have been written before Kristóf's journey in October 1656. The letter also refers to the author's own intentions. According to Nagyfalussy, he had been prompted to write the work by the unsatisfactory mental and physical progress of the young counts: "The young masters are not concerned with things of beauty as should become them. They do not like attending church and read only a little." In a reference to the prayer book published by Ádám Batthyány in 1654 and dedicated to his sons he laments that it was in vain that their father "had offered them a spiritual weapon...in the form of his beautiful book", since only daily use of it would bring about the desired results. He therefore suggests that Ádám Batthyány should have a few passages of King St. Stephen's *Admonitiones* read out to them in his presence. This, he argues, could perhaps help to shape their characters. It would also be advisable, he continues, if an experienced servant were to help them put into practice the theoretical side of their education.

Nagyfalussy was doubtless familiar with the entire text of the *Admonitiones*, since it had been inserted into the Hungarian Corpus Juris in 1628.[87] Nevertheless, in addition to part of the preface he paraphrased only six chapters out of the original ten. He chose to emphasise those admonitions that could be interpreted as valid for the relationship between fathers and sons in general. Bearing in mind the misdeeds of Kristóf and Pál, he naturally placed the chapters stressing obedience and a son's duty to follow the example of his forefathers at the beginning of the work. These chapters were followed by advice on the way to deepen one's spirituality, and on the importance of the church and of prayer, tolerance and temperance. Finally, piety, compassion and good deeds are praised and encouraged. The chapters on the duties of a king and on the responsibilities of clergymen, barons, soldiers and guests were omitted. This paraphrase is the first known translation of the Latin original.

In a last chapter Nagyfalussy also deals with Kristóf's further education. He rejects the idea of a grand tour in Germany, maintaining that only harmful things could be learnt in that country. He quotes István Csáky, who had said of his son: "What he learnt in Graz is worth far more than ten thousand thalers in my eyes, but I regret his stay among the Germans more than if I had lost thirty thousand." Nagyfalussy suggests that the young man should go instead to Transylvania, giving several reasons for his choice. He knew Transylvania well as he had resided, during a short period when he had intended to become a Jesuit, at the monastery of Kolozsmonostor in 1651.[88] He must also have been aware that Batthyány had relatives there.

However, Nagyfalussy's ideas concerning the education of young Batthyány were never realised, and it was Ferenc Nádasdy who came to have an increasing say in the young man's life. The idea was for Kristóf to marry his eldest daughter, Krisztina, and it was for this reason that Kristóf spent two years in Nádasdy's household.[89] Kristóf's only surviving letter written at this time is dated in Saibersdorf and mentions a pilgrimage to Máriacell that had had to be postponed due to the illness of György Homonnai.[90]

Krsitóf's long years of education ended with a grand tour in Germany, for which the journey to Prague had been a kind of preparation. Since Nádasdy had recently accompanied Pál Esterházy, his brother-in-law, on a tour in Germany in 1653, he was able to give Kristóf detailed instructions and offer companions for the journey. One of them kept a diary, which means that we have a wealth of information about the tour, which lasted from 12 November 1657 to 13 June 1658. The participants visited all the important sights of Germany and northern Italy. Not only did they see famous churches, monasteries, arsenals and theatres, they also established valuable contacts in the highest echelons of society. They drew on their earlier experiences and the etiquette learnt at the coronation in Prague and at the Vienna court. The editor of the diary suggests that Nádasdy also had political considerations in mind when organising this tour for Kristóf.[91] It was not unusual at this time to exploit tours made by young people for political purposes.

The young Count Batthyány made the acquaintance of several important figures in political life. In Frankfurt he dined with his relative, Prince Lobkowitz. He then met the Elector of Bavaria, the archbishops of Köln and Trier, the prince of Württemberg and the archbishop of Salzburg. He also met the prince of Pfalz-Neuburg who recalled his memories of Hungary and spoke of his friendship with Ádám Batthyány.[92] An equally long list of distinguished names could be cited from the Italian leg of the journey. In Venice Kristóf was the guest of the apostolic nuncio, and in Florence he visited practically all the members of the reigning family. In Rome his guide was the influential Cardinal Chigi. Pope Alexander VII granted him an audience as a matter of course. Furthermore, lest we lose sight of the academic aspect of the tour, it should be pointed out that he visited the Jesuit Collegium Romanum and was even received by Athanasius Kircher.

This extended tour represented the completion of Kristóf's education, and he was soon given an opportunity to put his experiences into practice.

THE YOUNGER BATTHYÁNY

While Kristóf was excused from further study, Pál was made to suffer anew. In August 1655 he was in Graz again, this time with a much smaller household. His only companions were Pál Selyei and the valet Herics. Following his brother's example, he tried to get out of his unpleasant situation by passive resistance. On 3 August 1655 he attempted to persuade his father by alluding to Cicero: "A troubled mind is unable to reach its own targets. What is the use of my staying here? I have no inclination to study and the time I spend here is in vain, since I am learning neither scholarly nor other disciplines but merely putting you to great expense."[93] Ádám Batthyány, who otherwise tended to be rather miserly, was not taken in and Pál had to remain in Graz. He was there at least until the spring of 1657. In the spring of 1658 he spent some time there again but felt the stay to be similarly useless. He asked two young German gentlemen what they were learning there. They replied that they were preparing for their exams and mocked him for not returning sooner. Pál wrote that there were only twenty Hungarians there at the most.[94] When the school year ended in September 1658 his trials must also have come to an end since the letter he wrote on 12 December was already dated from Csejte. This is his last surviving letter written in his father's lifetime.[95] Nothing is known of any tour arranged for him to compare with that undertaken by his brother.

THE SUBSEQUENT CAREERS OF THE BATTHYÁNY BROTHERS

The effectiveness of the brothers' education would best be judged by analysing the activities in which they were involved in later life. However, the lack of sources makes this impossible. While their father's life is extremely well documented, far fewer documents survive in connection with the two young men. Nevertheless, it seems clear that they held offices as a consequence of the family's social position and their father's ingenuity. It was he, for example, who succeeded in making the post of captain-general of the Transdanubian region hereditary in his family.[96] The brothers had few individual merits to boast of. Although there are reports of their initial bravery as soldiers, their fervour soon abated.

For some time Kristóf was supported by Count Ferenc Nádasdy, who saw him as his future son-in-law. However, this relationship did not last since the proposed marriage never took place. Krisztina Nádasdy's reasons for refusing to accept Kristóf as her husband can be deduced from a remark made by Archbishop Lippay. He alluded in a letter to Kristóf's tender feelings "not for his fiancée but for her mother".[97] Apparently he was unable to resist the famous beauty of Countess Julianna Esterházy, the wife of Ferenc Nádasdy. Relations between Nádasdy and Kristóf Batthyány were certainly distinctly reserved from that time on. Even distant acquaintances were aware of the situation. On one occasion Frater Nicolaus Donellanus wrote to Prince Portia about a matter of dispute between them. Their differences were also fostered by deputy captain-general János Sárkány, whose wife later also had an affair with Kristóf Batthyány.[98] Ironically, it was probably due to the poisoned relationship between Batthyány and Nádasdy that the former survived the conspiracy by a group of magnates in the 1660s that cost Ferenc Nádasdy and two of his friends their lives.

After the break with Krisztina, Kristóf married Annamária Palocsay, the daughter of Gábor Palocsay and Ilona Apponyi.[99] Their union was far from happy and the couple soon regarded one another with coldness. Only four years after their marriage, in 1665, Annamária asked Prince Lobkowitz to help bring about a reconciliation with her husband.[100] In 1669 she asked to be defended against his cruelty after he had broken two of her ribs and hit her over the head with a mace.[101] In spite of their troubled relationship they had two sons, Ádám and Boldizsár. Their father gave both of them a traditional education. Ádám attended the grammar school in Sopron before beginning his university studies in Graz in 1679. He graduated on 19 June 1680 with distinction.[102] In 1683 he took over the administration of the family's affairs from his father who had fallen into disfavour with the king, but he died, while still only a young man, in 1703. The younger brother, Boldizsár, studied poetry in Graz in 1690 and continued his studies at the Hungarian-Illyrian College of Bologna between 1699 and 1702.[103] He was then forced to return home due to illness. He spent the rest of his life administering his estates and died in 1743.

In early 1659 Pál Batthyány got engaged to Katalin Illésházy, the daughter of Gábor Illésházy and Éva Széchy. According to a letter written by Farkas Esterházy, Katalin, a rich countess, had other suitors besides Pál. One of the Csáky brothers and a wealthy magnate from Silesia were also talked of in connection with her.[104] In the end the marriage contract between Pál and Katalin was signed in 1659 but was realised only on 22 January 1662 in Trencsén.[105] The couple had two sons, Ferenc and Zsigmond. Since Pál died young, in 1674, they became orphans at a young age. Guardianship of the brothers was granted first to their uncle, and then to a cousin, both called Ádám Batthyány. Ferenc attended schools in Graz. He completed his schooling in 1687 with distinction and received a gold chain from the king in recognition.[106] The younger brother, Zsigmond Batthyány, began his studies in the syntax class in 1686. His preceptor, István Böjtös, usually gave good reports of his progress. Zsigmond was successful in his studies, was preparing for graduation in 1690, and had very good prospects of receiving the golden chain from the king.[107] Either the members of this generation were keener on their studies, or their social position was of greater consequence than in the case of the sons of Ádám Bátthyány I.

* * *

Members of the European aristocracy laid great stress on formal education from the sixteenth century onwards, since they wished to be equal to the challenge represented by the professional intelligentsia. To them, however, education meant more than merely studying at school. It involved dancing, playing musical instruments, etiquette, fencing and speaking modern languages. In addition to the traditional rhetoric and logic, formal school education included law and military disciplines such as fortification, mathematics and geometry for those who wanted to take up a military career.[108] The sons of Ádám Batthyány I, in contrast, received a traditional classical education. Besides their lack of modern languages, they suffered most of all in their future careers from the absence of any legal and military training.

Bearing in mind the conditions in Hungary, their upbringing cannot be called unsatisfactory. On the other hand, many of their contemporaries were raised according to far more modern standards. In 1654 Miklós Pálffy, for example, was a student in Rome, where horse riding featured among the many subjects he studied.[109] Pál Esterházy sent his two sons, Mihály and Gábor, to the Jesuit college in Parma where an emphasis was placed on the teaching of law.[110] Ferenc Rákóczi studied fencing, dancing, geometry, history and geography in Florence and Rome in 1693/94.[111] Zsigmond Széchenyi studied law, Italian and French, dancing and riding in Florence and Rome in 1699.[112]

However, the majority of young aristocrats were educated in the same manner as Kristóf and Pál Batthyány. They attended a secondary school and then university for a certain time. Kristóf was also sent by his father on a grand tour in Europe. As a royal chamberlain he had an opportunity to learn court etiquette. However, during his travels he did not receive formal education of any kind, unlike some of his contemporaries.

Within two generations of the Batthyány family, between 1610 and 1690, the education received by the highest dignitaries in Hungary underwent a significant change. Out of the thirty-seven most influential persons in the first half of the seventeenth century, fourteen attended university while the majority, that is, eighteen, did not. In five cases the educational circumstances are not known. Out of the seventeen persons who assumed office after 1650, the majority, twelve, had studied at university, three had not, and in two cases the educational circumstances are not known.[113] The difference between the two periods is remarkable. During the lifetime of Kristóf and Pál the level of individual erudition became an important factor in shaping individual careers. However, it should not be forgotten that the means of learning differed significantly, and profound knowledge could also be acquired in informal ways. The question remains as to whether it was the sons of Ádám Batthyány who lacked any interest in studying, or the schools they attended that failed to stimulate them intellectually.

Whatever the truth in relation to the Batthyány boys, there is one striking example in Hungary of the disparity between formal education and individual talent. Miklós Zrínyi was one of the most outstanding personalities of the seventeenth century and the hero of many battles against the Ottomans. He was the author of works on military theory and was the leading politician of his day. He also composed the first baroque epic in Hungarian and published a number of lyric poems. During his school years, however, his guardian, Archbishop Péter Pázmány—who apparently had some experience of the character of young people—claimed that Zrínyi lacked any intellectual capacity whatsoever.[114]

Notes

1 János Kanizsai Pálfi, a preacher from Pápa, to Ferenc Batthyány, 6 April 1625: Béla Iványi, "A körmendi Batthyány-levéltár reformációra vonatkozó oklevelei 1527–1625." In *XVI–XV századi szellemi mozgalmaink történetéhez.* Edited by László Szilasi, 29/1 (hereafter: Adattár 29/1): 317–318.

2 György Zvonarich, in his foreword to the volume of sermons written by his father, Mihály Zvonarich, referred to himself as the preceptor of Ádám Batthyány. *Magyar postilla*, Csepreg, 1627.

3 Mihály Lónyi to Ádám Batthyány, 1641: Hungarian National Archives (Magyar Országos Levéltár, hereafter: MOL): P 1314. Batthyány family archives, Missiles (hereafter: P 1314), No. 29386.

4 Ádám Batthyány to László Esterházy, 20 July 1648: P 124. Esterházy family archive, documents of Count László (hereafter: P 124), No. 396.

5 There are extant bills relating to the *Sword of the Soul*: P 1313. Batthyány family archive, main archive (hereafter: P 1313): Fasc. 267, f. 357 and Fasc. 269.

6 Tibor Koppány, "Batthyány I. Ádám építkezései 1629–59". *Történelmi Szemle*, 1984: 539–555.

7 Inventory of Rohonc, 1635: P 1322. Batthyány family central archive in Körmend (hereafter: P 1322), Fasc. 112, Inventories 76, No. 16.

8 His conversion has attracted much comment. István Fazekas, *Die Bekehrung Adam Batthyany im Jahre 1629*. Schlaininger Gespräche, 1994, is based on documents relating to the conversion that have not previously been investigated.

9 Auróra Formentini's family came from Görz. Ernst Heinrich Kneschke, *Neues allgemeines Adels-Lexicon III*. Leipzig, 1861: 199–300.

10 Batthyány family tree, Table I.

11 P 1314, No. 52415.

12 Ibid., No. 52409.

13 Ibid., No. 52417.

14 Ibid., No. 52418.

15 Quoted by Arnold Magyar: *Ein Beitrag zur Kultur- und Religionsgeschichte des Südburgenlandes bis zur Gegenreformation*. Graz, 1976: 152–153.

16 Notes made by Ádám Batthyány concerning his expenses, 1637: P 1336. Miscellaneous burnt notes, Box 15 (no number).

17 Household inventory: P 1322, Fasc. 48, No. 352, 4 June 1634—4 June 1635; 17 June 1638–17 May 1639; 17 May 1639–17 May 1640.

18 György Poletincz is mentioned in the notes as working as a preceptor between 1641 and 1645. The last mention of him is on 20 September 1645, when he received twenty forints: P 1322, 326/b bound fasc. 197. According to other data he accompanied the children to Sopron.

19 The contract with Ulrich Neumayr: P 1322. Fasc. 48. Book of contracts f. 57.

20 Inventory of Rohonc, 1650: P 1322, Fasc. 112.

21 After sixteen years in other types of service, Mátyás Pongrácz was appointed as the boys' steward on 12 July 1649: P 1322, Fasc. 46, No. 353,

f. 33v. Instruction to Mátyás Pongrácz, 12 August 1649: P 1315. Batthyány Family Archive, notes of Ádám Batthyány (hereafter: P 1315), Fasc.1, f. 39–41.

22 P 1322, Fasc. 52. Inventory, No. 893. f. 16; Ibid., No. 893. f. 18v.

23 György Borsiczky to Ádám Batthyány, 14 August 1651: P 1314, No. 7050; János Magnovith to Ádám Batthyány, 28 June 1650: P 1314, No. 30204.

24 Mátyás Pongrácz to Ádám Batthyány, 17 July 1649: P 1314, No. 37846.

25 Both László Esterházy and Borsiczky, a later prefect, made attempts to convert Pongrácz: György Borsiczky to Ádám Batthyány, 12 June 1651: P 1314, No. 7039; 16 July 1651: Ibid., No. 7047.

26 Memoirs of János Magnovith: P 1315, Fasc. 2, f. 67.

27 P 1314, No. 30199.

28 János Magnovith to Ádám Batthyány, 10 January 1651: P 1314, No. 30210.

29 János Magnovith to Ádám Batthyány, 21 May 1651: P 1314, No. 30222.

30 György Lippay to Ádám Batthyány, 13 May 1651: P 1314, No. 29318.

31 György Borsiczky to Ádám Batthyány, 19 August 1651: P 1314, No. 7051.

32 György Borsiczky to Ádám Batthyány, 22 July 1652: P 1314, No. 7077.

33 György Borsiczky to Ádám Batthyány, 8 September 1651: P 1314, No. 7060; 9 September 1651: P 1314, No. 7054; 11 September 1651: P 1314, No. 7055.

34 György Borsiczky to Ádám Batthyány, 10 December 1651: P 1314, No. 7065.

35 György Borsiczky to Ádám Batthyány, 13 June 1651: P 1314, No. 7041.

36 György Borsiczky to Ádám Batthyány, 28 March 1651: P 1314, No. 7087.

37 Béla Iványi, *A magyar könyvkultúra múltjából. Adattár XVI-XVIII. századi szellemi mozgalmaink történetéhez* 11. Szeged, 1983 (hereafter: *Adattár* 11): 280–281.

38 Kristóf Batthyány to Ádám Batthyány, 1 July 1653: *Adattár* 11, 284.

39 György Borsiczky to Ádám Batthyány, 8 January 1652: *Adattár* 11, 571–573.

40 György Borsiczky to Ádám Batthyány, 22 June 1655: P. 1314, No. 7093; Ludovicus Némethy, *Series parochiarum et parochorum archidioecesis Strigoniensis.* Esztergom, 1895: 509.

41 Instruction from Ádám Batthyány: P 1322, Fasc. 36, No. 320.

42 János Magnovith to Ádám Batthyány, 21 May 1651: P 1314, No. 30222.

43 György Borsiczky to Ádám Batthyány, 6 March 1652: P 1314, No. 7076.

44 János Magnovith to Ádám Batthyány, 29 January 1651: P 1314, No. 30214.

45 János Magnovith to Ádám Batthyány, 12 April 1651: P 1314, No. 30221.

46 P 1314, No. 7037.

47 P 1314, No. 7037.

48 P 1314, No. 7061.

49 György Borsiczky to Ádám Batthyány, 4 January 1652: P 1314, No. 7070.

50 P 1314, No. 7073.

51 György Borsiczky to Ádám Batthyány, 6 February 1652: P 1314, No. 7073.

52 János Magnovith to Ádám Batthyány, 24 January 1651: P 1314, No. 30213.

53 János Magnovith to Ádám Batthyány, 24 March 1651: P 1314, No. 30220.

54 György Borsiczky to Ádám Batthyány, 6 June 1651: P 1314, No. 7039.

55 György Borsiczky to Ádám Batthyány, 12 June 1651: P 7040.

56 György Borsiczky to Ádám Batthyány, 28 June 1651: P 1314, No. 7044.

57 György Borsiczky to Ádám Batthyány, 14 November 1651: P 1314, No. 7061.

58 János Magnovith to Ádám Batthyány, 22 March 1650: P 1314, No. 30197.

59 Georgius Széchenyi, *Concio funebris pro funere Illustrissimae Dominae Comitissae Aurorae Catharinae Formantin.* Vienna, 1654. Correspondence concerning the publication: *Adattár* 11, 294–398.

60 Mátyásné Pongrácz to Ádám Batthyány, 7 January 1654: P 1314, No. 34957.

61 Johann Andritsch, *Studenten und Lehrer aus Ungarn und Siebenbürgen an der Universität Graz 1586–1782. Forschungen zur geschichtlichen Landeskunde der Steiermark* 22. Graz, 1965 (hereafter: Andritsch): 83.

62 P 1322, Fasc. 36, Instructions, No. 323.

63 On the occasion of Ádám Batthyány's visit to Graz between 27 May and 2 June 1654, he had lunch twice with Prince Eggenberg, and on one occasion he dined with him: P 1315. Itinerary of Ádám Batthyány, f. 167.

64 P 1322, Fasc. 58, No. 1200. Inventories, 5 June 1654.

65 Ibid., No. 11187. Inventories, 12 March 1654.

66 Balázs Vasdinnyei to Ádám Batthyány, 21 April 1655: P 1314, No. 51131.

67 Pál Batthyány to Ádám Batthyány, 3 April 1654: P 1314, No. 5184.

68 István Pathay to Ádám Batthyány, 21 April 1654: P 1314, No. 35963.

69 István Pathay to Ádám Batthyány, 27 April 1654: P 1314, No. 35964.

70 István Pathay to Ádám Batthyány, 4 February 1655: P 1314, No. 35966.

71 Kristóf Batthyány to Ádám Batthyány, 7 September 1654: P 1314, No. 4784.

72 Pál Batthyány to Ádám Batthyány, 26 March 1655: P 1314, No. 5198; 9 April 1655: Ibid., No. 5202.

73 Ádám Batthyány's itinerary, 1654: P 1315, f. 167. At this time, with the year of mourning completed, Count Batthyány was considering the idea of remarriage. According to a letter from Mátyás Pongrácz's wife, dated 4 June 1654, one potential future wife was one of the Eggenberg princesses: P 1314, No. 37838.

74 P 1314, No. 35963.

75 Pál Batthyány to Ádám Batthyány, 9 April 1654: P 1314, No. 5186.

76 Balázs Vasdinnyei to Ádám Batthyány, 4 July 1654: P 1314, No. 61114.

77 Kristóf Batthyány to Ádám Batthyány, 23 December 1654: P 1314, No. 4786.

78 Balázs Vasdinnyei to Ádám Batthyány, 27 March 1655: P 1314, No. 51130.

79 Kristóf Batthyány to Ádám Batthyány, 31 March 1655: P 1314, No. 4798.

80 Kristóf Batthyány to Ádám Batthyány, April 1655: P 1314, No. 4793.

81 *Haus-, Hof-, und Staatsarchiv* (hereafter: *HHSta*), *Hofarchive, Zeremonialakten, Protokoll*, Vol. 1, 405. Ádám Batthyány was very much looking forward to the Diet. It is perhaps no coincidence that among the secular lords it was he who arrived with the largest retinue, including 600 horses (ibid., 176). Among his household the rumour spread that he had been elected palatine: Mátyás Pongráczné to Ádám Batthyány, 19 March 1655: P 1314, No. 37835.

82 *HHSta, Hofarchive, Zeremonialakten, Protokoll*, Vol. 1, 523.

83 *HHSta, Hofarchive, Oberhofmeisterakten Sonderreihe, Eidbücher*, Vol. 2, f. 144.

84 Ferenc Nádasdy to Ádám Batthyány, 14 August 1655: P 1314, No. 32477.

85 Letters written during the travels of Márton Nagyfalussy and Kristóf Batthyány: P 1314, No. 33501–33507; No. 4799–4808.

86 This piece of writing was preserved together with the letter of Kristóf Batthyány to Ádám Batthyány: P 1314, No. 4798.

87 Modern edition: *Scriptores rerum hungaricarum tempore ducum regumque stirpis Arpadianae gestarum. Edendo operi praefuit Emericus Szentpétery*, II. Budapest, 1938: 616.

88 Ladislaus Lukács, *Catalogus generalis seu nomenclator biographius personarum Provinciae Austriae Societatis Jesu 1551–1773*, II. Rome, 1988: 1077.

89 Ferenc Nádasdy to János Mednyánszky, 8 June 1657. Mednyánszky family archive, MOL P 497, Fasc. 2.

90 Kristóf Batthyány to Ádám Batthyány, 19 June 1657: P 1314, No 4810.

91 "Batthyány Kristóf európai utazása 1657–1658." Diary kept by László Szelestei Nagy. *Peregrinatio Hungarorum* 2. Szeged, 1988 (hereafter: Szelestei Nagy): 68.

92 Szelestei Nagy, passim. For further information about the journey see Ferenc Nádasdy to Joannes Bp. Marielli, the tutor of István Nádasdy, 1 August 1670: Zichy family archives from Zsély. MOL P 707, Fasc. 81. NB. Letters, No. 2024.

93 Pál Batthyány to Ádám Batthyány, 3 August 1655: P 1314, No. 5203.

94 Pál Batthyány to Ádám Batthyány, 17 July 1658: P 1314, No. 5205.

95 P 1314, No. 5206.

96 Decree of Leopold I, 18 May 1655: Joannes Paulik, *Genealogia illustris stirpis de Batthyán*. National Széchényi Library, Manuscript archives: Fol. Lat. 95. No. 59. Appointment of Kristóf on 7 April 1659: Ibid., No. 60.

97 György Lippay to Ferenc Wesselényi, 2 April 1659: MOL, Archives of the Hungarian Chamber E 199 a, II, 65, No. 38.

98 7 February 1663. *HHSta Ungarische Akten Speciali,* Fasc. 431, f. 180–181; Ágnes R. Várkonyi, "Zrínyi szövetséglevele. Europica varietas – Hungarica varietas." *Tanulmányok*. Budapest, 1994: 116.

99 Invitation from Kristóf Batthyány to Archduke Wilhelm Leopold, 2 September 1661. *Hofkammerarchiv, Familienakten* BP-66 Batthyány f. 26–27.

100 Lipót Óváry: *A Magyar Tudományos Akadémia történeti bizottságának oklevélmásolatai*, III. Budapest, 1901, No. 1389: 222.

101 Ibid., No. 1617: 259.

102 Andritsch, 101; Margarethe Rath, *Die Promotionen in disputatione sub auspiciis imperatoris an der Universität Wien. Mitteilungen des Österreichischen Staatsarchivs*, 1953 (hereafter: Rath): 139.

103 Endre Veress, *Olasz egyetemen járt magyarországi tanulók anyakönyve és iratai 1221–1864*. Budapest, 1941: 544, 646.

104 Farkas Esterházy to Pál Esterházy, 1 February 1659: P 125, No. 701.

105 The marriage contract of 20 March 1659: P 1313. Maioratus, Matrimonialia Lad. 34. No. 2.

106 Andritsch, 102; Rath, 139.

107 The letters of István Böjtös to Ádám Batthyány, 1685–1690: P 1314, No. 7626–27.

108 On the education of the Austrian aristocracy, which probably had a strong influence on the education of the Hungarian aristocracy, see Otto Brunner, *Adeliges Landleben und europäischer Geist. Leben und Werk Wolf Helmhards von Hohberg 1612–88*. Vienna, 1949; Gernot Heiss, "Bildungsverhalten des niederösterreichischen Adels im gesellschaftlichen Wandel: zum Bildungsgang im 16. und 17. Jahrhundert." In *Spezialforschung und "Gesamtgeschichte"*. Edited by Grete Klingenstein and Heinrich Lutz. Wiener Beiträge zur Geschichte der Neuzeit, Band 8. Vienna, 1981: 139–155; Gernot Heiss, "Standeserziehung und Schulenunterricht. Zur Bildung des niederösterreichischen Adeligen in der frühen Neuzeit." In *Adel im Wandel. Politik, Kultur, Konfession 1500–1700*. Niederösterreichische Landesausstellung. Rosenburg, 12 May-28 October 1990: 391–407.

109 Pál Jedlicska, *Eredeti részletek a Pálffy-család okmánytárához 1401–1653. A gróf Páffyak életrajzi vázlatai*. Budapest, 1910: 409.

110 István Fazekas, *Paul Esterhazy*. Bollwerk Forschtenstein. Katalog der Burgenländischen Landesaustellung 1993. Burgenländischen Forschungen Sonderband. Eisenstadt, 1993: 48.

111 Ferenc Rákóczi, "Vallomások." *Magyar Remekírók*. Edited by Lajos Hopp. Budapest, 1979: 48, 50.

112 Documents in relation to the Italian journey of Zsigmond Széchenyi, 1699–1700, have been published by Péter Ötvös. *Peregrinatio Hungarorum*, 1. Szeged, 1988: 32, 42, 53.

113 *Libri dignitariorum* I: MOL E 683.

114 Ferenc Hanuy, *Pázmány Péter összegyűjtött levelei*. Budapest, 1911, II: 513.

Epitaph of a noble youth by a seventeenth-century master
(Hungarian National Gallery)

Portrait of Count Ádám Batthyány I by a seventeenth-century master
(Hungarian National Museum)

Portrait of Júlia Esterházy by Benjamin Block
(Hungarian National Museum)

The castle of Sárospatak (photo by László Váradi)

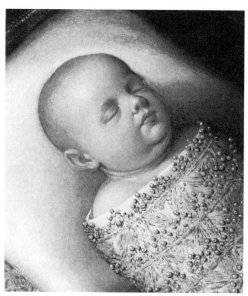

"Infant lying in state" by a seventeenth-century master
(Hungarian National Museum)

CHAPTER 4

THE MARRIAGE POLICY OF THE ESTERHÁZY FAMILY AFTER THE DEATH OF PALATINE MIKLÓS

THE FOUNDER OF THE DYNASTY

Miklós Esterházy was one of the most talented and influential members of the Hungarian political elite from the age of about thirty.[1] It was at this age that the king granted him a title. Later, in 1622, he was appointed lord chief justice. At the same time he was captain-general of Érsekújvár and lord lieutenant of three counties. He was without doubt an eminent politician, who had on several occasions proved his loyalty to the Habsburgs and his ability to carry out important duties. The events of 1625 proved to everyone the validity and popularity of his political position. He was elected palatine by the overwhelming majority of the Diet. The election took place in rather tense circumstances: the members of the Diet had made the election of the palatine a precondition for the coronation of the heir apparent.

The financial foundations for Esterházy's political career had been created as a result of his first marriage. By marrying Orsolya Dersffy, the widow of Ferenc Mágóchy, he had come into possession of several important estates in western Hungary. His only anxiety was the fact that he had only one son, a weak and sickly boy, who was just nine years old in 1625. Esterházy had been a widower for several years and his political successes had made his desire to start a new family even more urgent. However, he still waited five years before remarrying. Such a delay was not unusual—it was generally considered unwise to be over-hasty in such matters. This common attitude was expressed, among others, by György Thurzó, another famous and successful politician. According to Thurzó "marriage is not a minor issue in a man's life but the biggest thing. If you win by it you stand to win a lot, but if you lose, then even death would be preferable."[2] Miklós Esterházy managed to find a suitable partner in 1624, not long before his election as palatine.

Countess Krisztina Nyáry, his second wife, came from a wealthy and distinguished family. As her fiancé, Esterházy showered Krisztina with signs of his boundless affection. Once, in an extravagant gesture, he had his portrait painted and sent the picture to her as a present, unintentionally embarrassing even the rich heiress. What began as an obvious marriage of convenience finally became a genuine love match, and the couple lived in happiness.

The secret of their harmony lay in the fact that they each received what they wanted from their partner. Krisztina Nyáry was an ideal wife, a kind, obedient and understanding woman, who created a comfortable home for her husband. She does not seem to have had many interests herself and preferred to stay at home—something, which Esterházy regarded as one of her greatest merits. Far more importantly, Krisztina presented Esterházy with nine children in the space of seventeen years. Their first daughter, who died in infancy, was born in the first year of their marriage; the couple's last child, a boy, was born when Esterházy was fifty-nine.[3]

Miklós Esterházy bestowed on Krisztina Nyáry the love and affection she craved. He expressed his love and attachment to his wife day by day, something for which she had yearned. Her first husband, Imre Thurzó, had been talented and ambitious and was far more interested in politics than in his young wife. She had felt very lonely at that time and had often thought of her own parents, Kata Várday and Pál Nyáry, who had had a loving relationship and who had cherished their only daughter dearly.

The harmony in the Esterházys' marriage was most clearly visible in their relationship with their children. Whenever they mentioned István, Esterházy's son by his first wife, they called him "our son". They gave the children nicknames, and while this was not unusual in the seventeenth century Esterházy clearly started to do it only after his second marriage. Proof of this can be found in the wording of the various wills made by Esterházy. In the will written before he met Krisztina he referred to his only son using his full Christian name, István.[4] However, when Krisztina gave birth to a son, László, Esterházy prepared a new will taking account of the changes in the inheritance. In this new will he called his sons by their nicknames, Istók and Lackó.[5] He continued to refer to his children by their pet names even after his wife's death. These names can be found in the will he made in 1641, even though István was already a married man with a child of his own by that time.

Evidence that their married life was mutually satisfying can also be seen in the great care with which Esterházy followed his wife's pregnancies. We have a touching picture of the "old man"—as he mockingly referred to himself—eagerly awaiting the arrival of the "new guest" in the house. He promised his wife that he would be present at each of her confinements, and on those occasions when he was unable to be present he made all the arrangements beforehand. In 1628, for example, he gave orders for the baby to be christened in his absence. If it was a boy it was to be given his own name, and if it was a girl it was to be named after its grandmother.[6]

THE PALATINE'S HOUSEHOLD

Esterházy was very attached to his home and was keen to return to his family whenever his responsibilities allowed. When he was unable to be at home he promised to "run to you during the night if I have to".[7] He was frustrated at the slowness of his work and annoyed by the time-consuming talks in Vienna, and he longed to be able to reduce the number of his visits there. He even returned home several times during the Diet in Sopron where the greatest event in his career, his election to the position of palatine, took place. Of course, there was no great difficulty in getting home from Sopron since at that time his family estates were concentrated in the western part of Hungary.

After his election as palatine, the court that he established in Sopron County became the centre of the country. In the absence of a national royal court the palatine's court came to be the representative court of Hungary. It did not differ fundamentally from other aristocratic courts—there were merely more servants and personnel to meet the demands of the palatine's office.

The first high aristocratic court of the country was not just a centre of political life, it was also the place where the palatine's family lived. During the two decades in which Esterházy served as palatine, his court at Kismarton became the best known of his estates. However, whenever he bought or was granted a new estate or castle, he had it renovated and moved there with his family for a time. His son Pál was born in Kismarton, for example, while the youngest boy, Ferenc, was born in Sempte. The estate formerly owned by the Thurzós came into Esterházy's hands in 1639 as a pawn. The palatine had it renovated at once and soon moved there. The construction work must have been exciting for the older children, as must the reconstruction work carried out at Frakn贸. P谩l remembered it with delight even as an old man.[8] Esterh谩zy employed famous Italian architects who had worked for the emperor and for the Austrian aristocracy. The same group of architects worked for the Esterh谩zys, the P谩lffys, the Batthy谩nys and the N谩dasdys.[9] The renovated castles became symbols of social status, as did the gardens around them. Esterh谩zy was very proud of his gardens and often mentioned the plants and flowers to be found in them in his letters. In contemporary thinking, gardens reflected the accomplishment of their owners. A well-kept ornamental garden reflected the erudition of its owner and suggested his abilities in office.

The creation of a palatine's court, in the form of a high-level representative centre, was a historical enterprise in a Hungary left without an independent centre of state life. These courts sent out envoys and received diplomats regularly, so they had to function according to European standards. As the first political dignitary of the country, Esterh谩zy had to receive his guests in circumstances worthy of his office. He was well known and highly respected, not only in Hungary and Vienna, but throughout Europe. In 1628 the king of Spain awarded him the Golden Fleece, making him a knight of this exclusive order that accepted only the highest elite of the time. The palatine maintained close relationships with several diplomats accredited in Vienna—he even invited a minister of the king of Spain to be the godfather of his son P谩l in 1635.[10] One of his daughters, Julianka, received a proposal of marriage from, among others, John Kasimier, the future king of Poland.

However, Esterh谩zy found it important to base the reputation of his court not only on finely reconstructed buildings and gardens, but above all, on efficient and well-organised activities. In his view, this demanded a fear of God and the observance of the proper regulations. Without these everything would be "confused" and "honesty and concord" would be lacking.[11] Esterházy's court was strictly regulated and organised rationally along hierarchical lines. He wished to create a community from among the persons of various social ranks—relatives, noblemen in his service and other employees living in his court—so that those standing higher on the social ladder would receive due respect, while those below them would not be treated with disdain: "The Master demands that there be concord and love among them…as if they were all kinsmen."[12] The lengthy court regulations drawn up by Esterházy also suggest his thriftiness. Despite the splendid external trappings, he was strictly economical and did his best to prevent wastefulness in any form.

Esterházy also regarded it as his duty to provide for the spiritual needs of those around him. The clergymen residing at his court played an important role in everyday life there. Esterházy preferred and supported above all the Jesuits and the Franciscans. His court was basically a Catholic one. Religious ceremonies formed the framework of its life. At eight o'clock in the morning everyone attended Mass. For the Catholics this was obligatory, while the followers of other denominations were free to pray in the chapel according to their own rites.[13] Esterházy had become a Catholic out of conviction in his youth, long before the great wave of re-Catholicisation that began in the 1630s, and he was proud of converting others. He was tolerant towards the Protestants at his court, while supporting the Catholic Church with generous donations.

Valets were supposed to "read some history or other books" to one another for an hour both before and after lunch,[14] a sign of how exacting Esterházy was in matters of culture. He himself regularly read the books in his library of several hundred volumes, and did his best to give his children the kind of education required by young Hungarian aristocrats.

ESTERHÁZY'S EDUCATIONAL PRINCIPLES

Esterházy had definite ideas about the education of his children. He followed the general practice of leaving them with their mother until the age of four or five.[15] Until that age the children were surrounded entirely by women—their mother, nurses and women servants. Before marriage daughters remained with their mothers, from whom they learnt how to run a household. If the mother died, the young girl would usually be brought up by older female relatives. Boys, however, were taken from their mother's care at an early age and their education arranged by their father or other male relatives. They were allowed to continue to live with their families for a few more years and were usually taught by preceptors. However, they were not separated from the adults and adult life—they took part in all family events and saw and heard things from which children today are generally protected. In a society where the margin between childhood and early adulthood was very narrow and where children started their independent life very early, this mixing with adult society proved useful, helping children to adapt to adult life. As in most aristocratic families, girls in the Esterházy family were often married at fourteen, after which they began an independent life in their own households.

Miklós Esterházy expected a great deal of his children, especially of his first-born, István. However, the boy must have been a disappointment to his father as a child. Esterházy wrote of him that he seemed somewhat backward, that he often left his mouth hanging open and did not listen to what was being said to him. István was three years old when he lost his mother and over eight when he was presented with a second mother. During those very years that are so important in the forming of a person's character he was left practically alone, since his father was often absent from home. However, these circumstances can hardly be regarded as a full explanation for István's troubles. His was a fate shared by many children—it was not unusual for the offspring of aristocratic families in those days to be brought up by people other than their own parents. Thus, in the absence of any detailed information about him, the causes of István's problems cannot be determined for certain. One of the possible reasons for his father's disappointment may have been that Esterházy, an exceptionally gifted man himself, judged everyone by his own capacities and simply expected too much from his son who had merely average, or even below average, intellectual abilities.

Esterházy did not consider István's condition to be without remedy. He was convinced that diligent study would eventually help make up for his setbacks. This was probably why he laid particular stress on István's education. In the will he wrote in 1623 he addressed the boy, then not quite seven years old, in a rather unusual manner, giving him moral and practical advice. He repeated this advice in the admonitions he presented to his son in 1634 when István was already eighteen years old: "I give this advice not to your preceptors now but to you yourself."[16] István carefully preserved the document. When he died at an early age in 1641 his relatives drew up an inventory of his belongings and the first item on the list was this letter, sent to him by his father, which was found in an iron chest.[17]

István's private tutors were well-known and outstanding Jesuit teachers, such as István Keresztesi, who was on good terms with Mátyás Hajnal, the Jesuit confessor of the Esterházy family. This fact makes Esterházy's lack of success in selecting tutors for his third son, Pál, all the more striking. Several tutors were appointed, since Esterházy had to dismiss a number of them on the grounds of cruelty.[18] Their qualifications were also poorer than those of the preceptors engaged to teach István. János Torday, for example, became an accountant in Sempte when he abandoned his career as a tutor.

As regards the schooling of Esterházy's sons, it was again István's situation that appears to have been especially favourable, even though his father had not yet been made palatine at the time he wrote the will in which he set down the principles for his son's education. The boy was sent to the Jesuit school in Nagyszombat with a whole household to serve him. "They should be twelve altogether—a master of ceremonies, a priest to set him a good example, a preceptor, two foot-boys and eight children of a similar age or a little older from noble families, possibly relatives", wrote Esterházy.[19] The younger brothers, László, Pál and Ferenc, had only three such schoolmates each to help them and one prefect to supervise their studies.

As to the length and quality of their education, however, no difference was made between the young Esterházys. All of them were to study in Nagyszombat until the age of sixteen, then for three or four years in Vienna. Through their free access to the emperor's court they were to become acquainted with the life of the elite and its rules. Finally, before taking over the administration of their estates, they were to complete their studies with a tour in Germany or Italy if they so wished.[20]

Miklós Esterházy's aims with respect to the boys' education are also reflected in his admonitions to István. He set down in writing the rules of behaviour he regarded as the ideal for a faithful Catholic. He wished not only István, but also his three younger sons, to follow these rules, and he himself tried to live up to them throughout his life. The advice he repeated constantly was that each of them should dedicate his time to useful work. Each child was to spend his days in such a way that he might rest peacefully at night: "...ask who you have been during the day and if you are found without great shortcomings, praise God. If not, beg God's forgiveness and ask Him to help you avoid such shortcomings in the future. Flatterers may call this clerical behaviour but you should dismiss them as people who are setting you a trap, for there is no better means of freeing yourself of your sins."[21]

Temperance and balance, wherever possible, were the primary values that Esterházy wished his sons to pursue. They were to treat others, strangers and acquaintances alike, with kindness and helpfulness. Distinguished personalities from abroad were to be honoured; they were to be addressed sensibly and childish talk was to be avoided. They were to be given proper answers to their questions and were to be received by the master of the house personally, as good manners demanded.

The young counts were to be particular about their appearance but were to avoid ostentation. Similarly, there were to be no displays of excessive emotion. The preservation of one's health was of extreme importance to Esterházy. Moderation in all things and cleanliness—which was far from being a commonly accepted requirement in those days—were the guarantees of good health. Everyone was to wash their hands before meals—the Esterházy family already used soap. Miklós Esterházy became an expert in the treatment of various illnesses. Members of his family often asked for his advice, but he was also ready to give advice without being asked. To István he wrote: "Take good care of your health, for that is nothing other than our duty, and be abstemious in what you eat and drink…or you will doubtless fall seriously ill as you fell ill once before, or you will die early from eating and drinking to excess. Reflect always on your conduct in matters of eating and drinking."[22] However, despite all such precautions, István often fell ill and died at the age of twenty-five, three years after his marriage and only a few months after the birth of his only child, a daughter.

BUILDING A DYNASTY

The political career of Miklós Esterházy was unequalled by any of his contemporaries. Within his lifetime he obtained what members of other aristocratic families managed to achieve only in the course of several generations. He seized every opportunity for advancement and strove resolutely to preserve the social and economic positions he attained. One of the most effective ways to increase power and wealth was by suitable marriages. In contemporary parlance marriage and good luck were virtually synonyms. Esterházy was well aware of this fact and acted accordingly where his children were concerned. His aim was to build up a powerful dynasty.

Miklós Esterházy's children had far greater advantages than he himself had enjoyed at their age. Born into the aristocracy, they were regarded as a good match by every family in the country. Their father selected their future partners carefully. He was thirty when he married for the first time, but his offspring were allowed to marry at a younger age. His sons were free to marry once they had completed their education at the age of twenty-two, while his daughters were married off at the age of fourteen, as was usual at the time.

However, only two marriages took place during Esterházy's lifetime. He saw only two of his children reach adulthood—István and Julianna, his elder daughter. When choosing partners for them the expansion of his family was uppermost in his mind. By that time, as a result of his two marriages he had connections with most of the country's aristocracy, while his own father had been a mere county official and had married Zsófia Illésházy before her brother had been made a magnate. Unquestionably a *homo novus*, Miklós Esterházy therefore wished to forge links with titled families of long standing. He was fully aware of the social differences within the aristocracy and had personal experience of them. As palatine of the country he was the first in rank and was also one of the first in terms of wealth. Nevertheless, when it came to social nuances he knew that members of ancient families would inevitably be placed before him. This was typical of contemporary values—the age of one's title was more important than one's individual abilities or financial status. It was even more important than the offices to which one had been elected or which had been bestowed by the ruler. Whenever a potential bride or bridegroom was mentioned in letters written in this period, their "good lineage" was stressed above all. It was considered more important than personal appearance, health and financial status.

In Esterházy's eyes there was only one attribute to equal a good lineage. He insisted that his children's partners be Hungarians. His closest relatives also deliberately avoided marrying foreigners. This was due mainly to Esterházy's political aims. His overriding ambition was to take his country's internal affairs out of the sphere of Viennese bureaucracy. It was in the 1630s that a group of young and talented aristocrats formed around him, who totally accepted his political aims and supported him in his desire to create an independent Hungarian administration. They represented the core of a party under Esterházy's leadership. A few years later all of them became outstanding politicians and military leaders. With the exception of Ádám Batthyány, the members of this group—Miklós Zrínyi, Ádám Forgách, László Csáky, György Erdődy, and Ferenc Wesselényi— were still only promising young men in the 1630s.

The most valuable person from Esterházy's point of view was undoubtedly Ádám Batthyány. There were two reasons for this, one sentimental and one rational. Firstly, Miklós Esterházy regarded Batthyány as a younger brother—he had once been on very good terms politically with his father, Ferenc Batthyány. On the other hand, the young people around him came from the circles of the Batthyány family. Zrínyi, Csáky, Forgách and the others were all relatives or close friends of Ferenc and Ádám Batthyány. It was for this reason that Esterházy endeavoured to reinforce the ties of friendship through marriage. Ádám Batthyány was twenty-eight years younger than Esterházy, but having married in 1632 his children were almost the same age as those born to Esterházy and Krisztina Nyáry. The two fathers agreed in the late 1630s that László Esterházy should marry one of Batthyány's daughters. The marriage took place after Esterházy's death.

Marriage was also a means of extending political influence. A striking example of this was the union of Julianna Esterházy and Ferenc Nádasdy, a man who can be regarded as the embodiment of Hungarian history. His great-grandfather, Palatine Tamás, was Esterházy's great hero, and his grandfather had become a legendary figure for his actions during the Fifteen Years' War. At the same time, Nádasdy was a man of ability who was highly respected in his own right. He was not a member of the Esterházy party when he proposed to the palatine's eldest daughter, Julianna. She had a number of other suitors, but Nádasdy was her father's choice and most probably her own. The only problem seemed to be that he was a Lutheran. However, since Esterházy's primary aim was to be able to number Nádasdy among his followers, he did not regard this as a fatal obstacle. Instead of refusing Nádasdy the hand of Julianna, he did everything in his power to convert him. He even prepared a lengthy work on Roman Catholic theological tenets for Nádasdy. His conversion in the autumn of 1643 was a great political success for Esterházy. He rewarded the young man by giving him his daughter's hand in marriage in 1644.

Esterházy's third aim in his marriage strategies was to keep any estates he could lay his hands on within the family. It was very difficult and expensive to obtain new property in the seventeenth century. However, there was an indirect, though complicated, method. Certain tactical moves and a modicum of good luck were required, and in two generations the new estates could be won. The first step was to marry a rich widow with young children. The new father would thus become the children's guardian and would thus gain control over their property, but he still had to prepare accounts detailing the income he had obtained once the children married or came of age. Thus guardians were only temporary administrators and did not become owners in any form. However, a marriage between members of the second generation could ensure that the estates remained within the family. There was nothing new in this method, nor was it at all exceptional, but the Esterházys were especially successful in its application.

Krisztina Nyáry had two daughters by her first husband—Erzsébet and Krisztina. When they arrived in the household of the palatine he had only one son, István, and the palatine immediately decided that István should marry one of the little girls. In 1625 he wrote the following to his wife in his will: "I ask you…with God's help, to bring up your children in such a way that one of your daughters becomes the wife of my son, István. If they, too, were to like one another, they would strengthen our union by theirs."[23] At the time, the elder of Krisztina's daughters was barely four and the other only three. In 1632 the younger, Krisztinka, died. The health of the two remaining children, István and Erzsébet, was equally poor. However careful their parents were, the children were nearly always ill. Esterházy still insisted on carrying out his plan and as soon as István finished his studies and reached the age of twenty-two the two young people were married, in September 1638. They lived together only a few years and had one daughter, Orsolya, in 1641. Her grandfather was proved right in his expectations. Several years later it was this little girl who preserved for the Esterházy family the immense wealth inherited by her father and mother from the Mágóchy, the Dersffy, the Thurzó, and the Nyáry families.

It was not only his own children whom Esterházy used to further his political and financial aims. He determined the fate of his brothers' and sisters' children in the same manner. Six of his brothers and sisters lived into adulthood. He had an elder brother, Gábor; two younger brothers, Dániel and Pál; and three sisters. He maintained regular contact with his two younger brothers especially. Following his example they both returned to the Catholic faith. Esterházy's main concern was to have all his family members around him. His relatives' children grew up in his household together with his own children. They all had their definite place in the court. Esterházy paid for the schooling of the boys and they acted as fellow students for the young counts. Many of the daughters belonging to the extended family also lived in the palatine's household. They looked after their uncle's younger children. One of Pál Esterházy's daughters, for example, was ordered to attend her ill cousins, after which she also became ill.

One of Esterházy's nephews, László Révay, remembered the day he arrived at the palatine's court: "I was taken by my poor father and mother to Zólyom, to the court of my lord Miklós Esterházy, on Shrove Tuesday in 1619, to be a valet. However, he valued me above my merit and gave me a higher post right away."[24] This was usually the case with young relatives. Esterházy trusted them with the most delicate problems and they, in turn, were proud of their position and did their best to meet his expectations. A few years later Esterházy wished to see Révay on an important matter, but circumstances prevented Révay from making the journey. He apologised as follows: "I should have wings made for myself and fly to you through the night but it is difficult to be on the road even by daylight."[25]

Esterházy undertook the task of choosing partners for his nieces and nephews when they grew up. The young members of his family were allowed to marry baronesses at best. The only exception was László Révay, for whom Esterházy chose a high-born young lady, Erzsébet, the daughter of György Homonnai Drugeth, who had been brought up in Esterházy's court after the death of her father in 1628. However, Esterházy's plan stirred up an unexpected whirlwind. There were serious objections to the proposed marriage on the part of the archbishop of Esztergom, Péter Pázmány. He protested against giving the highborn and hugely rich Erzsébet to Esterházy's young relative who had only modest means. However, he was unable to prevent the marriage, which took place in 1630.

Esterházy married his nieces to the most important members of the outer circle of his party in order to ensure their loyalty. Thus, the daughter of Dániel Esterházy was obliged to marry István Héderváry, while the younger sister of László Révay married Zsigmond Örsy, a captain at Esterházy's court. According to Révay's diary, not even the bride's father was given advance warning of the forthcoming marriage, since he objected to the idea of his daughter marrying a Catholic.[26]

KEEPING THE FAMILY TOGETHER

Several examples illustrate the internal cohesion of the Esterházy family. It was not only Esterházy's love for the various members of his family that made this family unique, but his relatives' feelings towards him. Révay's message, quoted above, is one example of this. Esterházy's relatives admired and respected him because they knew they were living with an exceptionally talented man. They were witnesses of the different stages in his political career and of his exemplary family life, and they accepted him as an absolute authority in his position as head of the family. His brother, Dániel, was the first to note down the deeds of Esterházy that gave rise later to various legends.[27]

The palatine's brothers were especially grateful to him since they knew that their social and financial advancement depended entirely on him. In order to help his brothers financially he renounced his inheritance from his father's family for their benefit. They even received their first larger estates from him. He gave Dániel Beckó and Pál the castle of Zólyom. He also helped them acquire property later on. These gestures resulted in the establishing of a clear hierarchy within the extended family. There are diary entries that leave us in no doubt about this. While Dániel, for instance, made notes about everything that happened within the extended family, especially concerning the family of his elder brother, a diary kept first by Krisztina Nyáry, then by her son Pál, mentions only their immediate family, especially the children.[28] There are no signs of submission or envy here; the relationships between the various members of the extended family appear normal—primarily because Esterházy had the good sense to ignore signs of excessive veneration. He was proud of his success but never boasted of it. His love for his relatives was sincere. As he stated in the admonitions written for his son István, he considered good relationships among the members of a family to be the basis for that family's survival.

Esterházy's character had a great impact on the younger generation. One of his nephews, Farkas Esterházy, proved to be the most receptive among the young people around Esterházy and grasped the importance of the palatine's policy of keeping the family together. Farkas was twelve when his father died in 1627, after which he went to live with his uncle.[29] He was brought up as a Lutheran initially, but later his uncle persuaded him to become a Catholic. By 1632 Farkas was attending the Jesuit College in Vienna. A few years later he studied law there. His conversion cannot have been forced on him, for he remained a faithful Catholic throughout his life. In 1643 he even visited Rome bearing the palatine's letter of recommendation.[30] He went on to travel around Europe. After completing his studies Farkas returned to Kismarton and entered the palatine's service, his experiences abroad having enhanced his respect for his uncle still further. He regarded his uncle as a role model. This highly educated and loyal young man was held in great esteem by the palatine. The outstanding role of Farkas within the family was generally recognised. Zsigmond Megyeri, for instance, a distinguished lawyer, appealed to him in a letter a few years after the death of the head of the family, asking not to be left out of the Esterházy circle. He wrote to Farkas: "My dear son and master, I ask you to look upon me as an Esterházianist as long as I live."[31]

ESTERHÁZY'S LEGACY

When Esterházy died in 1645 he was already sixty-three and had suffered from gout for many years, but his death was still unexpected. He left four orphans. His eldest son, László, was nineteen and returned from Vienna to be at his father's side before he died. Palkó was ten, Marianka seven, and Ferkó four and a half. Esterházy's granddaughter, Orsika, was also four, and had been living with her grandfather, who was her guardian, since the death of her parents.

Although László had not yet come of age, he already exercised several rights at that time. His responsibilities increased dramatically after the death of his father. His relatives helped him greatly. Their primary concern was to maintain the political and social relationships built up by Esterházy for the benefit of his children. They succeeded in preserving an influential circle of supporters around the orphans, in the persons of counts Ádám Batthyány, Zsigmond Forgách, Miklós Zrínyi, and also Pál Pálffy, who had been the last to join the group. The relationship between Pál Pálffy and Miklós Esterházy had not been particularly good. The guardians, however, and later László Esterházy, laid great stress on winning him over. Count Pálffy, a man familiar with the ways of the Vienna court, was able to give them confidential information and valuable advice. Pálffy was not a politician to be ignored. From 1646 he was lord chief justice, and from 1649 to his death in 1653 he was palatine. As such, he became a member of the council of guardians ex officio. In the end the Esterházy party accepted Pálffy as their leader—and this stands as his greatest achievement.

As to the relatives, in everyday matters concerning the orphans they relied chiefly on Ádám Batthyány. Not long after Esterházy's funeral, in early 1646, Dániel Esterházy sent Ádám a letter recommending them to his good will: "I ask you not to let my boy László Esterházy and his little relatives suffer need in anything, out of respect for their deceased father", he wrote to Batthyány.[32] Batthyány assured them of his benevolence but expected a service in return, namely, confirmation by the guardians of the agreement he had made with Esterházy regarding the future marriage of his daughter, Eleonóra Batthyány, to László Esterházy. The wedding was eventually planned for late 1648 by which time László would have reached the age of twenty-two. This had been the wish of the palatine himself, as recorded in his last will.

Some high Catholic Church dignitaries also belonged to the group of supporters. These included György Lippay, archbishop of Esztergom; János Püsky, archbishop of Kalocsa; and György Szelepcsényi, later archbishop of Esztergom, who was still a bishop when the children were minors. Ádám Szalkovics, the future canon of Esztergom, played a special role as the most intimate confidant of the family and as the teacher of Pál and Ferenc.

The guardians did their best to keep Esterházy's faithful followers—men such as Zsigmond Örsy, György Kürtösy and István Olasz Kolozsvári—in the service of the family. They were all Catholic noblemen who had been granted estates by the palatine in return for their services. They acted in confidential military, diplomatic and family matters. They were all middle-aged and had proved their loyalty to the Esterházy family on many occasions.

After the palatine's death, loyalty and reliability among his followers were essential. When György Kürtösy's term of office expired he wrote in a letter that he was no longer able to serve the family since he was hard of hearing, his eyesight had deteriorated, and his memory was failing.[33] In spite of this he was still asked to stay on, and he continued to offer faithful service to the Esterházys. There were no such problems with Zsigmond Örsy. He was Esterházy's brother-in-law and the palatine had appointed him as a member of the council of guardians. However, from the children's point of view, István Olasz Kolozsvári was the most important of the three. As a young man he had been László Esterházy's teacher, and the nephew of Péter Pázmány also remembered his old friend with affection.[34] He enjoyed the confidence of several generations of the family. As an administrator of the Fraknó castle after the death of the palatine he took care of the little Esterházys—Ferkó, Marianka and Orsolya—who were living there at the time. Some years later he also looked after Pál's children. On one occasion he was even asked for his opinion regarding a nurse the family intended to employ.[35]

It was this small group of people on whom the orphans' closest relatives—Dániel and Farkas Esterházy and László Révay—could rely in solving the children's problems.

The most serious difficulty that arose after the death of the palatine was due to the actions of another close relative, Ferenc Nádasdy, the husband of Júlia Esterházy. He went at once to Vienna and tried to take possession of the Esterházy estate of Kismarton. At the same time, only one month after the palatine's death, he applied to the king for the guardianship of Orsika. The little granddaughter of Miklós Esterházy was then not yet five, which suggests that Nádasdy had in mind a particularly profitable scheme. On learning of the moves that had been made by Nádasdy, László Esterházy naturally took action immediately.

King Ferdinand III decreed that the two young men should come to an agreement between themselves. Nádasdy offered to support his brother-in-law in his attempt to gain the lord lieutenancy of Sopron County, which had become vacant on the palatine's death; however, he was unwilling to renounce the guardianship of Orsolya. He even managed to win supporters at the royal court. In one of his letters, Bishop Szelepcsényi remarked that there were rumours circulating at court that Esterházy was about to obtain the office of lord lieutenant, and Nádasdy the guardianship of the little girl. Although the king, who was then staying at Linz, had promised Szelepcsényi that he would make no decision regarding the dispute until after Esterházy's funeral, the rumours that had already filtered out much earlier proved to be well founded. In his decree issued on 20 December 1645, Ferdinand III made Nádasdy Orsolya's guardian until László Esterházy came of age. However, this was clearly no more than a gesture towards Nádasdy, as László Esterházy came of age within a year. He took over the guardianship in 1646, and when he died in 1652 his only brother, seventeen-year-old Pál, was granted guardianship over Orsolya after just a few days.

THE EXECUTION OF THE PALATINE'S WILL

László Esterházy's primary obligation was to carry out the provisions contained in the palatine's will. However, this was no easy task because of the serious financial problems that arose. Miklós Esterházy left huge debts, and his children's forthcoming marriages were also to involve considerable expense. At the same time, László Esterházy himself had hardly any income. The royal treasury kept putting off the payment of his father's unpaid salary arrears and the repayment of loans he had provided to the king. In the words of one bishop in Vienna, the treasury did not pay its debts because they were old, and meanwhile it was busy making new ones that would also be old before long.

In order to improve the situation, Farkas Esterházy suggested to László that he should cultivate a better personal relationship with the court and that he should serve the king for a year there, after which time he would be better able to settle all his problems. "Your continuous service around the king and your close relationships and regular conversations with the lords at the court will be of greater help to you in straightening out your affairs than any sum of money."[36] Since László was in need of the goodwill and assistance of others it was advisable for him to appear generous and obliging and to give presents to potential supporters. "Nowadays even distinguished persons humiliate themselves...", was how Farkas Esterházy put it.[37] Whatever the ideal solution, it was certainly true that financial problems weighed heavily on the young count and his family.

The most important point for us to consider, however, is the extent of the orphans' suffering after the loss of their father. They had loved him dearly and were probably present at his funeral. Nevertheless, it is very difficult to establish people's real feelings from the conventional letters that were written at that time. It was rare for people to describe pain and emotion. There is a striking illustration of such contemporary attitudes from the life of Miklós Esterházy himself. On the death of his wife Krisztina he notified his acquaintances, and even his best friends, in matter-of-fact, unemotional messages, yet after her death we know that he had shut himself in his room for several days, howling with grief and banging his head against the wall. It was little Pál Esterházy, his father's favourite, who witnessed these scenes.[38] He was the only one whom the bewildered family dared to send in to him. Pál wrote of this in his memoirs. However, when writing about his father's death some years later, he too, refrained from describing his own feelings of grief.

After the palatine's death the younger children remained at home in Fraknó. They had their nurses and the entire household staff with them and were in the care of László's former preceptor, István Olasz Kolozsváry. Little information about their lives survives from this period. The letters refer mostly to their state of health and their frequent illnesses, as well as to the fact that Ferkó and Orsolya were studying.[39] Kolozsváry mentions in his memoirs that they went on frequent walks in the neighbourhood, which the children enjoyed very much. They were fond of István Kolozsváry, and the old man, in turn, was happy to spend time with them. Great care was taken over their diet. They were given light but substantial meals, their nurses being aware of the part played by poor nutrition in the development of illnesses. László allowed them to eat meat even during Lent.[40]

The three little ones were seldom together at Fraknó since Marianka spent a great deal of time with the Nádasdys in their castle or at their house in Vienna. They would have taken Orsolya with them too, but László did not allow her to leave Fraknó. The Esterházys took special care of the little girl since they had important plans for her. She had the least freedom of the three children.

Pál's life changed considerably when his father died. His relatives sent him almost at once to the Jesuit College in Graz. The choice of school was probably influenced by the plague epidemic in Nagyszombat. According to the palatine's will three young relatives, Gáspár, Mihály and Sándor, his brothers' sons, Dániel and Pál, were sent with him as fellow students.[41] The heir apparent, the future Ferdinand IV, was one of their school-mates in Graz. However, in late 1646 the boys were studying already in Nagyszombat.[42]

Pál was much more interested in comedies and school plays than in studying. In his memoirs he describes with enthusiasm the five plays in which he was given the leading role.[43] He was proud of having learnt hundreds of lines for these perform-ances. He had inherited his father's feeling for art and music and was keen to seize every opportunity to show off his tal-ents. During the Diet of 1647 his qualities as a dancer were displayed before the king and queen and those attending the Diet.[44] Pál succeeded in being a sociable young man without neglecting his studies. His prefect, Ádám Szalkovics, informed the family that Pál had made great progress in learning lan-guages. As can be seen in his later writings he learned to read and write fluently in Latin. He was not quite so successful with German, however. According to his father's will it was in-tended that he should continue his studies in Vienna on reach-ing the age of sixteen. In 1650, when it was time to change schools, both Farkas and Dániel Esterházy wrote to László that they considered the change advisable "for the sake of the Ger-man language".[45] Nevertheless, for financial reasons László refused to send his younger brother to another school. His edu-cation in Nagyszombat was cheaper, and thus the boy's schooling was undeniably restricted as a result of financial considerations.[46] Although he studied German in Nagyszombat he failed to make real progress. In a note written in 1652, Farkas Esterházy mentioned that reports written by German officials on the estate had to be translated into Hungarian for Pál.[47]

However, the most frequent subject of Ádám Szalkovics's letters was not Pál's education, but rather his clothing. Surprisingly, he had to ask László repeatedly for a new coat or cloak to be made for the boy.[48] He wrote that the boy was in great need, having only one or two decent items of outdoor clothing. On more than one occasion Szalkovics even had to lend the money for new garments for Pál. Relatively little money had been spent on the children's clothing even while Miklós Esterházy was alive, and similar complaints can be read in the letters of previous prefects. László seems to have followed this tradition, being extremely economical where his brothers' clothes were concerned. Nevertheless, he was extremely particular about his own clothing. The lavishly decorated garment that he wore over his armour in battle even attracted the admiration of a very rich friend of his, István Koháry, yet the expensive clothes and jewels needed by Pál for his acting were lent to him by Countess Thurzó.[49]

Apart from problems such as these, Pál was always treated with kindness by his family. Members of his family regularly visited him at the Nagyszombat college and wrote him letters. He spent the holidays at home, either at the castle in Lakompak, his favourite, or at one of the other castles. High holidays were usually spent at the family's palace in Nagyszombat. Horse riding was his favourite pastime on such occasions. His first horse had been given to him at the age of four by his elder brother István, and he was always delighted to receive a horse as a present. He made long journeys on horseback even as a child. Pál was a talented rider, proud of his ability to maintain his presence of mind in dangerous situations. In his memoirs he describes several occasions which had called for great courage on his part. The boy was fun-loving and enjoyed parties. He continued to like amusements and to make practical jokes even as an adult. On one occasion he made his sister very angry by his unsuitable behaviour at the table while they had company.[50] He refused to apologise for what he had done. On another, similar, occasion he said that his behaviour had been meant for his own amusement.[51]

THE MARRIAGE OF LÁSZLÓ ESTERHÁZY

With the wedding of Mária Batthyány to László, which took place at carnival time in 1650, the agreement made by the two fathers, Miklós Esterházy and Ádám Batthyány, was finally realised. The path had not been a smooth one. Despite the long-standing marriage plans there had been serious tension between Batthyány and László Esterházy since late 1647. On the surface, the bride's frequent illnesses were the cause of the delay. Mária was genuinely in poor health a lot of the time. In February 1648 it was reported that she was not expected to live and Ádám Batthyány had urged László to pay her a farewell visit. Mária survived but was delirious again early the following year.

On the other hand, the reactions of the Esterházy family suggest that there must have been deeper motives at play. Batthyány was apparently devising schemes for postponing the wedding. In October 1649, after László's letters urging for the wedding to take place had been ignored, he sent envoys to Batthyány, led by István Aszalay, to find out Batthyány's intentions and to ask for Mária's hand in marriage once again. Batthyány finally consented and fixed the wedding date for 21 November.[52] In fact, this amounted to a rebuff since there would not have been enough time to complete the kind of preparations necessary for the wedding of an aristocrat. Batthyány knew very well that the Esterházys would not accept his offer.

Batthyány's motives are not certain. There is nothing to suggest the presence of another suitor, which would have forced the father to play for time, although this possibility cannot be excluded. It is more probable that he could not, or did not want to, hand over his daughter's dowry immediately. Two years after the couple was married he admitted to having postponed the wedding deliberately.[53]

If anything, László only worsened his already difficult relationship with Ádám Batthyány by his behaviour. He was irrational and impatient, once forcing Batthyány to exclaim: "I find you a man who is very hard to please, as I come to know you better."[54] When the disagreement between László and Batthyány began to get out of hand, Dániel Esterházy decided to intervene. "The difficulties in the case of my young relative and your daughter are very real", he wrote, but he argued that they could be solved with a little willingness to compromise. He assured Batthyány that László was not likely to be any more amenable in the future, and asked him to take the reputation of the Esterházy family into consideration too.[55] In the letter that he wrote to László, however, he expressed his anger at Batthyány's behaviour: "This episode is bringing disgrace upon us..."[56]

The Esterházys kept their promise and did not go on making claims in the form of letters. They decided to use indirect methods. They asked Nádasdy for advice, and also talked with Pálffy and the archbishop. As a result, Palatine Pálffy and other friends went to Batthyány, in the middle of November, to ask for a third time for Mária's hand in marriage to be given to László.[57] The distinguished delegates could not be refused and the date of the wedding was fixed for 6 February the following year.[58]

However, yet another disagreement arose just before the wedding was due to take place. This time the dispute concerned the length of time the young couple was to spend with their guests at Rohonc and Lakompak, respectively. László wanted to stay at Rohonc, the home of the bride, for just two days before going to Lakompak, together with Batthyány, to meet the guests he had invited there.[59] He was afraid of missing certain important guests if he stayed longer at Rohonc. On the other hand, Batthyány did not want to leave so early since some of his guests would be coming to Rohonc just to meet him.[60]

To everyone's relief the wedding finally took place on the appointed day. However, the young husband's ordeal was just about to begin. László, who was one of the most masculine men of the day and whom everyone referred to as the "beautiful count", remained childless. The Batthyánys blamed him for the failure even when the doctors sent his barren and sickly wife to a medicinal spa. Batthyány wrote to him insisting that it was pointless to send her for such treatment in the hope she would conceive. According to him children came from God and a good husband.[61] Such unsolicited intervention by their parents doubtless contributed to the lack of harmony between the young couple. During the two and a half years of their life together, a considerable portion of which they spent apart, Mária wrote barely a dozen letters to her husband. Even these letters were in German, which is somewhat surprising. Although her mother had been a lady-in-waiting at the Vienna court, Mária had been brought up in Hungary to become the wife of a Hungarian magnate. She must have been familiar with the language of the country, but was perhaps more comfortable with German and unwilling to make any effort to meet her husband's expectations. The question remains as to whether he did, in fact, have any expectations of her. As far as the marriage was concerned, we do not know her side of the story. As for Laszló, he was doubtless dissatisfied with it. Not long after the wedding, for which he had pressed so vehemently, László preferred not to spend his time at home. His relationship with his parents-in-law also seems to have been problematic. He even neglected to pay the usual formal visits.

THE MARRIAGE OF MÁRIA ESTERHÁZY AND GYÖRGY HOMONNAI

The question of Mária's marriage arose six years after Palatine Esterházy's death, in the autumn of 1651. It was the duty of László Esterházy and other relatives to choose a suitable husband for Mária and to make preparations for the wedding. In his last will the palatine had expressed his wish that Mária should enter a convent, as her deceased mother had intended. However, the decision was left to her.[62] Her relatives travelled with her to Pozsony several times to show her the convent of the Poor Clares and to acquaint her with the religious life. However, although she had several friends and acquaintances among the nuns she decided against joining them. As one of Mária's aunts put it, "she is too fond of dancing to be a nun".[63] None of Mária's relatives attempted to force her to take the veil.

As a little girl she had loved to stay with her sister Julianna in the Nádasdy household. It was probably here that she had acquired her love of dancing and entertainments. The household of the highly educated Nádasdy was one of the wealthiest in the country. The family also liked to stay in their palace in Vienna. Once their disputes had been settled there was a good relationship between the Nádasdys and the Esterházys, and Marianka was allowed to visit her sister as often as she wished. However much she enjoyed being there, her brother-in-law had other important plans for her. His wish was to see Mária Esterházy married to György Homonnai Drugeth.

The young girl—she was thirteen in 1651—had two suitors that year besides Homonnai: Miklós Zrínyi and the Italian prince, Pallavicini. Count Zrínyi, a leading politician and man of letters, had also proposed to Miklós Esterházy's elder daughter, but when his wedding plans came to nothing he had married Mária Eusébia Draskovich on 11 February 1646. After four years he had been left a widower. When the year of mourning was over he again looked to the Esterházy family for a wife. Although the Esterházys would have welcomed him as a relative his marriage plans failed once again. According to László Esterházy, the problem lay in the excessive financial demands of Count Zrínyi.

In the case of Pallavicini, the refusal came from Marianka herself—or at least this was the reason given by the family. The prince held Dániel and László Esterházy responsible,[64] nor was he far from the truth: while they did nothing to prevent the marriage they did not actively support Pallavicini. As no member of the family had ever met him, the Esterházy's reservations with respect to the marriage could only have been due to Miklós Esterházy's dogmatic insistence that none of his children were to marry foreigners. Whatever the reasons for it, the letter of refusal was very politely worded.[65] It was not only the prince who had to be pacified—the feelings of General Pucheim, who had recommended him, also had to be considered. Johann Christoph Pucheim was a general of the imperial army and vice-president of the War Council. He was related to the Hungarian aristocracy through the marriage of his daughter to the brother of Count Pál Pálffy. He devoted much time and energy to his attempts to bring the Esterházy and Pallavicini families together, and he even met with the wife of Dániel Esterházy, who was staying in Vienna, to discuss the intentions of the family.[66] He also arranged for individual meetings with the Esterházys in an attempt to convince them.[67] The reply was always the same: "Our sister does not consider this marriage appropriate."[68] Although unsuccessful, Pucheim was not offended by the refusal, and his good relations with the Hungarian aristocracy and with the Esterházys did not suffer as a result. Later on he even tried to organise further marriages. The letter of refusal was taken to Vienna by a delegation, since Dániel Esterházy considered this to be right and proper.[69] Farkas Esterházy represented Count László, the head of the family, as well as the family as a whole, and he was accompanied by Ferenc Nádasdy. For the latter, the journey represented a personal success, since the remaining suitor was his candidate.

György Homonnai Drugeth was a close relative of Nádasdy. He was twelve when he became an orphan, and was sent to the Jesuit school in Graz in 1646, the same school that Pál Esterházy attended after his father's death. They also studied together in Nagyszombat. Thus Homonnai had been in contact with the Esterházy family since his childhood, and this was his greatest asset. Marianka had met Homonnai as a child and had liked him. When he appeared as a suitor for her hand she reacted favourably. Dániel Esterházy, however, was very much opposed to the match with Homonnai. "I do not think the young man is someone to whom I would gladly give my dear relative in marriage. Since I love her dearly I would like her to marry a man with whom she will surely be fully contented throughout her life."[70] He asked István Csáky and the archbishop of Esztergom for their opinion. On receiving no answer from Csáky he considered his reservations justified.[71] He warned László more than once against giving in and told him not to listen to Marianka's opinion since she had known György only as a child and had not met him since.[72]

László and Farkas Esterházy had a different view of the matter and did not entertain such a strong antipathy for Homonnai. László, the young head of the family, was in fact put under huge pressure by this situation. He had great respect for Palatine Pál Pálffy, who had taken it upon himself to represent Homonnai's proposal officially.[73] Nádasdy was relying on László's respect for the palatine, and was justified in doing so. By 17 December 1651 László had promised his younger sister in marriage to György Homonnai. The exchange of rings took place the same day.[74]

Nádasdy and Homonnai wanted the wedding to take place as early as possible. In order to achieve this they paid such frequent visits to Kismarton that László Esterházy often complained about his self-invited guests. In the end he was forced—as he put it in a letter to his father-in-law—to promise that the wedding would be celebrated as early as 28 April 1652.[75] He was extremely angry about having to do so since this left little time to make the necessary preparations.

In the end the marriage preparations were left to Farkas. He repeatedly warned László about the lack of time and the magnitude of the task. This was the first time they had organised a wedding in the family on their own, and they could not afford to look ridiculous.[76] The weeks of preparation passed amid enormous tension, and several things remained to be done only a month before the wedding. Many items had to be bought in Vienna and Holy Week was not an appropriate time for shopping. The two younger boys, Pál and Ferkó, had no suitable clothes for the occasion. Coats had to be made for them at the last minute. At Sempte, where the wedding was to take place, there were no doors or windows in the houses where the guests were to be accommodated. Chairs and tables were also needed, and these had to be transferred from other castles. Not even the oven was ready to use. Homonnai's invitations were written in early March and he sent his representatives to Vienna with Nádasdy to purchase the necessary items. Farkas Esterházy was annoyed and warned László that the Esterházy family would be left behind.[77] In the month before the wedding he devoted all his time to the preparations and reported every detail of the last-minute haste to László. The Nádasdys helped enormously by buying clothes for the bride, which meant that she spent much of the time with them in Vienna. A few days after the wedding they did not fail to submit an invoice for their expenses.[78]

The bridegroom arrived from Nagyszombat with his guests on the day of the wedding. Among those invited was László Révay, a close relative of Homonnai. As the archbishop of Esztergom was ill the couple was married by the bishop of Eger.[79] The wedding feast lasted for two days. On the third day László Esterházy delivered Mária's dowry and the inheritance that had been agreed on by himself and Homonnai at the betrothal on 17 December. The agreement seems to have been fairly reasonable. At the Esterházys' request a clause was added, according to which Homonnai was to observe the provisions of the palatine's will. This was doubtless due to the dispute between Nádasdy and László Esterházy over their inheritance.

THE SECRET MARRIAGE OF PÁL AND ORSOLYA

At the time of the Homonnai wedding, another union was already being planned in the Esterházy family—the marriage of Pál and Orsolya Esterházy. There was nothing extraordinary about their betrothal—in the seventeenth century it was not uncommon for members of the Hungarian aristocracy to marry close or more distant relatives. It was a marriage of convenience in order to keep Orsolya's extensive property within the family. The various stages leading up to the marriage are worth looking at in detail since the episode provides a clear illustration of family politics at work.

Everything was organised in the strictest confidence, although not all the details could be kept secret. The preparations were much more thorough than those preceding the marriage of Marianka. All letters were written by the correspondents themselves rather than by clerks and were delivered to their addressees by trusted servants. The whole episode remains rather obscure. Very few notes were made and messages were sent mostly by word of mouth. After being read the letters were usually destroyed. Farkas Esterházy, for example, asked Pál to "tear up these letters".[80]

The sources that do survive are therefore very valuable. Most of these letters were written by important characters in the events; we have the letters of Farkas Esterházy to László and Pál[81], as well as the memoirs of Pál himself. As the facts reported in these documents are not mutually contradictory they can be regarded as authentic. It thus emerges that Farkas Esterházy played a major role in the organisation of this marriage.

In Pál's memoirs, stories about his relationship with Orsolya are central. Wonders and prophecies seem to prove the fact that their marriage was concluded as a result of divine inspiration. The first person to refer to this revelation was an Italian Franciscan friar who visited Erzsébet Thurzó, the widow of István Esterházy, at Lakompak in 1642. "He did not say anything but was looking at Orsicska and me...Then he took me by the hand and said in German that this child would marry the little girl sitting on the bed and sit in his father's chair."[82] By this he doubtless meant that Pál would become a palatine like his father, a prediction which also came true. The second prophecy was uttered by the eminent Jesuit, Lamormain, at Heflány in 1654. He took Pál by the hand and led him before Dániel Esterházy, László Révay and other relatives, saying that the little boy was to marry the daughter of István Esterházy if the well being and survival of the Esterházy family was to be ensured.[83]

The names of those who related these events to Pál are not recorded, but they are not of great importance here. The most important point is that the idea of the marriage was supported by clergymen who stressed a rather secular point of view—concern for the survival of the Esterházy family. The Catholic Church did not oppose the marriage before it took place, even though the two were so closely related as to have presented a natural obstacle in normal circumstances.

Besides such representatives of the Catholic Church, Pál also mentions in his memoirs those relatives who supported the marriage. He refers to Farkas and Dániel Esterházy by name, and mentions all those, whose approval, according to contemporary customs, was necessary before his marriage with Orsolya could take place. Described in one of his vivid narrative passages, his vision of Orsolya's mother seems to suggest her dead parents' consent to the marriage. "It happened one day at Lakompak", he wrote, "that the nurse was holding Orsicska in her arms and was walking with her, between six and seven in the afternoon. As I was standing near them I saw my poor sister coming towards us from the direction of the gate of the inner castle, wearing the garment she had been dressed in as she lay on the catafalque. She came closer, put her daughter's hand into mine, and disappeared."[84]

His own father, the palatine, is not mentioned in Pál's memoirs in connection with this union. Although there is no certainty that the idea of the marriage had not been raised before 1645, it could not have assumed the form of a concrete plan at that stage. There is no mention of it in the will made by Miklós Esterházy. Everything seems to point to the fact that Miklós Esterházy was counting on the Batthyány family in his marriage policy.

Indirect proof of this emerges in one of Pál's remarks regarding László's marriage to Mária Batthyány: "The younger girl was recommended to me by my lord Batthyány's servants. Countess Borbála Batthyány was indeed very beautiful and not displeasing to me, either."[85] The other piece of evidence is the highly unusual reaction of Ádám Batthyány to the marriage plans of Pál and Orsolya.

The idea of marrying off the two children was most probably raised only in the years following the death of Palatine Miklós.

In late 1647 Farkas Esterházy was still wondering how they would be able to produce the huge dowry and inheritance within the eight years before Orsicska reached the age of fourteen.[86] It was doubtless he who realised the advantages of keeping Orsolya for themselves. Farkas acted following the example left by Miklós Esterházy—with determination and courage he arranged for the marriage of Pál and Orsolya in the interests of the Esterházy family.

By 1650 the marriage was a settled matter. Pál wrote in his memoirs: "On 12 August that year my lord Farkas Esterházy came to see me in Nagyszombat and recommended that I marry my niece Orsicska, for this marriage would benefit the whole Esterházy family."[87] Soon after that he went to Kismarton. According to the memoirs "there we reported the idea to my brother who was very glad and wrote to Rome at once…I spoke to my niece Orsicska in private about it and I sensed her love for me." He then writes that in 1651, during the holidays, his brother took Orsolya to Kismarton and "we exchanged engagement rings once again before him".[88]

These were important episodes in the relationship between the young couple, but the accuracy of the account is questionable. It is highly unlikely that Farkas spoke about his plans with Pál first and informed László, the head of the family, only afterwards. It is much more probable that the matter was discussed with László and Dániel before anybody else, and this would have been more consistent with contemporary customs. Relatives always decided matters of such great importance together. Thus the whole sequence must have taken place in the reverse order: Farkas went to Nagyszombat to talk to Pál after first having consulted with László and Dániel. It must have been Farkas's tact that made Pál think his own consent was the deciding factor. Farkas first had to convince the fifteen-year-old boy to accept the idea of marriage. This was not a straightforward task since Pál had leanings towards the priesthood at that time. He writes of this openly in his memoirs. Although no other sources survive to corroborate his statement, it was customary for aristocratic families with several sons to allow one or more of them to become clergymen. Pál refers to an episode from 1638, which bears this out. János Telegdi, archbishop of Kalocsa and bishop of Nyitra, visited Sempte that year and on meeting Pál addressed him as "Archbishop Pál".[89] At that time Miklós Esterházy's first-born son, István, was still living, and Pál was the youngest of the three boys. According to the family records Miklós Esterházy himself had thought of joining the Society of Jesus.[90] The Jesuit teachers in Nagyszombat might also have tried to convince Pál of the advantages of becoming a member of the Society. The sincerity of his religious disposition was proved many years later by his dedicating two of his own sons to the priesthood.

It took Farkas three weeks to convince Pál. According to Pál's memoirs "he was so much in favour of it that after three weeks of incessant pleading and talking I finally agreed to commit myself to this marriage".[91] Unfortunately, the arguments used by Farkas were not recorded. His tactics may have been to make the young man feel responsible for the family's future and to make him accept the idea that this marriage would serve the interests of the Esterházy family as a whole. It was very wise on the part of Farkas not to present Pál with a fait accompli, but instead to get him to decide for himself.

Pál's claim to have spoken about the matter with Orsolya also seems highly unlikely. There would surely have been little point in his discussing the plan with the nine-year-old girl before the ecclesiastical dispensation had been granted. In his memoirs Pál stated that their exchange of rings took place for the second time in 1651. At the same time, a letter written by Farkas Esterházy definitely proves that it took place only in late June or in July

1652. Thus the betrothal was arranged prior to the arrival of the dispensation. This letter also corroborates the fact that Orsolya knew nothing of the plans concerning her marriage with Pál and was persuaded to marry him only at the last moment. The following is an excerpt from Farkas's letter to László Esterházy dated 15 June 1652: "Would you please come and persuade the little girl, with fine speeches and presents, to give her hand to your younger brother and exchange rings with her on his behalf...Then send her to Frakno where she should be guarded even more carefully than before."[92] For emphasis, he even repeats his request: "Your Honour should conquer her by fair talk, promises, and presents."

Such were the tactics used to win over the eleven-year-old girl. Her voluntary consent was vital, as this was a requirement of both the ecclesiastical and the civil authorities. So the game was to be played, and a gesture or a smile, even the smallest sign of acquiescence, was to be taken as a token of consent. After the betrothal the little girl was guarded carefully at Frakno so that she would have no opportunity to withdraw her consent. "After exchanging rings with her you should tell her to put her ring in a place where nobody will see it", Farkas suggested.[93] Orsolya was not allowed to go anywhere, not even to visit her aunt in the convent in Pozsony—even though the aunt had promised László that they would not try to persuade the girl to join the convent herself.[94] Her relatives also thought it advisable not to allow her to attend Mária's wedding.[95]

The Holy See granted the necessary dispensation after two years. In 1650, when László Esterházy commissioned two Carmelites to procure the dispensation for the young couple in Rome, all the arguments necessary for the pope to give his consent had been collected. A family tree was also enclosed, as was usual in such cases.[96] It showed that Pál and Orsolya were related both on their fathers' and their mothers' side. Pál was Orsolya's uncle twice over. The report was sent to Pope Innocent X by the chancellor of the apostolic nuncio in Vienna. On 20 August 1652, after the request had been sent to the Holy See, Alexander a Jesu Mária, general of the Carmelite Order in Vienna, summarised the arguments in support of the marriage. These notes contained no new lines of argument but simply arranged the existing arguments in a new order. These were also sent to the pope.

In the 1650 document[97] the faithful Catholic character of the engaged couple and of the Esterházy family was stressed in first place, together with their generosity towards ecclesiastical foundations. The document called the pope's attention to the fact that mixed marriages were common in Hungary and that a positive decision to unite the two Catholics would prevent the couple from marrying "heretics". This was the more important argument, since both of them were wealthy and influential. The Carmelite general's version of the arguments[98] stressed the importance of the dispensation to the Esterházy family, since the proposed marriage would bring peace and harmony within the family while a possible refusal would sow discord among its members and give rise to endless lawsuits. Were this to happen, not only the Esterházy family but also the reputation of the church would be damaged. The version written by the Carmelite provincial also called attention to the fact that the applicants lived in a neighbourhood bordering on the Ottoman Empire and were exposed to much hardship, and as such they deserved to be granted the dispensation.

These arguments were not sufficient in themselves. A large amount of money was also needed. Pál mentions in his memoirs that László had sent money to Rome for the Carmelites' expenses.[99] They were paid several thousand forints during the two years of their mission. As regards the circumstances in which the permission was obtained, they informed László that they had given one thousand forints to the pope's influential sister-in-law, "since there was no other way".[100] After receiving the money, this lady took the petition to the pope in person. Nevertheless, the family had to pay a great deal more money in connection with the dispensation.

While the Esterházys' envoys were already working on obtaining the dispensation for Pál and Orsolya, a strange event took place, which is described in a letter written by Anna Franciska Csáky, a Poor Clare in Pozsony, on 7 October 1651, to her brother, István Csáky.[101] There is no other source to support her statement, but she was doubtless well informed about all the young aristocratic girls as potential nuns.

Anna Csáky informed her brother that Gábor Illésházy had promised Pál Esterházy his daughter's hand in marriage and had even fixed the date of the betrothal, allowing two years before the wedding was to take place. Although the text of the letter is rather confusing it makes clear that besides the close relatives of the Esterházys, Pál Pálffy and Archbishop Lippay had also heard of the matter. Although "Pali accepted the idea with pleasure", all the others had been against it and the matter had had to be dropped. The little Countess Pálffy was only nine at the time and two years later would still have been too young to marry. The other reason for the refusal, according to the letter, was Illésházy's religion. It seems that news of Gábor Illésházy's conversion had not reached the convent of the Poor Clares in Pozsony. He had "become a papist", in the words of László Esterházy to Count Batthyány, in Vienna about one year earlier.[102]

Thus without knowing all the details of the matter, Anna, with her fine sense of diplomacy, suggested leaving things as they were. This affair was merely one episode during the period in which the marriage of Pál and Orsolya was being organised. It certainly proves that the plans did indeed remain a secret and that the real reasons for the Esterházys' refusal of Illésházy's proposal were not disclosed. At the same time it is also obvious that Pál's feelings for Orsolya were far from unambiguous. It is very unlikely that he loved Orsolya and that he had accepted the idea of marrying so early, let alone that he was pressing for the union to take place.

After a seemingly uneventful period in Orsolya's and Pál's lives, Farkas Esterházy wrote to László on 15 June 1652, informing him with great bitterness about Batthyány's deviousness: "He and his wife are going to come to Hefflan *sub illo praetextu* of learning if my lady has profited by the medicinal baths. They intend to win the confidence of the little girl using fair words and fine presents and to carry her off in their coach as if they were taking her out for a pleasant drive." He claims that they also intended to convince their daughter, László's wife, to join them, "by the use of threats if need be", while László was staying in Pápa, and that they planned to keep Orsolya at Rohonc in their custody.[103]

Pope Innocent X signed the dispensation on 13 August 1652,[104] but by the time one of the Carmelite friars arrived with it in Fraknó, its addressee, László Esterházy, was dead. He had fallen in battle against the Ottomans together with three other members of the family. Their burial was the most elaborate funeral of the century with over five thousand people attending. The four Esterházy heroes were given a final resting-place in the Jesuit church in Nagyszombat, built by Miklós Esterházy.

The family's reputation was greatly enhanced by the countrywide respect for the four heroes. The new head of the family, seventeen-year-old Pál, took over the offices and titles of his elder brother without opposition. Two weeks after László's death Ferdinand III fulfilled all Pál's requests, appointing him captain general of Pápa on 13 September 1652 and lord lieutenant of Sopron county on 14 November. The latter office had been held by two generations of the Esterházy family before him. At the same time the king made Pál Orsolya's guardian.[105] However, the problems surrounding the little girl's inheritance were not solved as a result, since the guardianship lasted only until her marriage, at which time the estates and money were to be delivered into her hands.

It was obvious that although Batthyány and Nádasdy did everything they could to help the Esterházys in the preparations for the funeral, Batthyány would soon renew his efforts to get hold of Orsolya's property. His daughter, László's widow, owned half of the Kismarton estate. Wishing to strengthen her position further Batthyány intended to send envoys to Pál, just a few days after his son-in-law's death, to demand that the officials at Frakno swear allegiance to his widow.[106] When Farkas Esterházy heard about this plan he immediately hurried to the palatine, meanwhile warning Pál not to allow Batthyány and his followers access to the castle. He gave Pál precise instructions in order to prevent him from making any mistakes before his return from Palatine Pálffy: "Go and stand on the bridge in front of the gate and face them. Do not write or speak to them about anything other than that you are fully aware of your father's will. That will determined that should your brother die without an heir you would inherit the castle of Frakno immediately. Therefore you have entered the castle as your own and have made the officials and soldiers there swear allegiance to you."[107]

While preparations for the funeral were being made at Nagyszombat, Farkas Esterházy helped Pál organise his court and prepared the ceremony for the young man's installation into his new offices. The arrangements were extremely thorough. He organised a feast for the county officials and ensured that the deputy lieutenant would inform Pál about all important matters without delay. He also remembered that gifts were to be given on the occasion of Pál's installation as captain of Pápa, and he advised him on how to avoid becoming too dependent on his superiors.[108]

When the long-awaited dispensation, signed by the pope, arrived at Frakno, these problems were temporarily pushed to the background and the letters written to Pál centred around the new topic. The last letter from Farkas Esterházy to Pál before the wedding was written late on the evening of Friday 18 October 1652 at Széleskút, and was sent at once to the addressee. Farkas wrote that Canon Ádám Szalkovics was to go without delay to János Püsky, archbishop of Kalocsa, who was the last high church dignitary needed to give permission for the marriage in line with the pope's letter.[109] As Püsky had always been a patron of the young Esterházys he raised no objections. In fact, he had prepared the authorisation for Szalkovics, which allowed him to marry Pál and Orsolya, even before he arrived.[110] The canon married them at Frakno, between four and five in the afternoon on 21 October.[111] According to the provisions of the Council of Trent at least two or three witnesses were needed for a marriage to be valid. Thus István Olasz Kolozsváry and György Kürtösy, two of the staff at Frakno, and Farkas Esterházy who rushed there to be the third witness, were present at the ceremony. All unnecessary stir and commotion were avoided. Not even Dániel Esterházy travelled to Frakno.

The need for the wedding to take place during the time of mourning for his brother and relatives was explained by Farkas Esterházy in a letter to Pál. He maintained that any further delay might have prevented the marriage from taking place at all. Any breach of secrecy would have represented a great risk both to the marriage and to the future of the entire Esterházy family.[112]

According to the pope's dispensation the wedding had to take place in keeping with the provisions of the Council of Trent. However, the Council had made it possible for diocesan bishops to make exceptions where they considered appropriate without affecting the validity of the marriage. Archbishop Püsky was naturally willing to make an exception in this case, and the wedding was therefore able to go ahead in secret in the presence of three witnesses. However, this was a dangerous procedure even with the archbishop's consent, since the permission of the king was also required in marriages between such close relatives. In fact, relatives up to the fourth remove were forbidden to marry since their relationship was considered incestuous, and violations of this law were severely punished. In 1652 no such permission was sought from the king for Orsolya and Pál. Furthermore, Orsolya was only eleven at the time, and was thus well below the accepted age at which girls were allowed to marry.

In any case, the secret was kept well; the Chancellery did not initiate legal proceedings against the Esterházys, nor did the relatives protest. Nádasdy would certainly have done so, as he did in 1655 when the public wedding took place after the king's permission had been obtained.[113] He did not attend the wedding of 6 February and protested against the incestuous marriage[114] even though he had no chance of changing the situation, given that the consent of both the pope and the king had been successfully obtained.

THE MARRIAGE OF THE YOUNGEST BROTHER

The last chapter in the family's internal affairs was the division of property between Pál and his brother Ferenc in 1660 and the latter's subsequent marriage.

The first step was taken in 1657 when László Révay discussed with Ilona Illésházy's father the possibility of a marriage between Ferenc and Ilona. He wrote to Pál that Count Illésházy had told him of a similar proposal he had received from Count

Pál Csáky, but that he, Révay, had replied that the countess should be kept for the Esterházy family.[115] Illésházy had been delighted and had told Révay that although he had no objections he had sworn not to promise his daughter to anyone before she reached the age of twelve. The question was therefore postponed for two years. In early 1659, however, a dispute arose between the Esterházy brothers concerning their inheritance. Farkas Esterházy acted as a mediator. He also remained in contact with László Révay and took him a message sent by Pál Esterházy to Illésházy pressing for the marriage of Ferenc and Ilona.[116]

Ilona had several suitors and Farkas Esterházy warned Pál that this competition meant they were pressed for time. The other suitors were all from distinguished families and each owned substantial property.[117] Illésházy's position was thus extremely favourable; while Ferenc Esterházy was his preferred choice he was in a position to lay down conditions. After all, he could not give his daughter to a man whose finances had almost been ruined by his elder brother. Furthermore, he laid down the condition that Sempte should be given to Ferenc when the two brothers finally divided the family property between them.[118]

According to Miklós Esterházy's will Sempte belonged to Pál, who naturally insisted on keeping it. Nevertheless, Sempte was not the central issue when it came to the division of property. The problem was that the machinations of the past decades had created a very complex situation, and the actual ownership of the family's estates had now to be established.

Both parties referred to their father's will. However, the situation in 1659–60 was very different from the situation in 1641 when the will had been made. For Ferenc the decision was critical, since the disagreement was threatening the possibility of his marriage with Illésházy's daughter. It was again Farkas Esterházy who tried to reason with Pál. He suggested having the father's will copied, as the original was very hard to read and marginal notes would have to be made.[119] He also urged him to come to a peaceful agreement with Ferenc as befitted loving brothers and in keeping with the spirit of their father's will. If they found it impossible to settle the dispute themselves, they should ask for their relatives' advice. Finally, Farkas tried to explain to Pál—in a very roundabout way for fear of offending him—that no inheritance by primogeniture had been laid down by the late palatine among his sons, but only among his future grandsons.[120] According to the will, in the event of László's death, his other two sons would inherit an equal share. However, the overwhelming reason for finding an amicable solution to the disagreement was, as László Révay put it, that a fair division of the property was a precondition for Ilona Illésházy's marriage to Ferenc Esterházy. Should the brothers be unable to agree Illésházy would not give his daughter to Ferenc in marriage. This would represent a great loss for him and he would undoubtedly seek legal compensation as a result.[121] Pál nevertheless continued to postpone the settlement and only came to an agreement with his brother on 24 November 1660, just a few days before the betrothal was due to take place. The order of inheritance between the two brothers was set down under five points and this document later became the basis of their descendants' division of the property.[122]

Ferenc Esterházy and Ilona Illésházy were married in early 1661, after they, too, had received the pope's dispensation.[123]

Although the most problematic period for Miklós Esterházy's heirs had come to an end with the public marriage of Pál and Orsolya in 1655 and the birth of their first child, the events surrounding the marriage of Ferenc are integral parts of this narrative. They demonstrate that the young Esterházys could rely at all times on the unselfish support of their relatives. From among the faithful members of Miklós Esterházy's family only his two nephews, Farkas and László Révay, were still living at that time, yet they were still successful in solving all the family disputes that arose. These relatives protected the Esterházy family's interests with great skill and tact. They remained true to the late palatine's spirit even if circumstances prevented them from acting according to his word.

Notes

1 Biographies of him include László Szalay and Ferenc Salamon, *Galántai gróf Eszterházy Miklós, Magyarország nádora 1–3*. Pest, 1863–1870; Csaba Csapodi, *Eszterházy Miklós nádor*. Budapest, 1942; Katalin Péter: *Esterházy Miklós*. Budapest, 1985.

2 György Thurzó to Szaniszló Thurzó, 6 February 1598: *Századok* 1894: 75.

3 Esterházy family tree, Table III.

4 Esterházy's first will, 11 June 1623: Hungarian National Archive (Magyar Országos Levéltár, hereafter: MOL). Esterházy family archive, P 108, Repositorium (hereafter: P 108) 4, Fasc. E, No. 33.

5 Esterházy's second will, 30 December 1630: P 108, 4, Fasc. E, No. 36.

6 Miklós Esterházy to Krisztina Nyáry, 31 July 1628: *Történelmi Tár* (hereafter: TT), 1901: 489. On 18 August 1628 a daughter was born to the Esterházys and was given the name Katalin after her mother's grandmother, Kata Várday.

7 Miklós Esterházy to Krisztina Nyáry, 12 October 1625: TT 1901: 374.

8 Pál Esterházy's memories of his youth: *Esterházy Pál Mars Hungaricus*. Published by Emma Iványi. Budapest, 1989 (hereafter: *Esterházy Pál*): 310.

9 Klára Garas, "Az olasz mesterek és a magyarországi barokk térhódítása (művészvándorlás, művészeti kapcsolatok)". In: *A magyarországi reneszánsz és barokk*. Edited by Géza Galavics. Budapest, 1975.

10 *Esterházy Pál*, 305.

11 The court regulations of Palatine Count Miklós Esterházy, c. 1630: *Magyar Gazdaságtörténelmi Szemle* 1901: 224.

12 Ibid.

13 Ibid.

14 Ibid., 228–229.

15 Orders given by Miklós Esterházy, 14 March 1625: P 108, 4, Fasc. E, No 35.

16 Miklós Esterházy's letter of admonition to István Esterházy, 18 October 1634: P 108, 60, Fasc. A, No. 1 (hereafter: Letter of Admonition).

17 Inventory, July 1641: P 108, 12, Fasc. Q, No. 638.

18 *Esterházy Pál*, 306.

19 Orders given by Miklós Esterházy to István's tutor, 11 June 1623: P 108, 4, Fasc. E, No. 33.

20 Ibid., and the will of Miklós Esterházy, dated 14 August 1641. Published in Zsigmond Bubics and Lajos Merényi, *Herceg Esterházy Pál nádor, 1635–1713.* Budapest, 1895 (hereafter: Bubics-Merényi): 268–271.

21 Letter of Admonition: P 108, 60, Fasc. A, No. 1.

22 Ibid.

23 P 108, 4, Fasc. E, No. 35.

24 The diary of László Révay: *Magyar Történelmi Tár* 1857: 245.

25 The letters of László Révay to Palatine Miklós Esterházy, 1644: TT 1909: 307.

26 The diary of the Révay family 1555–1667. Published by Arnold Ipolyi. *Új Magyar Múzeum,* 1857: 447.

27 Archives relating to the Esterházy family and its side branches. Compiled by Count János Eszterházy. Budapest, 1901 (hereafter: Eszterházy): 105–106.

28 The family diary of the counts Esterházy. Published by Sándor Szilágyi. TT 1888: 209–224.

29 On the birth and christening of Farkas Esterházy, see *Alsósztregovai és rimai Rimay János államiratai és levelezése.* Edited by Arnold Ipolyi. Budapest, 1887: 200.

30 László Berényi: "Emlékezés egy elfelejtett Esterházyra". *Turul* 1993/3: 25.

31 Zsigmond Megyeri to Farkas Esterházy, 31 August 1647. P 123. IV. d.

32 Dániel Esterházy to Ádám Batthyány, 15 February 1646: MOL P 1314. Batthyány family archive, Missiles (hereafter: P 1314), No. 11902.

33 György Kürtösy to László Esterházy, 27 November 1650: MOL P 124. Documents of László Esterházy (hereafter: P 124), No. 660.

34 Miklós Pázmány to István Olasz Kolozsváry, 22 April 1655: P 125. Documents of Pál Esterházy (hereafter: P 125). No. 6409.

35 Orsolya Esterházy to István Olasz Kolozsváry, 13 April 1657: P 125, No. 6906.

36 Farkas Esterházy to László Esterházy, 13 December 1647: P 124, No. 156.

37 Farkas Esterházy to László Esterházy, 3 March 1652: P 124, No. 177.

38 *Esterházy Pál*, 307.

39 István Olasz Kolozsváry to László Esterházy, 23 June 1651: P 124, No. 877.

40 István Olasz Kolozsváry to László Esterházy, 4 February 1651: P 124, No. 875.Eszterházy, 211.

41 *Esterházy Pál*, 311.

42 István Olasz Kolozsváry to László Esterházy, 18 September 1646: P 1314, No. 12099.

43 *Esterházy Pál*, 312–314.

44 Ibid., 312.

45 Dániel Esterházy to László Esterházy, October 1649: P 124, No. 76; Farkas Esterházy to László Esterházy, 23 May 1649: Ibid., No. 160.

46 Mihály Miticzky to László Esterházy, 28 October 1651: P 124, No. 758.

47 P. 124, No. 1714, fol. 28–32, sine dato.

48 Ádám Szalkovics to László Esterházy, 25 September 1651: P 124, No. 1210; 26 November 1651: Ibid., No. 1214; 3 March 1652: Ibid., No. 1215.

49 *Esterházy Pál*, 317.

50 Júlia Esterházy to Pál Esterházy, 26 December 1658: P 125. No. 724.

51 *Esterházy Pál*, 314.

52 Ádám Batthyány to László Esterházy, 28 September 1648: P 124, No. 270.

53 Ádám Batthyány to László Esterházy, 21 March 1652: P 124, No. 339.

54 Ádám Batthyány to László Esterházy, 22 December 1649: P 124, No. 289.

55 Dániel Esterházy to Ádám Batthyány, St. Stephen's Day (26 December) 1648: P 1314, No. 11915.

56 Dániel Esterházy to László Esterházy, 10 October 1649: P 124, No. 74.

57 Ibid., and Pál Pálffy to László Esterházy, 17 November 1649: P 124, No. 944.

58 Dániel Esterházy to László Esterházy, 10 October 1649: P 124, No. 74.

59 László Esterházy to Ádám Batthyány, 27 January 1650: P 1314, No. 12200; and 1 February 1650: Ibid., No. 12201.

60 Ádám Batthyány to László Esterházy, 31 January 1650: P 124, No. 293.

61 Ádám Batthyány to László Esterházy, 29 May 1652: P 124, No. 381.

62 The will of 1641: Bubics-Merényi, op.cit., 272.

63 Mária Magdolna Esterházy to László Esterházy, 23 April 1651: MOL P 124, No. 196.

64 Dániel Esterházy to László Esterházy, 15 December 1651: P 124, No. 131; László Esterházy to Ádám Batthyány, 19 December 1651: P 1314. No. 12288.

65 Dániel Esterházy to László Esterházy, 5 December 1651: P 124, No. 126.

66 Judit Rumy to Dániel Esterházy, 5 December 1651: P 124, No. 1601.

67 Dániel Esterházy to László Esterházy, 5 December 1651: P 124, No. 126; György Lippay to László Esterházy, 13 November 1651: Ibid., No. 694.

68 Dániel Esterházy to László Esterházy, 2 December 1651: P 124, No. 125.

69 Dániel Esterházy to László Esterházy, Ibid., and 5 December 1651: P 124, No. 126.

70 Dániel Esterházy to László Esterházy, 2 December 1651: P 124, No. 125.

71 Dániel Esterházy to László Esterházy, 5 December 1651: P 124, No. 126.

72 Dániel Esterházy to László Esterházy, 2 December 1651: P 124, No. 125.

73 Pál Pálffy to László Esterházy, 20 July 1651: P 124, No. 981.

74 The marriage contract drawn up between László Esterházy and György Homonnai Drugeth, on the latter's engagement, 17 December 1651: P 108, 3, Fasc. B, No. 25; Rep. 7, Fasc. D, No. 50.

75 László Esterházy to Ádám Batthyány, 16 February 1652: P 1314, No. 12264.

76 Farkas Esterházy to László Esterházy, 8 March 1652: P 124, No. 178; 13 April 1652: Ibid., No. 181.

77 Farkas Esterházy to László Esterházy, 8 March 1652: P 124, No. 178.

78 Ferenc Nádasdy to László Esterházy, 5 March 1652: P 124, No. 831; Júlia Esterházy to László Esterházy, 4 May 1652: Ibid., No. 24.

79 György Lippay to László Esterházy, 25 April 1652: P 124, No. 700.

80 Farkas Esterházy to Pál Esterházy, 30 June 1661: P 125, No. 705.

81 Farkas Esterházy to László Esterházy: P 124, No. 150–185; Farkas Esterházy to Pál Esterházy: P 125, No. 685–720.

82 *Esterházy Pál*, 305–320.

83 Ibid., 308.

84 Ibid., 311.

85 Ibid., 309.

86 Farkas Esterházy to László Esterházy, 13 December 1647: P 124, No. 156.

87 *Esterházy Pál*, 315.

88 Ibid.

89 Ibid., 314.

90 Eszterházy, 191.

91 *Esterházy Pál*, 315.

92 Farkas Esterházy to László Esterházy, 15 June 1652: P 124, No. 184.

93 Farkas Esterházy to László Esterházy, 20 June 1652: P 124, No. 185.

94 Mária Magdolna Esterházy to László Esterházy, 1 June 1651: P 124, No. 197.

95 István Olasz Kolozsváry to László Esterházy, 22 March 1652: P 124, No. 882/a.

96 Family tree, P 108, 3, Fasc. A, No. 3–4.

97 The general's documents: P 108, 3, Fasc. A, No. 2. Arguments for the marriage were eventually put in writing by Pál as well: *Brevis informatio in causa matrimonii Pauli et Ursulae nobilium personarum*: P 125, No. 11770, sine dato.

98 *Motiva Dispensationis, Anno 1650*: P 108, 3, Fasc. A, No. 1.

99 *Esterházy Pál*, 315.

100 Ibid., 319.

101 Anna Franciska Csáky to István Csáky, 7 October 1651: Farkas Deák: *Magyar hölgyek levelei 1515–1709*. Budapest, 1879: 285.

102 László Esterházy to Ádám Batthyány, 25 August 1650: P 1314, No. 12085.

103 Farkas Esterházy to László Esterházy, 15 June 1652: P 124, No. 184.

104 P 108, Rep. 7, Fasc. A, No. 10–11, sine dato.

105 Royal decrees: P 108, Rep. 7, Fasc. A, No. 4.

106 Farkas Esterházy to Pál Esterházy, 7 September 1657: P 125, No. 685.

107 Ibid.

108 P 108, Rep. 7, Fasc. A, No. 4, sine dato (1652).

109 Farkas Esterházy to Pál Esterházy, 18 October 1652: P 125, No. 686.

110 17 October 1652: P 108, Rep. 3, Fasc. A, No. 6.

111 21 October 1652: P 108, Rep. 3, Fasc. A, No. 7; TT 1888.

112 Farkas Esterházy to Pál Esterházy, 18 October 1652: P 125, No. 686.

113 The royal permission, 16 January 1655: P 108, Rep. 3, Fasc. A, No. 11.

114 The protests of Ferenc Nádasdy and his wife, Júlia Esterházy: P 108, Fasc. A, No. 9. At the same time, Pál's other sister, Mária Esterházy, and György Homonnai also protested, but after her husband's death Mária withdrew her protest: P 108, Fasc. A, No. 15.

115 László Révay to Pál Esterházy, 15 September 1657: P 125, No. 3666.

116 Farkas Esterházy to Pál Esterházy, 1 February 1659: P 125, No. 701.
117 Farkas Esterházy to Pál Esterházy, 17 March 1659: P 125, No. 702.
118 Ibid.
119 P 108, Rep. 7, Fasc. E, No. 71.
120 Farkas Esterházy to Pál Esterházy, 17 March 1659: P 125, No. 702.
121 László Révay to Farkas Esterházy, 22 March 1659: P 125, No. 6438.
122 P 108, Rep. 7, Fasc. E, No. 76.
123 The marriage document: P 108, Rep. 3, Fasc. C, No. 29.

GENEALOGICAL TABLES

THE BATTHYÁNY FAMILY
Table I/1

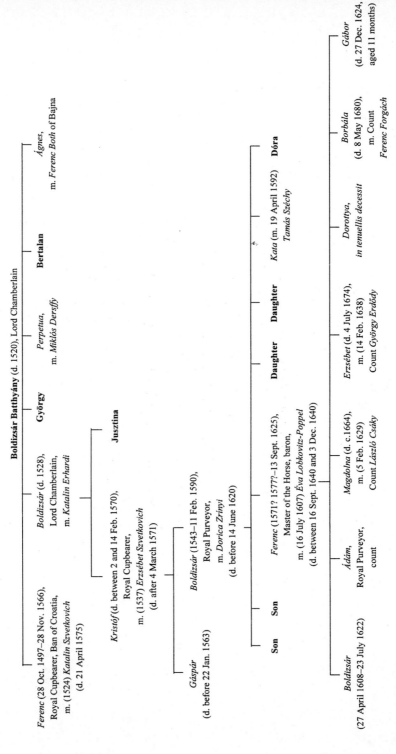

Boldizsár Batthyány (d. 1520), Lord Chamberlain

Ferenc (28 Oct. 1497–28 Nov. 1566),
Royal Cupbearer, Ban of Croatia,
m. (1524) *Katalin Szvetkovich*
(d. 21 April 1575)

Boldizsár (d. 1528),
Lord Chamberlain,
m. *Katalin Erhardi*

György

Perpetua,
m. *Miklós Dersffy*

Bertalan

Ágnes,
m. *Ferenc Both* of Bajna

Kristóf (d. between 2 and 14 Feb. 1570),
Royal Cupbearer,
m. (1537) *Erzsébet Szvetkovich*
(d. after 4 March 1571)

Jusztina

Gáspár
(d. before 22 Jan. 1563)

Boldizsár (1543–11 Feb. 1590),
Royal Purveyor,
m. *Dorica Zrínyi*
(d. before 14 June 1620)

Ferenc (1571? 1577?–13 Sept. 1625),
Master of the Horse, baron,
m. (16 July 1607) *Éva Lobkovitz-Poppel*
(d. between 16 Sept. 1640 and 3 Dec. 1640)

Son

Son

Daughter

Daughter

Kata (m. 19 April 1592)
Tamás Széchy

Dóra

Boldizsár
(27 April 1608–23 July 1622)

Ádám,
Royal Purveyor,
count

Magdolna (d. c.1664),
m. (5 Feb. 1629)
Count *László Csáky*

Erzsébet (d. 4 July 1674),
m. (14 Feb. 1638)
Count *György Erdődy*

Dorottya,
in tenuellis decessit

Borbála
(d. 8 May 1680),
m. Count
Ferenc Forgách

Gábor
(d. 27 Dec. 1624,
aged 11 months)

Table I/2

Ádám (14 Feb. 1610–15 March 1659), Royal Purveyor, count, m.
1) (3 Feb. 1623, Vienna) Countess *Aurora Formentini* (30 Dec. 1615–15 April 1653)
2) (15–17 Aug. 1655) *Katalin Wittmann* (later wife of Niklas Königsberg)

With first wife:

Mária Eleonóra
(1 March 1633–21 Oct. 1654),
m. (6 Feb. 1649)
Count *László Esterházy*

Ferenc (13 Nov. 1635–
May/June 1636)

Pál (5 Nov. 1639–11 May 1674),
m. *Katalin Illésházy*

Daughter (d. before
25 Aug. 1644)

Zsigmond (d. Feb. 1649)

Daughter
(d. before 23 July 1639)

Kristóf
(before 4 March 1637–6 March 1687),
Royal Cupbearer,
m. (1661) *Mária Palocsay*
(1644–7 Aug. 1686)

Borbála Terézia
(1640/1642–after 31 March 1692),
m. (1659?) Count *Péter Széchy*

Twin girls
(before 12 June 1645–1 Aug. 1646)

Boldizsár (d. 1741)

Ádám (13 Sept. 1662–26 Aug. 1703),
Lord Chief Justice,
m. (1692) Countess *Eleonóra Strattmann*
(1678–1741)

Ferenc (d. 9 March 1717), Royal Cupbearer, m.
1) Countess *Rozália Esterházy*
2) *Erzsébet Czehentner*

Zsigmond (1673–1728), Royal Purveyor,
m. Countess *Izabella Gallenberg*
(1668–1 July 1731)

With second wife:

Júlia Anna (b. 1656), nun

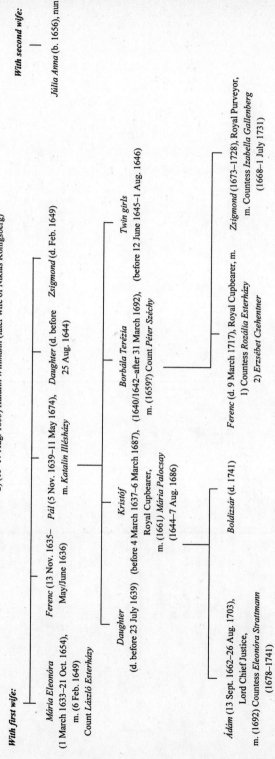

THE CSÁKY FAMILY

Table II/1

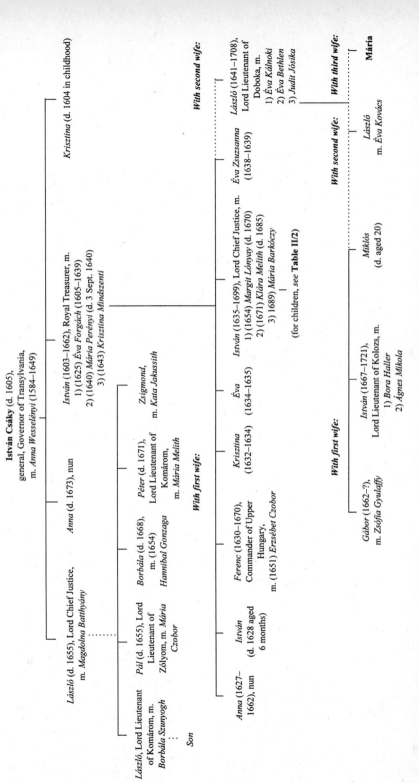

István Csáky (d. 1605),
general, Governor of Transylvania,
m. *Anna Wesselényi* (1584–1649)

Krisztina (d. 1604 in childhood)

László (d. 1655), Lord Chief Justice,
m. *Magdolna Batthyány*

Anna (d. 1673), nun

István (1603–1662), Royal Treasurer, m.
1) (1625) *Éva Forgách* (1605–1639)
2) (1640) *Mária Perényi* (d. 3 Sept. 1640)
3) (1643) *Krisztina Mindszenti*

László, Lord Lieutenant
of Komárom, m.
Borbála Szunyogh

Son

With first wife:

Pál (d. 1655), Lord
Lieutenant of
Zólyom, m. *Mária
Czobor*

Borbála (d. 1668),
m. (1654)
Hannibal Gonzaga

Péter (d. 1671),
Lord Lieutenant of
Komárom,
m. *Mária Melith*

Zsigmond,
m. *Kata Jakussith*

With second wife:

László (1641–1708),
Lord Lieutenant of
Doboka, m.
1) *Éva Kálnoki*
2) *Éva Bethlen*
3) *Judit Jósika*

Anna (1627–
1662), nun

István
(d. 1628 aged
6 months)

Ferenc (1630–1670),
Commander of Upper
Hungary,
m. (1651) *Erzsébet Czobor*

Krisztina
(1632–1634)

Éva
(1634–1635)

István (1635–1699), Lord Chief Justice, m.
1) (1654) *Margit Lónyay* (d. 1670)
2) (1671) *Klára Melith* (d. 1685)
3) 1689) *Mária Barkóczy*

(for children, *see* **Table II/2**)

Éva Zsuzsanna
(1638–1639)

With first wife:

Gábor (1662–?),
m. *Zsófia Gyulaffy*

István (1667–1721),
Lord Lieutenant of Kolozs, m.
1) *Bora Haller*
2) *Agnes Mikola*

Miklós
(d. aged 20)

With second wife:

László
m. *Éva Kovács*

With third wife:

Mária

Table II/2

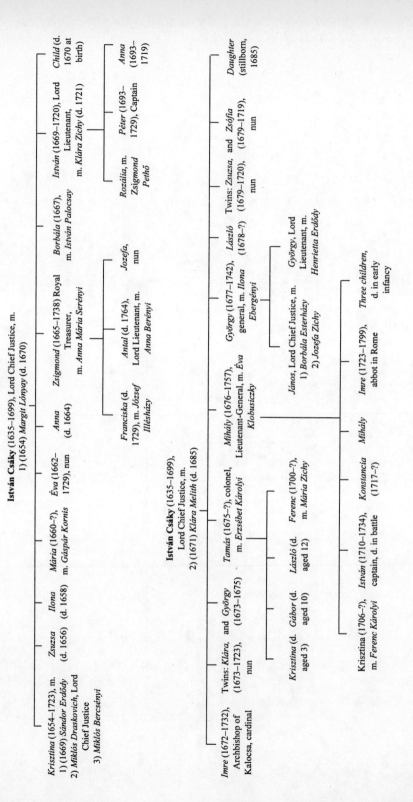

István Csáky (1635–1699), Lord Chief Justice, m.
1) (1654) *Margit Lónyay* (d. 1670)

Krisztina (1654–1723), m.
1) (1669) *Sándor Erdődy*
2) *Miklós Draskovich*, Lord Chief Justice
3) *Miklós Bercsényi*

Zsuzsa (d. 1656)

Ilona (d. 1658)

Mária (1660–?), m. *Gáspár Kornis*

Éva (1662–1729), nun

Anna (d. 1664)

Zsigmond (1665–1738) Royal Treasurer, m. *Anna Mária Serényi*

Franciska (d. 1729), m. *József Illésházy*

Antal (d. 1764), Lord Lieutenant, m. *Anna Berényi*

Jozefa, nun

Borbála (1667), m. *István Palocsay*

István (1669–1720), Lord Lieutenant, m. *Klára Zichy* (d. 1721)

Rozália, m. *Zsigmond Pethő*

Péter (1693–1729), Captain

Anna (1693–1719)

Child (d. 1670 at birth)

István Csáky (1635–1699), Lord Chief Justice, m.
2) (1671) *Klára Melith* (d. 1685)

Imre (1672–1732), Archbishop of Kalocsa, cardinal

Twins: Klára, (1673–1723), nun *and György* (1673–1675)

Tamás (1675–?), colonel, m. *Erzsébet Károlyi*

Krisztina (d. aged 3)

Gábor (d. aged 10)

László (d. aged 12)

Ferenc (1700–?), m. *Mária Zichy*

Krisztina (1706–?), m. *Ferenc Károlyi*

István (1710–1734), captain, d. in battle

Konstancia (1717–?)

Mihály (1676–1757), Lieutenant-General, m. *Éva Klobusiczky*

János, Lord Chief Justice, m. 1) *Borbála Esterházy* 2) *Jozefa Zichy*

György, Lord Lieutenant, m. Henrietta Erdődy

Three children, d. in early infancy

Mihály

Imre (1723–1799), abbot in Rome

György (1677–1742), general, m. *Ilona Ebergényi*

László (1678–?)

Twins: Zsuzsa, (1679–1720), nun *and Zsófia* (1679–1719), nun

Daughter (stillborn, 1685)

Table II/3

István Csáky (1635–1699), Lord Chief Justice, m.
3) (1689) *Mária Barkóczy*

Ádám (1691–?)

Erzsébet (b. 1693, d. in infancy)

János (b. 1695, d. aged 3 days)

Ferenc (1697–?)

Miklós (1698–1757), Archbishop of Esztergom

Table III/1 THE ESTERHÁZY FAMILY
Ferenc Esterházy's Branch

Ferenc Esterházy (1533?–1604), Lieutenant of Pozsony, m. (1566) Zsófia Illésházy (1547–?)

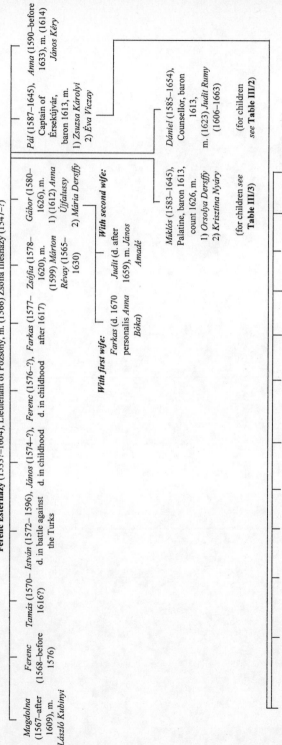

Magdolna (1567–after 1609), m. *László Kubinyi*

Ferenc (1568–before 1576)

Tamás (1570–1616?)

István (1572–1596), d. in battle against the Turks

János (1574–?), d. in childhood

Ferenc (1576–?), d. in childhood

Farkas (1577–after 1617)

Zsófia (1578–1620), m. (1599) *Márton Revay* (1565–1630)

Gábor (1580–1626), m. 1) (1612) *Anna Újfalussy* 2) *Mária Dersffy*

Pál (1587–1645), Captain of Érsekújvár, baron 1613, m. 1) *Zsuzsa Károlyi* 2) *Éva Viczay*

Anna (1590–before 1633), m. (1614) *János Kéry*

With first wife:

Farkas (d. 1670) personalis *Anna Bóka*

With second wife:

Judit (d. after 1659), m. *János Amadé*

Miklós (1583–1645), Palatine, baron 1613, count 1626, m. 1) *Orsolya Dersffy* 2) *Krisztina Nyáry*

(for children see **Table III/3**)

Dániel (1585–1654), Counsellor, baron 1613, m. (1623) *Judit Rumy* (1606–1663)

(for children see **Table III/2**)

Ferenc (1617–1652), Captain of Gyarmat, d. in battle against the Turks

Erzsébet (d. 1668), m. *István Héderváry*

Zsuzsa (d. in childhood)

Rebeka (d. 1645)

Zsófia, m. *György Berényi*

Miklós (d. 1669), Lord Lieutenant, m. *Ágnes Perényi* (d. 1674)

Magdolna, (1635–after 1700), nun

Sándor (d. 1679), m. *Erzse Morócz*

Ilona (d. 1651)

Gábor (d. in early infancy)

Péter (d. in early infancy)

Dániel (d. in early infancy)

Table III/2 THE ESTERHÁZY FAMILY
Dániel Esterházy's Branch

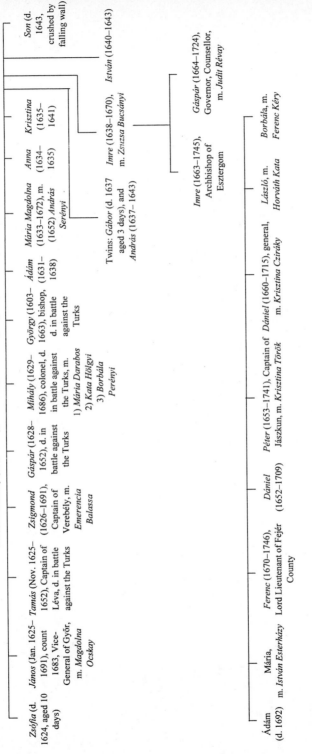

Dániel Esterházy (1585–1654), Counsellor, baron 1613, m. (1623) Judit Rumy (1606–1663)

Zsófia (d. 1624, aged 10 days)

János (Jan. 1625–1691), count 1683, Vice-General of Győr, m. Magdolna Ocskay

Tamás (Nov. 1625–1652), Captain of Léva, d. in battle against the Turks

Zsigmond (1626–1691), Captain of Verebély, m. Emerencia Balassa

Gáspár (1628–1652), d. in battle against the Turks

Mihály (1629–1686), colonel, d. in battle against the Turks, m. 1) Mária Darabos 2) Kata Hölgyi 3) Borbála Perényi

György (1603–1663), bishop, d. in battle against the Turks

Ádám (1631–1638)

Mária Magdolna (1633–1672), m. (1652) András Serényi

Anna (1634–1635)

Krisztina (1635–1641)

Son (d. 1643, crushed by falling wall)

István (1640–1643)

Imre (1638–1670), m. Zsuzsa Bucsányi

Twins: Gábor (d. 1637 aged 3 days), and András (1637–1643)

Imre (1663–1745), Archbishop of Esztergom

Gáspár (1664–1724), Governor, Counsellor, m. Judit Révay

Ádám (d. 1692)

Mária, m. István Esterházy

Ferenc (1670–1746), Lord Lieutenant of Fejér County

Dániel (1652–1709)

Péter (1653–1741), Captain of Jászkun, m. Krisztina Török

Dániel (1660–1715), general, m. Krisztina Cziráky

László, m. Horváth Kata

Borbála, m. Ferenc Kéry

Table III/3 THE ESTERHÁZY FAMILY
Miklós Esterházy's Branch

Miklós Esterházy (1583–1645), Palatine, baron 1613, count 1626, m.
1) (1612) *Orsolya Dersffy* (after 1583–1619)
2) (1624) *Krisztina Nyáry* (1604–1641)

With first wife:

With second wife:

István (1616–1641),
m. (1638) *Erzsébet
Thurzó* (1621–1642)

Magdolna
(1625–1627)

László (1626–1652),
Lord Lieutenant of
Sopron, Captain of Pápa,
d. in battle against the
Turks, m. (1650)
Eleonóra Batthyány
(1633–1654)

Katalin
(1628–
1630)

Anna Júlia
(1630–1669),
m. (1644)
Ferenc Nádasdy
(1623–1671)

Mihály
(1632–
1633)

Krisztina Mária
(d. 1634 aged
11 weeks)

Pál (1635–1713),
Palatine, Prince 1687, m.
1) (1652) *Orsolya
Esterházy* (1641–1682)
2) (1682) *Éva Thököly*
(1659–1716)

Mária (1638–1684),
m. (1653) *György
Homonnai Drugeth*
(1635–1661)

Ferenc (1641–1683),
Counsellor, Lord
Lieutenant, m.
1) (1661) *Ilona Illésházy*
(1646–1669)
2) (1670) *Kata Thököly*
(1655–1701)

Orsolya (1641–1682),
m. (1652) *Pál
Esterházy* (1535–1713)

(for children,
see **Table III/4**)

With second wife:

Mária Rozália (1672–1689),
m. *Ferenc Batthyány*

Antal (1678–1722),
General, m.
1) *Julianna Erdödy* (d. 1696)
2) *Mária Nigrelli*

Krisztina, nun

Franciska, nun

József (1682–1748),
Lord Chief Justice, m.
1) (1710) *Mária Eck*
2) (1740) *Antónia Saur*

Borbála, nun

Ferenc (1683–1754),
Royal Treasurer, m.
Szidónia Pálffy

Table III/4 THE ESTERHÁZY FAMILY
Pál Esterházy's Branch

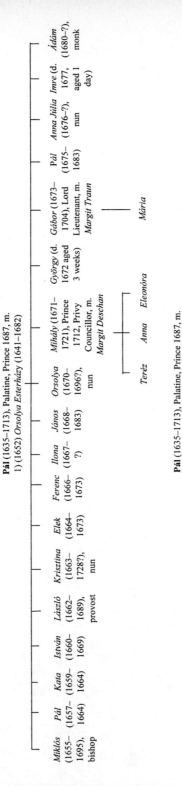

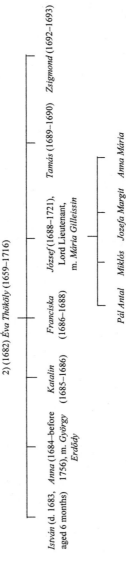

Pál (1635–1713), Palatine, Prince 1687, m.
1) (1652) *Orsolya Esterházy* (1641–1682)

Miklós (1655–1695), bishop — *Pál* (1657–1664) — *Kata* (1659–1664) — *István* (1660–1669) — *László* (1662–1689), provost — *Krisztina* (1663–1728?), nun — *Elek* (1664–1673) — *Ferenc* (1666–1673) — *Ilona* (1667–?) — *János* (1668–1683) — *Orsolya* (1670–1696?), nun — *Mihály* (1671–1721), Prince 1712, Privy Councillor, m. *Margit Deschan* — *György* (d. 1672 aged 3 weeks) — *Gábor* (1673–1704), Lord Lieutenant, m. *Margit Traun* — *Pál* (1675–1683) — *Anna Júlia* (1676–?), nun — *Imre* (d. 1677, aged 1 day) — *Ádám* (1680–?), monk

Teréz — *Anna* — *Eleonóra*

Mária

Pál (1635–1713), Palatine, Prince 1687, m.
2) (1682) *Éva Thököly* (1659–1716)

István (d. 1683, aged 6 months) — *Anna* (1684–before 1756), m. *György Erdődy* — *Katalin* (1685–1686) — *Franciska* (1686–1688) — *József* (1688–1721), Lord Lieutenant, m. *Mária Gilleissin* — *Tamás* (1689–1690) — *Zsigmond* (1692–1693)

Pál Antal — *Miklós* — *Jozefa* — *Margit* — *Anna Mária*

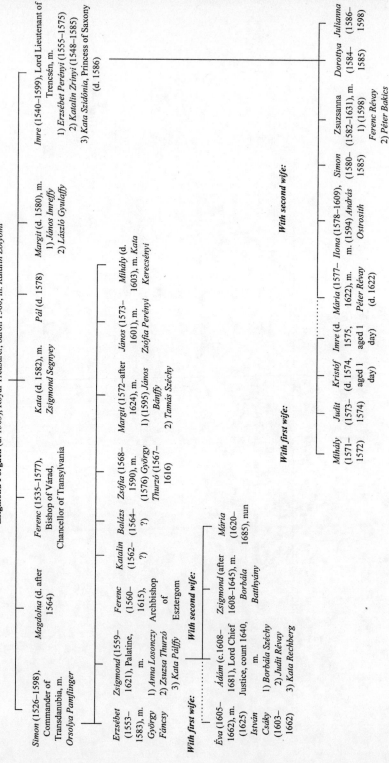

Table IV THE FORGÁCH FAMILY

Zsigmond Forgách (d. 1563), Royal Treasurer, baron 1560, m. Katalin Zólyomi

Table V THE RÁKÓCZI FAMILY

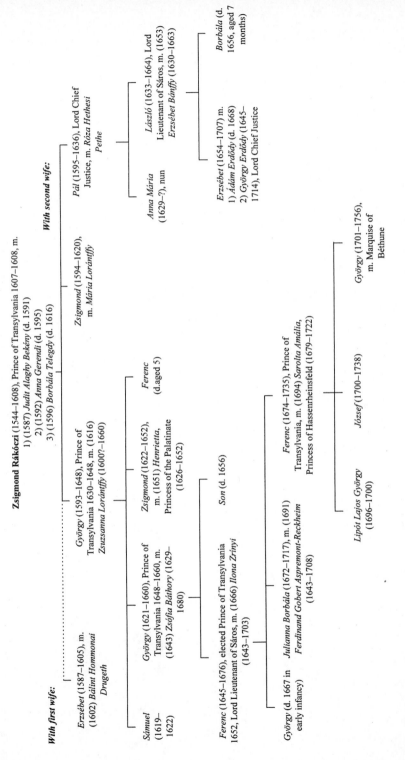

Zsigmond Rákóczi (1544–1608), Prince of Transylvania 1607–1608, m.
1) (1587) Judit Alaghy Bekény (d. 1591)
2) (1592) Anna Gerendi (d. 1595)
3) (1596) Borbála Telegdy (d. 1616)

With first wife:

Erzsébet (1587–1605), m. (1602) Bálint Hommonai Drugeth

György (1593–1648), Prince of Transylvania 1630–1648, m. (1616) Zsuzsanna Lorántffy (1600?–1660)

Zsigmond (1594–1620), m. Mária Lorántffy

Sámuel (1619–1622)

György (1621–1660), Prince of Transylvania 1648–1660, m. (1643) Zsófia Báthory (1629–1680)

Zsigmond (1622–1652), m. (1651) Henrietta, Princess of the Palatinate (1626–1652)

Ferenc (d. aged 5)

Ferenc (1645–1676), elected Prince of Transylvania 1652, Lord Lieutenant of Sáros, m. (1666) Ilona Zrínyi (1643–1703)

Son (d. 1656)

Julianna Borbála (1672–1717), m. (1691) Ferdinand Gobert Aspremont-Reckheim (1643–1708)

György (d. 1667 in early infancy)

Ferenc (1674–1735), Prince of Transylvania, m. (1694) Sarolta Amália, Princess of Hassenheinsfeld (1679–1722)

Lipót Lajos György (1696–1700)

József (1700–1738)

György (1701–1756), m. Marquise of Béthune

With second wife:

Pál (1595–1636), Lord Chief Justice, m. Róza Hethesi Pethe

Anna Mária (1629–?), nun

László (1633–1664), Lord Lieutenant of Sáros, m. (1653) Erzsébet Bánffy (1630–1663)

Erzsébet (1654–1707) m.
1) Ádám Erdődy (d. 1668)
2) György Erdődy (1645–1714), Lord Chief Justice

Borbála (d. 1656, aged 7 months)

Table VI THE ZRÍNYI FAMILY

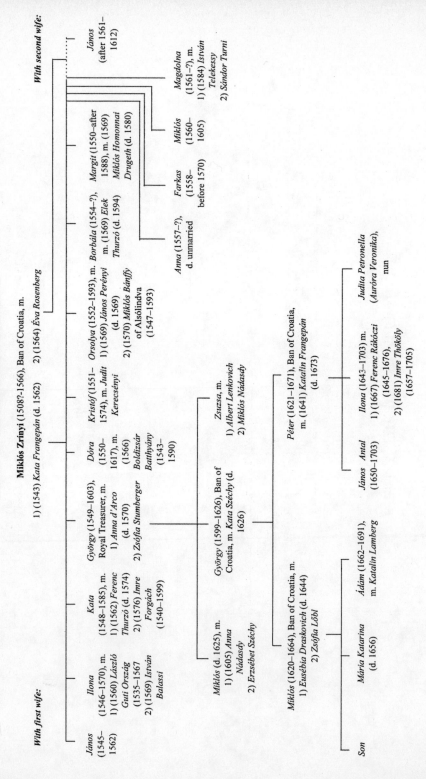

Miklós Zrínyi (1508?–1566), Ban of Croatia, m.

1) (1543) *Kata Frangepán* (d. 1562) 2) (1564) *Éva Rosenberg*

With first wife:

János
(1545–
1562)

Ilona
(1546–1570), m.
1) (1560) *László
Guti Ország*
(1535–1567
2) (1569) *István
Balassi*

Kata
(1548–1585), m.
1) (1562) *Ferenc
Thurzó* (d. 1574)
2) (1576) *Imre
Forgách*
(1540–1599)

György (1549–1603),
Royal Treasurer, m.
1) *Anna d'Arco*
(d. 1570)
2) *Zsófia Stumberger*

Dóra
(1550–
1617), m.
(1566)
*Boldizsár
Batthyány*
(1543–
1590)

Kristóf (1551–
1574), m. *Judit
Kerecsényi*

Orsolya (1552–1593), m.
1) (1569) *János Perényi*
(d. 1569)
2) (1570) *Miklós Bánffy
of Alsólindva*
(1547–1593)

Borbála (1554–?), m.
1) (1569) *Elek
Thurzó* (d. 1594)

Margit (1550–after
1588), m. (1569)
*Miklós Homonnai
Drugeth* (d. 1580)

With second wife:

János
(after 1561–
1612)

Anna (1557–?),
d. unmarried

Farkas
(1558–
before 1570)

Miklós
(1560–
1605)

Magdolna
(1561–?), m.
1) (1584) *István
Telekessy*
2) *Sándor Turni*

Miklós (d. 1625), m.
1) (1605) *Anna
Nádasdy*
2) *Erzsébet Széchy*

György (1599–1626), Ban of
Croatia, m. *Kata Széchy* (d.
1626)

Zsuzsa, m.
1) *Albert Lenkovich*
2) *Miklós Nádasdy*

Miklós (1620–1664), Ban of Croatia, m.
1) *Eusébia Draskovich* (d. 1644)
2) *Zsófia Löbl*

Péter (1621–1671), Ban of Croatia,
m. (1641) *Katalin Frangepán*
(d. 1673)

Mária Katarina
(d. 1656)

Ádám (1662–1691),
m. *Katalin Lamberg*

Son

János Antal
(1650–1703)

Ilona (1643–1703) m.
1) (1667) *Ferenc Rákóczi*
(1645–1676),
2) (1681) *Imre Thököly*
(1657–1705)

Judita Petronella
(*Auróra Veronika*),
nun

INDEX